"You Gotta Believe"

THROUGH
MY
EYES

Steve A. Balsamo

CREATIVE IDEAS PUBLISHING CO.

Through My Eyes
"You Gotta Believe"

Nicole Balsamo Winn - Co-Editor
Gary James - Co-Editor

Creative Ideas Publishing Co.

PAPERBACK ISBN: 978-0-9844140-1-7
HARDBACK ISBN: 978-0-9844140-3-1

Brooklyn boy makes good. There are plenty of stories about gangsters, drug addicts, etc. that come out of the streets of Brooklyn but this one is about the child growing up in that atmosphere and how he survives it.

It's a true story about a boy from Brooklyn who makes it big despite the odds stacked against him. It's a story about love, passion, success and all the trials and tribulations that come along the way.

Through My Eyes is a book that is sure to move you; it will inspire, motivate and entertain you. It's a rags-to-riches story, an underdog story, an Italian story and a love story all rolled into one man's life.

* * *

I like to dedicate this book to Chocolate the love of my life, my family & friends, and everyone who has touched my life along the way - without all of you there would be no story to tell. And let's not forget God who paved my way and the good old USA for allowing us the freedom to be all we can be.

But most of all I need to dedicate this book to Walter, because without Walter I may have given up on myself a long, long time ago. Walter gave me the inspiration to "never give up and never give in."

FOREWORD

Stephen Anthony Balsamo is my father and for most of my life that's the only way I saw him. As a dad. My dad. The best dad. It took 30 years for me to fully realize that he's so much more – a husband, entrepreneur, son, brother, leader, visionary, godfather, carpenter, uncle, friend, and now, a writer. Unfortunately, it will probably take another 30 more for me to fully appreciate all that means and all he's accomplished.

For someone who grew up without a strong father figure, my dad did everything right. It was right because it was the best he could and it was better than most fathers ever do. All my sister and I ever had to do was utter the words, "I want…" and our wish was granted. Just like that. It didn't matter if it was a clown for a birthday party, a pony, puppy, new pool, college education, vacation of a lifetime, dream wedding, or a piece of art. If we could dream it, dad would find a way to deliver it. He's always been really great at showing love through possessions and I suppose that's pretty obvious but when it comes down to it, there's so much more that matters.

Through his "Stevisms" my dad imparted great wisdom onto his girls but it was through his example that he taught us how to be successful, honorable, and passionate women. While other little girls went to dance class, I spent hours riding the forklift around the Creative Ideas factory. My Girl Scout troop consisted of 100 Hispanic men who all thought of me as their daughter or little sister. It was on those afternoons that I learned not to judge a book by its cover but instead, to identify a person's real character before I pass judgment.

Being a business owner isn't all it's cracked up to be. There is no quitting time; days run into nights and Fridays run into weekends. Quality time with your family is spent crammed in a big rig driving up the coast to a tradeshow. Sacrifices become a way of life and the term, "A means to an end" is all too familiar. Looking into my dad's tired eyes after a sleepless night is where I learned that success does not come easy and anyone who thinks it does is for sake of simplicity, a fool. Success requires perseverance, passion, time, and patience. It means not always being liked but constantly commanding respect. It means finding what you love and doing it the best you can, and it means learning from your weaknesses to improve your strengths. Using my dad as a model, I learned to be a leader.

Owning a vast amount of real estate brings with it the great responsibility of acting as landlord. I watched my dad spend years collecting rent from a family of four and every time he arrived to pick up their check he brought a gift with him. A teddy bear for one of the little girls, new dining room set he found at a garage sale, toys, household appliances, it didn't matter. I suppose we weren't the only ones who had our wishes granted over the years. This is where I learned that when someone is in need it's not simply my responsibility, but my honor to stop and help to the best of my ability.

Sharing your life with someone isn't easy and it involves a great deal of compromise but somehow, my parents made it seem like the simplest thing in the world. Over the years, I've watched them push each other to achieve their greatest potential and never for a second did they stopped dreaming - together. As busy as they've ever been, they always found the time to play and laugh with one another and they kiss all the time. Growing up in my household is where I learned that loving someone means wanting their happiness more than your own. That it's imperative to continue doing the little, thoughtful gestures for one another because they add up and get you through the rough times. It means operating as a team while maintaining an understanding of self, and it means never forgetting that you had a choice and you chose to commit yourself to this one person. By watching my mom and dad, I learned many of the habits I incorporate into my own marriage today.

But as a daughter, what I draw from most aren't all of the lessons but the memories. What stands out were the car rides singing Billy Vera and the Beaters together, the Saturday morning father-daughter dates to the carwash, looking out at every school play, graduation or recital and seeing my family in the front row, splashing around the hotel pool in Hawaii, Christmas mornings, first days of school, Sundays at the beach, and the feelings of love and faith that underscored it all.

I know my dad wishes he had similar memories from his own childhood and the sad reality is, he never will. The remarkable fact is, however; that he broke the cycle. He was the father he never had, the husband he never knew he could be, and the star he used to wish upon. It took reading this book for me to learn who my father really is; Stephen Anthony Balsamo – an unstoppable force of nature.

With enduring love and devotion,
Nicole Balsamo Winn

CONTENTS

CHAPTER 1
THE BEGINNINGS

My wonderful wife loves to call this, ***"The son of a sharecropper"*** story. She will tell you that every time someone asks how I got started I take them way back to the beginning of time. She usually gets a sly grin on her face whenever I tell my story. However, it's a story worth telling; it has something for everyone. Hopefully, it will inspire, motivate and entertain you. It's a love story, an against-all-odds story and a rags-to-riches story. It's a compelling story about blind faith, never giving up, ambition, passion and sheer determination. It's a story about a boy growing into a man and making the best of every situation along the way. It's a total success story! It's my story and maybe partly your story.

* * *

I was born **Stephen Anthony Balsamo** on Dec. 20, 1953 in Brooklyn, New York. I was named after my mother's father, Stephen, and my dad, Anthony. And oh, how I always wanted my first name to be Anthony; Tony, just like my dad. That would have been so much cooler than Stephen. I didn't hate being Stephen but let's face it, real Italians were never named Stephen. Name me just one gang-ster in "The Godfather" movies with that name? I've seen them all many times and I don't recall any Stephens as prominent figures in any of them. But Stephen it was, so I learned to deal with it. In Brooklyn, they cut it short to Stevie or Steven, but I always went by Steve.

Coming into this world just five days before Christmas had its drawbacks. Let's just say it's not the best time of year to be born. I always had to share my birthday and Christmas presents because no one could afford to buy for both occasions. People constantly reminded me what a *"pain in the ass"* it was to celebrate a birthday so close to Christmas. A bit of a guilt trip for a kid, wouldn't you say? December is also a very busy time of year with all of the holiday hustle

1

and bustle so you can easily get lost in the shuffle.

I didn't know it just then but I had an older brother named *Vito Stephen Balsamo*. Vito was born one year and five days before me on Dec. 15, 1952. So, that made things especially tough around the holidays and in the present department. Now they had to buy for two.

I grew to hate my birthday because I always felt it was such an inconvenience and a strain for everyone. It took me some 50 years to really begin to celebrate the fact that I was born and enjoy my birthday.

Unfortunately for our family, my brother, Vito, named after my dad's father and Stephen after my mom's, was born mentally challenged. He had what they now call Down syndrome. Nowadays, we have fancy names, treatment, understanding and tolerance for such unfortunate souls but back in the early '50s, people were very ignorant of such things.

In a neighborhood where a grade school education was a major achievement and immigrants were the norm, people's understanding and tolerance for the handicapped was limited at best. Instead, having a handicapped child was an embarrassment. It was something to be ashamed of - a disgrace, if you can imagine that. Understanding was replaced with gossip and name-calling. People looked, stared, pointed and laughed. They made comments under their breath. Tolerance was replaced with impatience and fear. Parents pulled their little ones away from my brother like he was leper.

Back then, there were no treatment centers, no schools, no help; parents were on their own. It made it very tough on a young family. It made it almost unbearable on ours.

Thank God, things have changed over the years. Thanks to the Kennedys and many others, today we are better educated and have much more patience and tolerance for the mentally handicapped. Is it enough? Probably not, but at least we've improved. It's a start.

* * *

My parents, *Anthony Dominick Balsamo* and *Noreen Ann Hoffman*, were married in a small Catholic church on Feb. 24, 1951. Visitation Church to be exact, located in the Red Hook section of Brooklyn. They met when my mom's family lived in the projects in Red Hook - a very scary neighborhood to say the least. The projects are a series of large apartment buildings built close together in the older neighborhoods which generally cater to the poor. Most projects have more than their share of crime, drugs, gangs and violence. Mom and dad met when they were just 16 years old at the Red Hook Public Pool. They started dating, fell in love and were married at the tender age of 19. By the time they were 20, my brother, Vito, was born and they were well into life's journey together.

* * *

Let's start with my mom - ladies first. Mom is the oldest of three children born to Stephen and Mary Hoffman. Stephen Hoffman, was born Stephen Macco but was adopted and raised by his stepfather which is where the Hoffman name came from. Grandpa was part Italian and maybe part German and lord knows what else. We however, we would only claim the Italian part. Back then, you weren't highly regarded or respected if you were a mixed breed. And forget anything to do with being German with World War II still fresh in everyone's mind. My grandmother, born Marie Capotosto, was a full-blown Northern Italian. Funny, but our extended families and others looked down their noses at that also. Lord knows, Northern Italians can't cook and they're snobs unlike us Sicilian Italians.

Mom had a younger sister and brother - my Aunt Joan and the baby boy of the family, my Uncle Billy (William). My Aunt Joan was a pretty blond with big boobs and a tough exterior but deep down inside she was a sweetheart. Just don't cross her because she might just give you a piece of her mind or kick your ass. Aunt Joan was once the girlfriend of Joey Gallo (Crazy Joe), the mobster who tried to take over Brooklyn and start the Sixth Family - not his best idea.

Aunt Joan later married Uncle Johnny (John Fezza) and they had two children, my cousins, Melanie and Kenny. After several tumultuous years, Aunt Joan divorced Uncle Johnny because he was a broken down drug addict and a thief and married my Uncle Philly (Phillip Garofolo). Uncle Phil was the cream of the crop. Even though he was involved in the rackets, he loved and took very good care of his family and made a pretty good living. They went on to have four more children together - two girls, Phyllis and Tina, and two boys, Frankie and Steven. Uncle Phil also had an older daughter, Connie, from a previous marriage who lived with them for a while. Aunt Joan was one of my mom's best friends and they spent a lot of time together. Unfortunately for them, they also shared many of life's hardships.

As for my Uncle Billy, he and my grandfather didn't get along very well - or so I'm told. Looking for a way to escape, he lied about his age and joined the Air

Force at the age of 17 and was stationed in California. He later married my Aunt Donna and they had a son, Danny. I don't think I remember my Uncle Billy at all until I was much older. He turned out to be our link to California but that comes later, much later.

* * *

One funny thing about my childhood in Brooklyn is that everyone seemed to have an *ie* or a *y* at the end of their name. Like Billy, Tony, Vinnie, or Paulie. I don't know for sure if that was just a Brooklyn thing or an Italian thing. I like to think it was a loving way to show affection for those close to you. It wasn't - but then hey, this is my story.

Another funny thing about my childhood in Brooklyn is that most adults seemed to have nicknames. Now mind you, they were not always the most flattering or endearing nicknames. No, by no means, in fact, if you had a major flaw or an odd career this might just spark your tag for life. Things like: Tommy Two Toes because he lost three toes on one foot, Fat Vinnie because he weighed 400 pounds, or Bobby the Butcher because he worked as a butcher. I think...I hope? We had a few good ones in our family also. We had Patty the Actor, one of my dad's best friends who had a few bit parts in the movies. My Uncle Red because he drank too much, had red hair and an even redder complexion. My cousin, Baby Vito, who was the youngest of the three Vito's named after my grandfather. Baby Vito was always a big eater and always overweight, even as a young child. So, to hear someone refer to a grown man who weighs over 350 pounds as Baby Vito is just silly. I still, to this day, refer to him that way. I can get away with it because he loves me but I wouldn't recommend it to strangers.

My mom got the tag, Bunny, from her girlfriends. It seems they all picked nicknames for each other as kids and Bunny stuck. My dad had the tag of Fish because he worked at my grandfather's fish market into his late teens. I don't think he liked that nickname very much, and I know my mom resented my dad's family for the Dizzy remarks also. I'm not sure exactly why but I think it had to do with her blond hair and fair skin. There were lots of wise cracks about dizzy blonds back then. However, when my dad called my mom Bunny, it was a loving thing. When he called her Noreen, watch out, he was probably mad. No one close to my dad ever called him Fish to his face. And to his family, he was known as Sonny, which was his mom's nickname for him. I remember calling my dad *"Pop"* once, which is what he called his dad. He quickly made it clear to me that would never happen again and it didn't.

It's funny the things you remember.

* * *

My mom's family seemed to be the better, more normal (whatever that is), wiser family as Italian families go. By the time I was born, Grandpa Hoffman owned a bar and grill in Brooklyn on Furman Street, right next to the highway and across the street from the docks. The Brooklyn Bridge was just up the street and it was and still is a majestic site to see. You know, every time I think of the Brooklyn Bridge or hear its name I'm reminded of a group, The Brooklyn Bridge and one of my favorite songs of all time, "The Worst That Can Happen." It's a sad love song and me, I'm a hopeless romantic, what can I say?

My grandparents' customers consisted of mostly truckers, longshoremen and wise guys who would come in to eat and drink their breakfast, lunch and dinners. Grandpa worked the bar, and grandma worked the kitchen. They both worked long hours and six days a week. I remember on Sundays, grandpa would close the bar and pick us up in his car and we'd go to their restaurant for dinner. Sometimes, it was just my grandparents, mom, Vito and I. But many times, Aunt Joan and my two cousins, Kenny and Melanie, would join us and then it seemed like a big party.

I'm not sure why but my dad and Uncle Johnny never seemed to be invited but back then, we kids didn't seem to mind. We'd eat dinner and play all over the bar and restaurant. I used to love helping grandpa bring up the cases of soda and beer from the cellar. That was my first job and it felt good being such a big help.

After dinner, we would go upstairs to their apartment and we'd watch grandpa's new, giant 24 inch color TV. Now that was the treat of the day! Every Sunday night, we'd watch "Bonanza" with Hoss and Little Joe and the "Wonderful World of Color by Walt Disney." Color TV, wow! What an incredible invention. And who could forget watching "The Wizard of Oz?" Afterward, grandpa would load us all in the car, pick up a newspaper at the St. George Hotel and then drop us off at home. Grandma always slipped my mom some money when grandpa wasn't looking. I never knew or asked why and I didn't care. Sundays were good, peaceful, happy days most of the time.

Grandpa and grandma started out poor and raised their kids in the projects in Red Hook. To come from nothing, escape the projects and end up owning a business was quite an achievement back then. In fact, it is at anytime. My mom, Aunt

Joan and Uncle Billy all went to grade school and on to some high school, which was also a major achievement. Later, they all held jobs! So the Hoffmans were an advanced Americanized type of family back in the 1940s and '50s. They were living the American dream. They were fairly educated; they owned a business, a car and a home. They worked for a living and they saved for a rainy day. They could hold their heads up high because they did it all legally. It looked like a great start for the Hoffman side of the family.

* * *

My dad's side of the family was another story altogether. My great grandparents were honest, hard-working, uneducated Sicilians who escaped to America from a small fishing village in Licata, Sicily. My great grandfather had and four brothers and it's said that one of them may have been the very first Godfather in Brooklyn but we don't talk about that very much so who knows for sure? Besides, back then that kind of talk could get you *whacked*.

Vito and Grace Balsamo, my grandparents, weren't immigrants so they spoke some broken English. However, they preferred to speak Italian most of the time and at home. Because of this, all of their children spoke both English and Italian fluently. Difficult as it must have been for my grandparents, they did their best to raise their six children. They lived in an old, small, three-bedroom apartment on Union Street in Brooklyn above a restaurant. Mom referred to it as a railroad apartment. That's when all the rooms are in a straight line and you have to pass through one to enter another without hallways.

My grandpa, Vito Balsamo, (one of five brothers and seven sisters) owned a small fish market right across the street from their apartment. At that time, Union Street was a very busy part of town. He later owned a second fish market on Court Street that was run by my dad and Uncle Red.

I remember all the shops and markets that lined both sides of Union Street - fish markets, pizza parlors, restaurants, fruit stands, Italian bread and bakeries. I used to love how there was always a steel barrel on fire with the shop workers huddled around it for warmth in the winter. As you walked down the street, you could smell the fresh bread baking and the pizza, oooh the pizza.

I can still hear my dad telling me stories of how he and my grandpa used to get up at four in the morning to go to Fulton Street Fish Market and buy the catch for the day. From his stories, I can envision them working together with their white, blood-stained aprons and a cigarette hanging out of their mouths as they loaded the stands with ice and fish. I can hear as they yelled out, *"Fresh fish, get your fresh fish."*

My grandpa was a very hard-working, honest man and as the story goes, he worked and smoked himself to death. By the time I was born, grandpa had already died of throat cancer. He was a whopping 44 years old. This was the start of the downfall for the Balsamo family, especially the boys who were now quitting school and were out of control.

The Balsamo family consisted of four boys and two girls. The family started with my Uncle Dominick, the oldest, then Aunt Rosie (Rose), Aunt Mary (Maria), my dad, Uncle Sally (Rosalino) and the baby, Uncle Joey (Joseph). This was a very dysfunctional family at best. Most of them never finished grade school and never learned to read and write. The brothers were in and out of trouble most of their lives, and the sisters were pregnant and married way too young.

My grandma, born Grace Incorvaia, was the leader of the family. She was a small, round, tough Italian woman and man, could she cook. She, too, could pack a wallop. She would think nothing of jumping up and slapping one of her sons if he displeased her. Grandma passed away at the ripe old age of 49. She died of a massive heart attack but most claim it was from a broken heart. Her heartache was partly due to losing the love of her life so young and partly from all the heartaches her children (mostly my dad, so they say) bestowed upon her.

My Uncle Dominick married his first cousin, Aunt Francie (Francis Morello), which is a sin by most counts us being Catholic and all. But they fell in love and did it anyway. He was by far, the most educated of all the Balsamos. He went the furthest in school and he could read and write with no problem. He was a World War II hero and a big hunter and fisherman. Later in life, he built a beautiful restaurant in Long Island (The Mermaid) and became a self-made millionaire. He and Aunt Francie had seven children together: Six girls, Gracie, Lenore, Denise, Janet, Rosemarie and Barbara, and then finally the baby boy, Billy (William). We Balsamo's are very persistent and don't give up easy. Uncle Dominick insisted on having a son so he just kept on trying.

I've heard rumors over the years that he also had a mistress and two other children with her but that's another story - his.

Next came my Aunt Rosie, She married Uncle Sammy (Salvatore Russo) and they had two children a boy, Butchie (Salvatore), and Nina (Philomina), my first wife. I'll tell you about that later. For some reason, Uncle Sammy and the Russo clan did not see eye to eye with the Balsamo clan. It's been said that the Russos were better educated and looked down their noses at the Balsamos. The Russo brothers were also big shots down at the docks, bosses or something like that. Back in the day, a longshoreman was a pretty good job, let alone being a boss, and so it seemed that the Russos always had the upper hand on the Balsamos. You might say they just did not get along at all. There were way too many arguments and fights to remember but Uncle Sammy was always in the middle of all of them.

Truth be told, it all started with a fist fight on the docks. One of Uncle Sammy's brothers, a big-time boss and a *made man,* slapped my Uncle Joey in the face and Uncle Sally came to his rescue, flattening the Russo brother. There is an unwritten law that no one can lay a hand on a made man without permission from the upper ranks in the family. There was talk of killing the Balsamo boys over this. However, the Balsamo's were a big well-connected family and peace was agreed upon. But there were always hard feelings after that.

My Aunt Mary was my favorite. She helped me through some of the toughest years of my young life. She was a blessing to me but she cussed like a drunken sailor and oh, what a temper. She was a big, burly, Italian woman and might have been the toughest member of the whole Balsamo family. And believe me, they were all pretty tough. I can remember my Aunt Mary throwing a neighborhood *shylock* down a flight of stairs for getting nasty with her. The poor fellow was just trying to collect the money she owed him but that didn't stop her. And with the Balsamo boys as her brothers, well, he just kind of accepted it, which was the lesser of two evils.

Aunt Mary married my Uncle Red (Santo Garafolo) at a very young age, 16 I think. He was, as they referred to him, *"a piece of bread."* This is a term of endearment that meant he was an easy-going, nice, gentleman. Not the wise-guy type like the rest of our family. Uncle Red was truly a hard-working, honest, good guy. He took a lot of shit from my Aunt Mary and the Balsamo family. Maybe that's why he drank so much. They had three children, two boys and a girl. The first was my cousin, Donny (Dominick), who was my idol, and then there were Vito and Sandra.

Next, came my dad. He and mom had us two boys and later on, came the baby of our family, my sister, **Jacqueline Rose Balsamo**. By the time Jackie was born I was already nine, a young man of the world. Lucky me, now I had a pain-in-the-ass baby sister to worry about.

Uncle Sally, born Rosalino, hated his name and changed it to Sal. Believe me, no one was allowed to ever say the name Rosalino. I get nervous just thinking

8

about it. He married Aunt Jeanie (Jane) and they had two boys and a girl. Baby Vito was the oldest, followed by Gracie (Grace) and Larry (Laurence). My Uncle Sally was the hardest working of all the Balsamo brothers. He was a longshoreman and worked on the docks for many years. He also may have been the least-educated and meanest of the brothers. I can't ever remember him smiling or being in a good mood. He scared the shit out of all of us and he would beat the crap out of my cousin, Vito - often.

Uncle Sally went on to own a car service on Court Street and he did very well for himself and his family. My aunt was nicknamed Jeanie by my grandma who couldn't pronounce Jane so Jeanie it was; whatever grandma wanted became law. Aunt Jeanie (another blond) and my mom became very good friends and would spend a lot of time together over the years. They, too, shared a lot in common and bonded together to fend off the Balsamo sisters, who could be cruel to them at times.

Last but not least, was my Uncle Joey, another of my favorites. Uncle Joey came along later in life for my grandparents and was just a baby when his dad died. Uncle Joey and my cousin, Donny (Aunt Mary's eldest), were so close in age that they were best of friends as kids. With my grandfather dying so young, my dad claims to have helped raise Joey but then so did Aunt Mary and Aunt Rosie. Either way, whoever did, they didn't do a very good job; he was a bit of a terror. Uncle Joey ran around with Crazy Joe Gallo, the man who tried to start the Sixth Family ("The Mad Ones" by Tom Folsom is the title of a book about him).

In New York, there were only *Five Families*, one for each borough (Brooklyn, Queens, the Bronx, Staten Island and Manhattan). Joey Gallo and his outlaw crew had other ideas and the five families didn't agree with them. That started one of the worst mob wars in New York history. As it turns out, Uncle Joey was one of the few lucky ones who lived to tell about it. He married Aunt Yvonne and they had a daughter, Joette. Of all the brothers and sisters, only Uncle Joey ever divorced and then remarried. Aunt Debbie came along later in life for him but she was never really accepted into the family. Seems back then, divorce was frowned upon. She seemed to make him very happy and, for some of us, that's all that mattered. They never had any children of their own. But they had a condo in Brooklyn, a home in New Jersey and a house in Florida - all paid in full. Not bad for a low-ranking mobster.

After years of all the crazy gangster stuff, Uncle Joey would go on to run a very successful shylock business in Brooklyn, which Uncle Sally lent him the money to start. This is the business of lending money to those who can't borrow from a bank at a very high interest rate. So, he was a banker so to speak, just one you always wanted to pay timely. ***Or else!***

* * *

So there you have it - lots of family, lots of cousins, lots of second and third cousins, aunts and uncles. It was all very confusing when we would get together for holidays. Way back when, family tradition was everything. You named your children after your parents, brothers and sisters so we had many Vitos, Gracies, Dominicks, Marys and Tonys. Not that many Stevens, Hmmm? Whenever someone would call out a name, six people would answer.

The dinners were big, loud and had lots of great Italian food. Everyone in our family was a great cook, and everyone pitched in. The lasagna, meatballs, sausage, the soup, it was all so good we ate until we almost exploded. Then, the Italian coffee and desserts, wow. The crowds were always loud and hearty. It all seemed to be just one, big, happy family. Little did I know at that time. I think I loved that part of my childhood the most but I really can't remember all that much. As a young child, the first five years are mostly a blur. The memories I have are mostly all good. They consist of family gatherings, holidays, toys, love, caring and ***no fear***.

We were taught it was great to be a Balsamo. It was great to be an Italian, and it was great to be a New Yorker. I was, and still am to this day, very proud of that.

* * *

And then my young life took a turn for the worse. I started to grow up. I had to grow up way too young. I started the first grade at five years old. That's when it all started to change for me. I started to understand things that I would soon come to regret. When you're just a baby, life seems to protect you from the horrors of the real world. You just don't understand what's going on around you nor should you have to. No children in this great world should have to endure pain, fear, worry or hunger. That's why we have our parents, uncles and aunts. The adults to protect us, the innocent.

* * *

This is my story; it's ***"Through My Eyes" as I've seen it through each stage of my life growing up.***

My great grandfather Dominick Balsamo (seated), my Grandpa Vito (far right) and his four brothers.

Grandpa's Fish Market on Union Street.

Mom and Day's wedding: best man George, maid of honor Aunt Joan, Mom, Dad and Uncle Joey as a boy.

The Hoffman family: (left to right) Uncle Billy, Aunt Joan, Grandpa (Steve) and Grandma (Mary).

The Balsamo family: Uncle Dominick, Grandma (Grace) and Uncle Sally.

The Balsamo family: Aunt Rosie, Grandma and Aunt Mary.

CHAPTER 2
THE FORMATIVE YEARS

Let me start out by saying that although I remember a lot of things over the next five years, putting them in chronological order is a bit challenging. After all, this was between the time I was five to ten years of age, so excuse me if I get things a little out of sequence. Also, I'd like to point out that I spent most of my life trying to forget my childhood; it wasn't very pretty. So now I'm putting the bits and pieces back together one by one. I'm telling you, the beginning of my story through a child's eyes, *my eyes.*

As children, we seem to remember the worst of things, the scariest things and the very best things. All the rest in the middle seems to fade away. I'd also like to throw in that some of my memories may not be exactly as others in the family might remember them so please excuse me. I was just a child, it was a long time ago and I would never want to hurt or offend any of my relatives or friends. I love and respect them all very much.

Another thing I'd like to point out is that there are two ways to write your own story. First, you can tell what pleases you - like your accomplishments, achievements and all the good things that have happened in your life. These are the events that make you look and sound great and I've had more than my share.

And then there is the second way, which is how I chose to write my story. It's where you let it all hang out, the good, the bad and the ugly. You have to let yourself go completely and be totally honest and vulnerable. You tell the truth as you know and believe it to be and let the pieces fall where they may. After all, we're human and if you're going to write your own autobiography then you owe it to yourself and your readers to be up front and honest, even if it hurts.

I also must admit, I have never written much of anything in my life. My education was very limited. I can't spell or type very well so I hunt and peck with two fingers and thank God for computers and spell check. I will say, as I'm writing, I'm self-educating and learning a lot along the way. I've read more books in this past two years than in the past ten combined.

One last thing. Some of the terms and language used throughout this book are **not** *politically correct*, and they are **not** meant to be. They're also not what I feel or believe but reflect the nature of the times, so please no offense intended. I also took the liberty to change most of the names (other than family and close friends) to protect the guilty.

OK, enough excuses; I just wanted set the record straight. Now, back to my story…

* * *

New York, in the 1940s and '50s, was the melting pot for the world. Immigrants from all over the world would arrive in New York City, and many of them ended up in Brooklyn. Talk about a strange, scary, yet wonderful place to grow up. We had it all but let's start with the strange and scary and the crazy things we learn.

First we have *discrimination.* If you were different, we hated you. It was just that simple. In our neighborhood, we had the Italians, the guinnies, the wops, many who couldn't speak a word of English but somehow we thought we were superior to the rest. We had the Blacks, spades, niggers, (the "N" word, a truly ugly term for anyone). They were the real troublemakers, wanting equal rights and all that. We had the Jews, the kikes, they were going to take over the world and own everything, and how did they get so rich anyway? They didn't even believe in Jesus and what was with those sideburns and funny little caps? Next, we had the Puerto Ricans, spics, filthy people who were going to ruin the neighborhood and spoke Spanish of all things. Throw in a few of the Irish drunks, some German Nazis, some Asian chinks and a few Japs and this is what we called the neighborhood. We had a derogatory name for everyone and everything. Heck, we were equal opportunity racist. We were a bit prejudiced to say the least. It's enough to scare anyone to death, let alone a child.

How did we become so ignorant?

* * *

Now I have my own theory on racism. It seems to me that 99 % of the people on this planet are at least a bit racist or prejudiced *if* they would never admit it to themselves. The problem is most of us deny it and lie to ourselves and everyone else. Like an alcoholic who has to work at being sober every day the rest of their lives, the first thing you have to do is admit you have a problem. Only then can you work on it and let the healing begin. All too many of us say we're not this or that but we are. We're all just a little guilty, black and white and everything in between. If we honestly looked into our hearts, really looked and tried, this world would become a better, safer place for everyone. I hate the fact that we have the words: bigotry, prejudice and racism in our language. They are nasty words, words we could all do without. But hey, what do I know? Maybe I still see things through the eyes of a child. Okay, off my soapbox.

* * *

In the neighborhood, everyone had their own little pocket, their turf so to speak. So at a very young age you were taught not to go here or there because those *undesirables* lived and hung out there. It's funny how quickly children learn and adapt to such ugly things. How we learn to hate others at such a young age because we're a little different from each other. I, on the other hand, didn't hate anyone but I was sure scared to death of everyone who was different or strange to me. We hear all these nasty terms battered around and they just become a way of life. We think it's normal to point, to stare, to hate. It's not! It's a shame that people can't just get along, but they never have and I'm afraid they never will.

Next, you had all the really *bad guys*. These were the Italian gangsters, the mobsters with names like wise guys, the Mafia, the Family, the Black Hand. But, somehow we Italians, well, we were okay with them. I guess we gave them a pass because they were like us - Italians, family. After all, they were protecting our neighborhood from the other races trying to move in and take over. Heck, they could be your uncle or cousin and they usually were in most cases. Just don't get in the way of a stray bullet or a getaway car.

Then you had the *drug dealers* and the *drug addicts* these were very scary people - blacks and Puerto Ricans according to the popular view. They were screwing up the good name of booze, prostitution and gambling with all that drug trafficking. And let's not forget what they were doing to our neighborhood; they were ruining it by trying to take over.

Now, look out for all the *young gangs*. You had brass knuckles and Garrison belts, pipes and bats, switchblade knives and zip guns. For crying out loud, a guy could get his head handed to him if he wasn't careful. The streets were a very dangerous and scary place, especially at night. At night, the alleys were dark, cats cried out, dogs howled and the drunks hovered in dark corners. As a young boy, if I were out after dark it was to go to the store for milk or cigarettes. I would run down the middle of the street so I wouldn't get jumped (yes, back then a kid could buy cigarettes for their parents and we did). I learned at a very young age that if you ran fast and were already running, you'd have a big head start and nobody could catch you.

* * *

Now, at the ripe old age of five, I was starting on my journey to school. I was very young to be going into first grade because I was born very late in the year, December. Most of my classmates were already six, a full year older and bigger than me. I remember that being the hot topic of discussion in our family at that time. I think mom wanted to get me out of the house and off to school as soon as possible so she could have a little peace and just tend to my brother. Having two boys a year apart and one with a serious learning disability was a major challenge. We were wild kids. My parents couldn't take us anywhere. It got so that we weren't welcome in people's homes, let alone nice restaurants or movie theaters.

I remember one time, my Grandma Hoffman babysat Vito and I so my mom and dad could go out for the evening. Somehow, we convinced her to sit in a chair and play Cowboys and Indians with us. We managed to tie her to the chair and stick her in the arm with a fork until she bled. Needless to say, when my parents came home and found my grandma tied to the chair and crying, we got the beating of our lives.

Another time, my brother and I took turns throwing a hard ball at my dad's beautiful fish tank that sat on top of our console TV. Well, I guess the ball won because there was fish, glass and water all over the place. I think I threw the winning shot but I blamed Vito just the same. Let's face it; being slow, he was an easy target. We made a mess of the apartment below us and ruined their ceiling and floors. I think we got our butts kicked once again.

My poor mom would get into many fights with the neighbors over us and the crazy things we did. I remember Vito and I sitting in the doorway of our apartment watching mom and the neighbor, Ginger, go at it over us making noise with our rocking horses. Seems we were disturbing her sick mom while she slept in the apartment below us. She gave my mom a pretty good beating. She pulled her hair and scratched her face. My Grandma Balsamo was visiting her sister-in law, Aunt Netty, one floor below us. When she heard the commotion she rushed out into the hall and beat the heck out of that lady. It's been rumored that she was pregnant and miscarried shortly after that. Nowadays, someone would go to jail or there would be a lawsuit but not back then. It just quietly went away.

I think my brother and I got the crap beat out of us often but we never seemed to get the message. Vito couldn't learn and I was young and full of piss and vinegar so we made quite a pair. Mom never could seem to control us and dad wasn't around all that much. I think we were part of the reason he went out so much - at least that's what mom would tell us.

Vito was always getting into trouble and he was a little dangerous to himself and others. He was a real fire bug and loved to play with matches. He'd also hang out the windows and one time he almost fell out but my Uncle Johnny caught him by his feet and pulled him back in. It's a good thing because we lived four stories up. My dad had safety bars installed on the windows after that but that didn't stop Vito. He had no fear and he would climb down the fire escape or get up early and sneak outside in his underwear. I think he was trying to break out but he always got caught. Maybe he wanted to go to school?

* * *

Talking about Vito and almost falling out a window just gave me a thought. Windows! Most of us, throughout this great country, don't give windows a whole lot of thought. We cover them with drapes, blinds and shutters. We stick furniture in front of them and every now and then we open one up to get a little fresh air.

In Brooklyn, windows are the *eyes of your home,* the gateway to the neighborhood. Through our windows in our apartment we could see Clinton Street from the front, the side alley from the side windows and the back alley through the rear windows. As a kid, I would run from window to window to see if my friends were outside playing. When we were babies, mom would only open them from the top so we couldn't fall out. Funny, but as we got a little older, she would open them from the bottom. Maybe after getting to know us a little better she was hoping we'd fall out.

Our front windows were used for many things like watching the kids play, talking to the neighbors, checking the traffic or the weather, tossing down coins for ice cream or just taking in the sunset and relaxing. I have seen people arguing with each other from windows, calling up the kids for dinner or just waiting to see their guests arrive. Sometimes, you found a parking space from the window. The sweet kids we were growing up, we used windows to throw all kinds of things down at the passing cars or neighbors' kids. Things like marbles, candy, water balloons or eggs. We thought that was real funny but we always got caught and got our butts whipped.

Our side windows were a real kick. From these windows, you could see right into the neighbors' apartments, which helped with sex education. I had a girl from my class who lived next door and she would pass me the homework from her window so I could copy it. I was always trying to sneak a peek at her or her older sister dressing. All of these side windows had clothes lines and everyone would hang out their wash to dry. We always knew what kind of underwear the neighbors wore and we snickered about that a lot. One time, mom spotted a giant owl sitting on our clothes line, which about scared her to death. Another time, I had a monkey looking in my bedroom window at me. Yes, a monkey. It seems one of our neighbors was monkey-sitting (if you can believe that) so they just tied a rope around its neck and let it climb all over the outside of our building.

From the rear windows, you could see the back alley and many more apartment buildings and windows. What I would've given for a pair of binoculars back then. These rear windows had the fire escapes so in case of an emergency you could get out and down to the street. But somehow, we managed to find all sorts of uses for them. Like monkey bars, we played on them. Some people used them to hang clothes or just to hang out listening to music under the moonlight with your best girl. I've seen plants and trees (and pot) growing on them, people having a beer or a smoke and let's not forget the barbeques. I think in Brooklyn, we find many uses for everything. We seem to cover all the bases.

* * *

Going to school was kind of cool in the beginning. There were lots of kids and it looked like a great place to be. I went to a Catholic school, Sacred Hearts of Jesus and Mary, which belonged to the St. Stevens Church. It was a large four-story building with a big concrete yard out back and a block wall that surrounded the yard. All of the boys and girls had to wear *"the uniform,"* which made us seem the same but we weren't. The boys wore gray, bell-hop pants with a burgundy stripe down each leg. We also wore a white, collared, dress shirt with a burgundy tie that had the schools initials on it. Burgundy leather shoes, a burgundy belt and a burgundy sweater - also with the school's initials on it completed the ensemble. I guess burgundy must have been the hot color for that school, and having the initials on everything never let us forget where we belonged. I looked cute in my uniform. I remember wanting the sweater so bad when I first started school but it took a while for mom to afford it. Later on, we got the blazer as we graduated to the upper grades.

The girls wore a plaid gray and, you guessed it, burgundy skirt, a white blouse with a burgundy kind of bow tie, white knee high socks and burgundy shoes. They wore the same sweaters as the boys and trust me, they looked hot. Even today, when I see a woman in a plaid skirt with knee high socks and a sweater, I go crazy.

Our school went from the first to the eighth grades so you had a lot of different ages of kids together. Five-year-olds mixed in with teens was not the best plan. Back in Brooklyn, we didn't have middle school or junior high. We went straight from grade school to high school, right into the ninth grade. I remember an older girl in the building next door to us used to walk me and her kid sister to and from school the first year. By second grade, I was going to school by myself. Now, as I remember it, I had to walk two miles each way through rain, sleet and snow. Trust me, I really believed that for many years. When I was about 40, my wife and I went back to Brooklyn and only then did I realize that it was actually only five blocks. Even today, it still seems like two miles to me. I guess that's the way some things look to a child, larger than life.

As time passed and I grew more aware of my surroundings and my life, things started to deteriorate for me. I always wondered why I got to go to school while my older brother stayed at home. It was then that the term *retarded* started to have some real meaning to me. At school, a lot of the kids would make fun of my brother because he was what they used to refer to back then as *Mongoloid*. This is a form of mental retardation that makes many of those who have it look very similar. The best way I could describe it through my young eyes was a round head with kind of slanted eyes and a pug nose. He was really very cute, why couldn't they just see that?

In a school full of Catholic white kids, mostly Italian or Irish, all from a radius of about 20 city blocks, everyone gets to know everything about everybody. It's amazing what kids pick up from their parents and how cruel they can be in repeating it. Let's face it, teasing has been and always will be a part of a kid's life. We all do it. By now, I started to understand the real differences between me and my big brother who was starting to become smaller than me. Another flaw in Down syndrome is not only does the mind not seem to grow but the body seems to slow also. Vito, my big brother, the kid I slept with night after night for many years, my hero, was now becoming a major distraction and problem in my life.

I never could understand why people had to make fun of him and the way he looked. So, at a very young age I started to defend him. Fights at school were becoming more and more frequent. The same kids who were my friends just hours before were quickly becoming my tormentors and enemies. And just when I thought things couldn't get worse, I started to notice that my dad and mom were beginning to have problems also. Dad would just go missing from time to time.

* * *

Anthony Dominick Balsamo. My dad, Tony, *"was as cool as the other side of the pillow."* He was tall, about six feet, and for Italians, that's pretty tall. He also had a nice built. He had a head full of wavy black hair and a fairly dark complexion. My dad was a handsome man (the Dean Martin type) and he knew it and flaunted it. Dad was one of the best-dressed men in all of Brooklyn. He wore hand-tailored suits, fedora hats, the best Italian leather shoes and belts money could buy and I'll never forget his full-length camel's hair coat. Dad was a real ladies' man and a man's man. The women loved him and the men emulated and respected him. His hands were always well manicured and he was always clean shaven, by a barber no less. All his clothes were dry cleaned and sharply pressed. Dad had rings, watches and a gold chain around his neck. He always drove a brand new convertible Cadillac, his favorite car for life. Money spilled freely all over town. He was your stereotypical cool wise guy.

We lived at 387 Clinton St., Brooklyn 31, New York. Top floor left, to be exact. That address was drummed into me as a very young child. In Brooklyn back in the 1950s, Clinton Street was the high end of the neighborhood. All of the buildings had higher rents, are larger apartments, and the bottom floors were reserved for professionals, such as doctors, lawyers and dentists. Heck, you could see the New York City skyline from our windows and rooftop. The neighborhood library was across the street, and the police station was right around the corner. We had a large, three-bedroom apartment with a living room, formal dining room, kitchen, bathroom and a house full of fine furniture. Oh, and that dreaded dumbwaiter and fire escape.

* * *

You just can't believe how I hated that dumbwaiter and the fire escape. They were two of the scariest things in life to me. Somewhere in my younger years, I heard stories of how the crooks would come up the dumbwaiter or the fire escape in buildings and break into apartments. I never forgot them. Finally, one day my worst fear became reality. We had gone out to dinner and when we got home, our front door was locked from the inside and someone was robbing our house. The really frightening part was that we could hear them inside. Sure enough, they came up the fire escape and escaped the same way. It scared the living crap out of me and I was never the same after that. Dad wasn't around all that much so that made things worse. I always feared someone would break in at night and hurt my family.

You know, now that I mention it, I was scared of a lot of things. We had to go up three flights of stairs to our apartment, down small halls that were kind of dark and narrow. Sometimes, the bulb would be out, and it would be really dark. We lived just below the stairs to the rooftop and I always believed someone would come down that way. We had a glass back door in our living room that had a crappy little lock on it and I hated that door. I'll bet I checked the lock at least once a day even though no one ever used it. I also didn't care much for looking out the windows four stories up. I was afraid I'd fall out. Let's see: buses, the subway, nighttime, strange men checking out my mom, the cellar in our building, the rooftop, bullies, drunks, bums, drug addicts - you name it and I feared it. Everything except the wise guys, I was fascinated by them and even looked up to them, I think we all did. After all, they were the real men in the neighborhood - not the poor slobs who worked hard for a living. Nah, they were the suckers.

* * *

What did my dad do for a living to afford to live on Clinton Street? Well, not much. My dad worked for his father in the fish market for most of his childhood years. Work and my dad didn't agree much so soon after my grandpa died, dad went on his merry way to become a wise guy. He had a small restaurant with his mom for a short time and the fish market with his older brother, but neither lasted long. Dad loved the life of the wise guy. If you don't know what a wise guy is then see the movie "Goodfellas." That was my family to a T, at least through my eyes. I don't think there were any Stevens in that movie either, were there? Oh well, sometimes you just have to accept things for what they are.

Dad hung out with many wise guys, some of whom were very important people in the neighborhood. Because of his personality, my dad was one of the most popular guys around town. Everybody knew Tony. He was well-connected, well-liked and everybody's best friend. My dad was loved by one of the most powerful Godfathers in all of New York and, because of this, he was making a $1,000 a week booking numbers, when most longshoremen were working 50 hours and making a $100. My dad ran the numbers business in Brooklyn for the under-boss and his mentor, no names please. He hung out in the best clubs and restaurants. He ate well, drank well and partied way too much. He was living large. Tony was king.

When I was very young, dad would wake me up in the middle of the night to ask me to give him *"three numbers."* These were the numbers he would play the next day, kind of like the lotto except the game was illegal and run by the mob. I would always give him numbers that were either threes or multiples of three. He hit the numbers (which meant he won) a few times on 3-3-3 and 3-6-9, numbers I gave him.

Today, my favorite number is *three*. Hmm, I wonder why. I remember even in first grade, I was the third kid in line, the third seat in class and the third named called when they took roll. I never figured out that it had something to do with my last name starting with a B. Throughout my life, I've always looked for the number three in everything I do; I still believe it's my lucky number to this day.

* * *

Now, back at the ranch I could see my mom and dad were beginning to have some real problems. At first, they seemed to be simple arguments but then they grew into full knock-down brawls. Most of the knocking down was done by my dad to my mother but mom was a game fighter and always came back for more. By the time I was six or seven years old, I can remember standing between them pleading with them not to hit each other. Dad, you see, would go away for days at a time. Mom didn't seem to like this so she would get into big fights with him. In some small defense of my dad, it was my mom who would always start with the hitting. Then dad would always finish it off by giving her a beating and my brother and I would scream and cry for them to stop. Then dad would get cleaned up and dressed and use that as an excuse to go out again. I remember standing in front of the front door crying, trying to block his way as he pushed past me to leave. I'd beg him not to go but he always did...

Dad, I guess, would go on binges with girlfriends and my mom just couldn't take the embarrassment and humiliation of it all. I guess she would rather walk around with big, dark sunglasses on to cover up the black eyes but there wasn't much she could do to hide the bruises and fat lips. I couldn't believe a man could hit a woman with such fury, let alone his wife, someone he loved. I hated, feared and resented my dad very much for this. This is one of the first of many valuable lessons I would learn from my dad at a young age.

* * *

I swore I would never raise a hand to my wife. I never have and I never will.

* * *

Noreen Ann Hoffman. My mom was a beautiful, young, intelligent woman. She was 5'2, thin, with blond hair, hazel eyes and a great shape. She, too, dressed very well and very stylishly. Unlike most Italian women of the day, mom had the makeup, the manicured nails and toes and the latest hairdo for the time. Everywhere we went, men's heads whipped around as she passed. And like most Italian women, she had a serious temper and could let it fly.

Mom worked before marriage. She had an office job which she liked but once married she was no longer allowed to work. My dad wouldn't hear of it. To him and his kind, that would be a disgrace. I don't think mom could ever understand why my dad had to go out with other women when he had such a prize at home. To top it off, he left her home trapped, as she would remind us often, with two young, wild, uncontrollable kids to deal with. He was out living it up in fine restaurants and clubs with his buddies and girlfriends spending money like there was no tomorrow while she was home attending to two boys 24 hours a day, seven days a week. I think she subconsciously resented us for that. I remember that Vito would be sick a lot also and that was an added burden on her. Mentally handicapped kids seem to get sick a lot. Their immune systems just don't work as well as ours and they catch everything and it lasts longer. It seemed Vito was becoming a major problem for everyone. Little did I know?

* * *

People used to say that the neighborhood had *eyes.* In Brooklyn, we had relatives or friends on just about every block, so word traveled very rapidly. The Balsamo family tree branched out to the Batistas, the Russos, the Morellos, the Incorvias and the Garofalos among others. These were all very large, prominent families known throughout the neighborhood. If my dad was seen on the street with another woman, it didn't take long for my mom to hear all the dirty details. If mom was seen with another black eye, everyone knew about it in short time. And Vito, for crying out loud, everything he did became a front-page story. The whole family and neighborhood knew every detail of our lives. So with my dad and the Balsamo family being so well known and popular, it was a bit of a curse.

Gossip, another of the wonderful things we learn all too young.

* * *

Still, most kids will never have some of the experiences that we were afforded growing up in a small city neighborhood. I know it was scary at times but it was also very safe at the same time. At five years old, you were outside playing on your block with all the neighbors' kids. Moms hung out the windows watching and chatting with each other as we played. The neighbors watched out for all the kids, and everyone knew everybody. Women walked the streets freely with their strollers or sat on the stoops with their infants. Today, you can't do that in the safest of neighborhoods. Parents are afraid to leave their children unattended for a second with all of the dangers in the world. It's a darn shame the world has come to that. When we were kids, the biggest fears our parents had were that we would get lost, hit by a car or get a skinned knee while we were playing.

And the games we played: Ring-a-Levio, Tops, Skelizes, Freeze Tag, War and Hide-and-Seek. All you needed was your imagination and a friend or two. Little did I know how much an imagination would save me as time went on but we'll get to that soon enough. We had more fun with a bag of marbles, a yoyo, some baseball cards or a few bottle caps then kids today with all their computer games and cell phones put together.

I loved to roller skate and ride my bike all over the neighborhood. If you wandered too far it never failed that you would run into a relative or family friend who would chase you home. I loved to run into my Uncle Dominick. He always gave me a $10 bill and told me to get lost. We hitched rides on the back of buses to get around town. We went to the candy store and bought penny candies when a dime would buy you a bag full. Today, there are no candy stores and no penny candies. I think they were all replaced by liquor stores, and now a candy bar costs close to a dollar at the market. My favorite foods in the world were rice balls, a meatball sandwich and a slice of pizza. My favorite drink was a Manhattan Special (coffee soda) or an egg cream. Guess what? They still are.

When we were growing up in Brooklyn, we didn't have the nice grass ball parks like kids have today. We didn't know about Little League or Pop Warner but we didn't care. We played in the street. We made up our own games. We played stoop ball and most people today don't even know what a *stoop* is. It's the steps leading up to your apartment building, so there. We played fist ball, stick ball, and hand ball; we used manhole covers and car door handles as bases. Out of bounds was a building or a sidewalk. All we needed was a rubber ball; gloves were optional.

On real hot summer days, we would run and play in the *Johnny Pump* also known as a fire hydrant. If you had a wrench and an empty tomato sauce can, you could have a ball until the fire department or police came around and shut down the water. Minutes after they left, we'd turn it back on. We collected stamps, coins and baseball cards. We played with chemistry sets and spiders and heck, we even had a library card. The girls in the neighborhood played house, jump rope, hula hoop or hop scotch. They had Barbie dolls and record players and they giggled a lot.

We hung out on corners, at candy stores or at the pizza parlor. We went on dates to ice cream parlors, movie theaters or roller skating rinks as we got older. These were simple times that provide some of my fondest memories. Kids today just don't do these types of things. I miss all of that. I wish the world would stop changing so fast. It's changing and not always for the best.

But then, ***"That's life, what can I tell you."***

This quote is a *Stevism,* one of the many sayings I use in my life. I love that saying. It's a quote from one of my favorite movies "Meet Joe Black," spoken by Sir Anthony Hopkins. I've always said that,

"If wisdom had a voice, it would be that of Anthony Hopkins." Another *Stevism.*

Get used to them. I've adopted plenty of them over the years and I've used them to help shape my life. Not having much of a formal education, I would hear sayings, clichés for lack of a better term, that I would find a deeper meaning in and I would use them to build my belief system. My dad was famous for having a saying, a cliché, for just about everything and I learned many things from him (and his sayings). 'Til this day, whenever we move into a new house or office we throw salt over our shoulder and buy a new broom. When anyone in our family gets a new car, we put something red in it for good luck. Dad had more theories and superstitions than most. However, most of my life lessons I can attribute to my dad. From his preaching, I learned some really good things and, from his actions, I learned a lot of things in life not to do, too.

* * *

Another great thing about our neighborhood was all the great food and delivery men. I think if you owned a phone you could have almost anything delivered - from pizzas to groceries to drugs. We had the mailman, the Fuller brush man, the milkman, the Drakes Cake man, the watermelon truck, the fruit and vegetable carts, the ice cream man, the Italian ices cart, the vacuum cleaner salesman and the newspaper boys. Heck, even the butcher delivered and so did the fish markets. As a matter of fact, when we got sick, the doctor would come to the house and for haircuts, the barber made house calls also. Let's not forget the organ grinder and his monkey and the neighborhood gypsies. We even had trucks that drove around the neighborhood with rides on them. Yeah, rides! Like a Ferris wheel or spinning tea cups. For a dime or a quarter, you could have a blast.

We enjoyed lots of church processions, bazaars, feasts and street fairs. I loved to go to them with all the food, games and rides. My favorites were the red candy apples and the cotton candy. I just loved all the excitement; it was a blast. I would beg my mom to take me everyday they were open but most days, she would say "*no*." So I would go down to the corner, climb up on the mailbox where I could see the fair going on one street down. It's there, I'd sit and cry because I couldn't go.

* * *

Okay, let's get back to reality. Must we? I was having so much fun. But yes, we must, because life isn't always fun; life is hard, it's work and painful. People are mean and hateful. Someone is always out to get you, use you or take advantage of you. More of the wonderful things we're taught all too young. He's black, she's Hispanic, he has only one leg, she's a whore, he's a drunk, she's gay, they're homeless. And it seemed to me that everyone was bad and scary for one reason or another.

I think we just made shit up as we went along.

* * *

By the third grade, I dreaded going to school. On Sunday nights, when mom would say, "*Get to bed, you've got school in the morning,*" I would get sick to my stomach, literally sick. I knew that tomorrow I'd have to figure a different route to school to avoid this one or that bully. I couldn't go down that street because that's where the public school was and that's where all the bad kids were. I couldn't go that way because all the junkies hung out there and forget going this way because that's where all the card clubs and gangsters hung. So remember when I said earlier that it seemed like a two-mile walk to me? Well, that's because most days, it was.

Once I got to school and the safe haven of Catholic kids, priests and who could forget the nuns, things didn't get much better. I was falling behind. I was very distracted. I was teased in the hallways and bathrooms. It got to a point where I wouldn't use the restrooms in school at all. I tried to travel through the halls as quickly as possible. I would forget to do my homework. That's not true I just didn't do it. I could never read and study at home. I just didn't know how and I couldn't concentrate there anyway. I started to become the class clown because if they were laughing with you, it was better than having them laugh at you. I thought this might make the other kids laugh and like me, but it didn't help much.

Needless to say, the nuns didn't appreciate my humor much. I had to make many trips to the hall where they would slap my face and then tell me to go back inside and sit down. Now, if that wasn't humiliating enough, sometimes they would have me stand in front of the class where they would beat my bottom with a large wooden ruler while everyone watched. One time, I had to kneel on my hands under the teacher's desk in front of the whole class. It seemed like hours but now my best guess is it was probably 15 minutes. Man, minutes can last an eternity when you're young and embarrassed. After school and at lunch it was more of the same - the teasing, the taunting, the bullying. Kids can be so cruel.

I remember when I couldn't wait for lunch break to get out to the school yard for a great game of fist ball with the guys. We'd eat our sandwiches between innings while our teammates batted. The girls would hang out and watch and giggle as we got a hit or made an out. Sometimes, we'd go down the street and if we had lunch money we'd get a great big meatball, sausage or tuna sandwich and a Manhattan Special at this house that became a store only at lunch time. Oh, those were the good ole' days.

You shouldn't have good ole' days at that tender age; they should all be good days. On the way home from school, I'd look for a different route because it seemed to me that my old friends were just waiting for me to turn the next corner. The teasing never stopped and the bullies were everywhere but most days I made it home in one piece. And then one day one of my best friends in the world hit me in the face with a dose of reality.

* * *

Paul Cammarie was my best friend and we called him Paulie (big surprise). He was one of the coolest kids around and I loved him. He was a star to me. He had the perfect life, the perfect family. His folks owned the Cammarie Bakery on the corner of Henry and Sackett streets about a block from my house. This is the very same bakery made famous in the movie "Moonstruck" with Nicolas Cage and Cher. (Again, no Steves in that movie either, what's up with that?) I grew up playing in and around that bakery for what seemed like years. I can still smell and taste the fresh Italian bread his dad would give to us in the basement of that store.

Paulie was a little bigger than me, a good-looking Italian boy. He was always the captain of everything. I would just die when he would choose me to be on one of his teams. He was my *"bestest good friend"* to quote Tom Hanks from the movie "Forrest Gump." Paulie and his family lived in the apartment above the bakery. His cousin, Nicky, and his family lived in the apartment next door. It was truly a family affair.

I remember the first time I ever really kissed a girl (if you can call it that), Paulie and I were on a double-date. We were about 11 years old and we took our dates for a slice of pizza and then down to the park to make out. I'll never forget that day for as long as I live. Her name was Vince (short for Vincenza). She was a really cute Italian girl and she didn't speak very good English but I couldn't care less. I was in love. We went behind the bathroom building for some privacy and then I kissed her. It was going great until she started opening her mouth and I couldn't figure out why. I'm thinking, doesn't she know how to kiss?

Well, Paulie got a real kick out of that story on the way home and I got a great lesson. I needed to learn how to French kiss. It sounded disgusting to me but I was ready and willing to make the sacrifice. For some reason, Vince never did give me the chance to try with her again and I was heartbroken. My good buddy, Paulie, must have taken mercy on me that day. He never mentioned it to anyone as far as I knew. Thank God, they both took mercy on me.

I was on my way over to Paulie's house one afternoon to see if he wanted to come out and play catch. Little did I know but my whole world would come crashing down around me that day. As I approached the bakery, Paulie, his cousin Nicky and some of our friends were out front playing ball. All of a sudden, it happened. Paulie told me that his parents didn't want him to hang around with me anymore and I was to stay away from them, the bakery and their street. I was shocked. *"Why?"* I asked. The rumor was that my dad was a *"drug addict and a thief"* and they didn't want my kind around anymore. *"My kind,"* I thought. What did I do? I was crushed and in denial. How could Paulie, my pal, make up such a story just to hurt and humiliate me in front of everybody? And why? I told him he was an f---ing liar and I ran away. I had nowhere else to go so I went home.

* * *

Suddenly, things started to make a little more sense to me. I now looked at everything differently. I noticed that lately, my dad wasn't going away as much and mom and dad fought over different things, mostly money. I started to pay closer attention when I was home. As a kid, you tend to ignore the dirty little details of your parents' fights. You mostly just want it to stop and please, no hitting. Funny thing, I can only remember my dad ever hitting me a few times in my life, mostly when I would try to break up their fights. But mom, now that was another story.

This was the beginning of a new era for me. Things went from difficult to impossible. All of a sudden, I was aware of things changing rapidly. When you're that young the only things you should be aware of are food, fun and school. But not me! Little things that I never noticed were now hitting me in the face like a frying pan.

I had never understood why my mom and dad would have to take me to see Father Del Vecchio at the church office before every new semester at school. You see, Father Del Vecchio was the head man of the church and the school. I'd wait in the outer office and mom would go in for a while and when she would come out it was obvious she'd been crying. I'd always thought it was just church stuff. I mean, hey, after sitting through mass for an hour every Sunday for eight years I know I wanted to cry. But somehow, I found out through the rumor mill that she would go in and beg the good Father to allow me to go to school another semester without paying the tuition. I guess it worked because I went to that school for eight long years and graduated.

You see, to attend a fine Catholic intuition like Sacred Hearts you had to pay tuition, buy uniforms, Christmas cards, candies, chance cards and take part in many other functions that all cost money. Money, that all of a sudden we didn't have. I hated the fact that we had to beg for anything. *I hated being poor.*

As a kid, I went out for the local church baseball team, football team and the Cub Scouts. I would hang out until enrollment days when I had to pay for the uniforms and entry fees. I never took that stuff home; I'd just trash it and never go back. I knew we didn't have the money for such things and I was getting old enough to know better than to ask mom. I knew it hurt her to always have to say, *"We can't afford it,"* so why cause her the unnecessary pain?

I wasn't very good at sports anyway because I didn't get much practice; it's hard to learn team sports when you have no team. Besides that, my dad never taught me how to play catch, he never took me to a baseball game and we never went horseback riding. In fact, he never did anything with me at all, never. He promised it all but never delivered. I really missed out on all of that and it's one of those things you can never recapture. I find that very sad to this day. I missed not having a dad but hey, that's life, you can't have it all. Or can you?

I received my first Holy Communion around this time. I remember getting all duded up in a white suit, white shirt, white tie, white socks and white shoes. For crying out loud, white! Of all things! Then, if that wasn't bad enough, to top it off mom made me wear shorts with pulled up knee socks. I felt like the laughing stock of the neighborhood. Lucky for me, I guess many of the other mothers shopped in the same store because a lot of my buddies had on the same outfit.

Frank's Department Store was the neighborhood clothing store on Union Street and it was right across the street from my grandparents' house. It was small but it had everything and my friend, Joseph Socko's dad, owned the store. I never understood why a store so small would be called a department store. There were no departments, just a store. Believe it or not, it's still there and I stopped in and reminisced with the owners not long ago. Funny, but they still remember my pretty blond mom and our family.

My dad seemed so proud of me that day. He took me all over town to visit everybody. His aunts, his uncles, cousins and friends, the wise guys at the card clubs, all the shop owners, the barber, the druggist; we went up and down, street after street. We drove out to Flatbush and Bensonhurst. Everywhere we went people kissed me and gave me money. The fives and tens were flowing like water from a sink. Somehow, at the end of that very long day, all I ended up with was a soda, a candy bar, a few coins and a very dirty white suit. I never saw that suit again, thank God. Looking back, all the money and the reason for going all over town that day makes sense to me, dad...

My confirmation was more of the same, only worse. I was older and knew more. I asked Batista (Benny) Balsamo, my dad's cousin, if he would do me the honor and be my sponsor. We called it *"Godfather"* back then. He accepted and I was thrilled and proud. Benny was a very important man around the neighborhood, a "Made Man" whatever that meant (wink, wink). I just knew that he was well-respected man about town and he was my Godfather and I was excited and proud.

My new name was: **Stephen Anthony Batista Balsamo.** You see, you add your sponsor/godfather's name to yours after you're confirmed. My godfather must have been rich because he bought me a brand new, red, ten-speed bike as a confirmation present. I couldn't wait to get home from the money tour that day to ride my bike. I think I rode it for an hour or so before it got dark and I had to come in. I wanted to bring it upstairs to our apartment but my dad wouldn't let me. He said it was too heavy to lug up three flights of stairs. My dad and I locked it up in this big dark closet in the cellar where no one would find it. All night long, I waited for morning to get downstairs and ride my new bike. Needless to say, that next morning, it was gone. Dad took it and sold it for drugs. I hated him then more than ever.

The very same thing happened when I graduated grade school. For a graduation present, my parents took me to Sears where they had a revolving credit card. I was able to pick out my own present so I chose a 14k gold tiger's eye ring similar to one my dad used to wear. I was thrilled. This was my first real piece of jewelry. That night, I made sure I slept with the ring on my finger and my fist clenched so tight that no one could steal it. When I awoke the next morning, all I had left was the memory. Mom made payments on that damn ring for months, I had it only a few hours but my dad got his next fix.

* * *

Around the house, things were also changing and starting to disappear. Mom's fine china, gone. The holiday silverware was gone. Some of our nicer knick-knacks and wall hangings were gone. The telephone for crying-out-loud, gone. It was ripped out of the wall by the police of all things. Mom's wedding rings, her fur, even some of the furniture was all disappearing. We now had some empty drawers and closets that used to be full of stuff.

I noticed that dad had changed a lot also. He'd lost a lot of weight, his nails were long and unruly, his fingers yellowed from cigarettes. His hair was graying and it hadn't been cut lately and he needed a shave most of the time. His nice clothes and all the jewelry were gone. He was beginning to look like a bum. The doctor and the barber didn't come to our house anymore and we couldn't afford the milkman or the other deliveries.

On an average day, we'd wake up, dad would fight with mom and then he'd disappear for most of the day. He walked everywhere now; the Caddy was gone also. When he came back, he and mom fought some more and then he usually crashed on the couch. He smoked a lot, Pall Malls, no filters. He also nodded off with cigarettes burning and mom would scream at him all the time that he was "*going to burn down the house.*" Great! That's just what I needed, something else to worry about as if my life wasn't full of enough troubling things already.

From then on, if we were home at the same time I'd stay close to him so I could keep an eye on him. He'd lie on the couch and I'd play on the floor nearby with my toy soldiers (my favorite toys of all time). Dad never did burn the house down but we sure had a lot of holes and burn marks on the furniture and hardwood floors. I guess I'd fall asleep and lose sight of my self-appointed duties all too often.

A couple of times, I think my dad almost overdosed on the drugs he was taking. I remember one time he was in the dining room when he started convulsing. He fell to the floor and his eyes rolled back in his head. He was shaking uncontrollably and white foam started coming out his mouth. Mom was screaming and trying desperately to help him. I was freaking out, screaming and crying but what could I do? I don't remember what happened after that but he survived and so did I.

It's a shame, but I have way more bad memories like these of my dad than good ones. I just know there had to be some good memories, too. I mean really, life can't be all that bad, can it? I just don't recall the good times as vividly as the bad and that makes me very sad. For most of my life, many of my dreams were nightmares about my dad.

As time marched on, mom also started to change. Some mornings she seemed grouchier than normal and she would get sick. It seemed like she was gaining weight. Well, several months later we had a new addition to our family, my baby sister, Jacqueline Rose Balsamo. *Jackie* was born on March 21, 1962. Jackie was named after Mrs. Kennedy, our president's wife at the time, and Rose after her godmother, our Aunt Rosie. Another mouth to feed, great! And there goes our playroom. Thank God it wasn't in December. Lord knows, I had to share that month with enough people already. Seems Grandma Hoffman's birthday was Dec. 21.

* * *

Thinking about Mrs. Kennedy reminds me that as a young boy of eight, I loved President John Fitzgerald Kennedy. He was my hero in every sense of the word. In fact, Aunt Mary bought me a picture of the president and I hung it over my bed. The highest honor of my young life was when I was picked to play the lead in a school play called PT boat 109. I got to be JFK, can you imagine? By the way, that was the first part I ever had in a play and sadly, the last. My acting career was short but sweet.

My first real understanding of death came on Nov. 22, 1963. I was just nine years old but I was devastated when word spread that President Kennedy had been shot and killed in Texas. I sat on the mailbox on the corner and cried.

* * *

After my sister Jackie was born, everyone seemed happy for a few weeks. But as always, trouble started up again soon enough. My brother, Vito, was getting older and harder to manage. By the time Jackie was two, he was sick all time and trying to escape more than ever. Mom was scared to death that he would hurt the baby. He could be quite rough sometimes but he loved his baby sister and would never hurt her intentionally. One day, mom was washing clothes and she left a cup of bleach on the counter. Something happened and she went to attend to Vito. When she returned, my sister was choking. Jackie thought the bleach was juice and drank a mouthful. Luckily, dad was home, flopped on the couch as usual and he rushed her to the hospital. Thank God she was fine. Mom, not so much.

I think this really scared my mother and made her realize that Vito was getting to be more than she could handle. Mom was at her wits end with all of this. And then one day, the biggest change ever happened. I came home from school and my brother, Vito, was gone. Mom sat me down and tried to explain that she just could not handle taking care of Vito, the baby, me and everything else without any help.

I think dad was in jail at the time. He'd go there often, sometimes for weeks, sometimes for months. On and off, dad would take these little trips and when he was gone, life was good. We'd have food, get some new clothes, the bills were paid but most of all, there was peace, no fighting. Sometimes, I wished that he would never come back. But he always did. I loved my dad but I hated him at the same time. When he would return, he and mom would start up all over again. The arguments, then the fights and then the hitting. They gave me nightmares.

When dad would first arrive after one of his little trips, he would look great. He'd gained weight and his hair, skin and nails looked like the old days. And there was always the promise that, *"This time things will be different."* But that promise was never kept. Another of the many things I learned from my dad at a very young age.

* * *

"Whenever I make a promise to anyone, I keep it, especially my wife, kids and family."

* * *

Vito never did come back. He was sent to Willowbrook State School in Staten Island. Willowbrook was like the projects for the mentally handicapped only worse, more like a bad prison. To get there, we'd have to all load up in grandpa's car on Sundays and he'd drive us across this new bridge called the

Verrazano Bridge. It seemed like it took hours. My dad never went except maybe one time. Once there, I'd see hundreds of kids and adults that all looked like my brother. Mom tried to explain to us that this was the best thing for him and that he would be happy here with people like himself. But I could never understand why he'd cry so much every time we'd leave. Every Sunday, for a long time, we went to see Vito. Sometimes, Aunt Joan, Melanie and Kenny would come with us and then the car was really crowded.

I remember mom and Aunt Joan getting into big arguments with some of the staff there. It seemed that every time we went to see Vito he had another injury. A black eye, a busted lip, missing teeth, stitches, broken nose, you name it and it went on and on. The staff always blamed it on the other patients but mom believed that the staff was beating these kids for misbehaving. Aunt Joan was sure of it and just wanted to kick someone's ass. As for Vito, he just wanted to come home. Me, I just went somewhere else in my mind.

* * *

You know, I don't know what God was planning for people like Vito, but I think he may have lost his way when he made these helpless little souls. Not only do they look different but they have trouble eating, talking, dressing and going to the restroom - all the things we're so blessed to take for granted everyday. To top it off, they age rapidly. They're sick more often and longer than most. My brother started losing his sight at seven and was legally blind by his early teens. He was already showing signs of arthritis and other ailments that attack the elderly. For crying out loud, he loved his long hair and even that was thinning rapidly. Can't a guy catch a break? I guess not if you're unlucky to be born that way.

I loved and missed my brother everyday and I will carry some of the guilt to my grave. I didn't know what I did wrong but I believed that I must have been really bad to be punished like this.

* * *

So, Paulie and the rest of my friends turned out to be right. My dad had become a drug addict, the kind of person that I had always feared and hated. His vice was heroin. A nasty, very addicting drug that ruins more lives than it ever helps. This had been coming on for a few years but the dirty little secret was kept quiet for as long as possible. You see, when the wise guys want to keep a secret in the neighborhood, it's kept. Nobody ever did find out what happened to Jimmy Hoffa, right?

Not to mention, the Balsamo family was a large, well-respected and connected family in Brooklyn so no one dared to embarrass them.

My dad was a player in their game. He made them a lot of money and he was very well liked. So they put up with his bullshit and he tried his best to stay on the straight and narrow but eventually, he went too far. It was okay when he ran around with other women. They didn't care if he drank, smoked or gambled. But when he started stealing their money for drugs and losing money gambling that he couldn't pay back, well, then the party was over. The money dried up and he was ousted. They no longer wanted anything to do with him. Once that happened, everyone else was able to speak about it freely and they did. Everyone knew.

Everyone but me. How could I have been so blind, so naïve? I guess I saw things through the eyes of a child. Well, no more, those days were over for good.

* * *

Somewhere along my journey, I learned of "The Secret life of Walter Mitty," a book by James Thurber, written in 1939. I think I must have read it in school or seen the movie starring Danny Kaye, I can't remember. *Walter Mitty* was just an average man who had a vivid imagination. He'd always daydream about being someone or somewhere else. Anyway, I realized I had become a Walter Mitty somewhere back in time. I somehow developed an incredible imagination at a very young age.

I could go places where others couldn't see or hurt me. Everything I did, I would imagine I'd be doing something else. At work as a stock boy, I'd pretend to be the store owner. Riding my bike, I was a race car driver. I was a detective, a soldier, a gangster, my good dad, a drummer and a singer, just to name a few. I played baseball in the World Series with the Yankees and Mickey Mantle. My professional basketball name was Slam-Dunkin DuCannon. Batman had nothing on me. I carried a gun most of the time. I rode in planes and sailed on ships (mostly on top of the corner mailbox).

I started thinking that maybe I was crazy and maybe I was. Sometimes, you'd have to call my name several times just to get my attention. I think this helped me get through a lot of the loneliness and fear.

An imagination is a great tool to have in life. It can help you get through the toughest of times and help you plan for the best of times. I learned how to use it for both and it would come to serve me well. As I write this book, I imagine you reading it, maybe getting something positive out of it for your own well-being. I imagine it being picked up by some big publishing company and becoming a best seller. I see a movie in the future, an interview with Oprah, an Academy Award and on and on.

Walter never stops and I never want him to, he's always been there for me and always will.

* * *

Now don't get me wrong, I had a lot of friends as a kid, maybe more than most but they never lasted very long. I'd go from block to block making new friends but sooner or later, they would either tease me about Vito or my dad. I began to get very angry. I was getting bigger and tougher (plus I had my super powers) and fighting was becoming a way of life. But that just caused me more problems. The other kid's parents would chase me off and warn me not to come back as soon as they realized that I was Tony's son.

And God forbid if I ran into my dad while I was out with my friends. That was really horrifying because by now most kids in the neighborhood knew what a junkie was and looked like. Dad looked as bad or worse than most. He had a really bad habit. And he was always with other junkies who looked just as scary. I followed him one day to a really bad part of town. He went into a house for a while and when he came out he was really messed up, really high. I was scared and curious at the same time. I wanted to call the police and report this place as a drug house but we learn very early on that, *"You mind your own business, you look the other way. You never rat on anyone."* That's a good way to end up dead. I kept my mouth shut and followed as my dad stumbled home and back onto the couch. This became his way of life.

How did this happen? Why did this happen? I wanted to know. My dad was cool, a wise-guy, a Balsamo. He was a big shot around town, a member of the *family*. Money was never an issue. Well, shit happens and sometimes it just keeps happening. My life as well as that of my whole family became a living hell. We never knew what the next day would have in store.

I began to realize that our only money streams were welfare and food stamps, most of which my dad would steal for drugs. We never had food in the house anymore and it started to make sense why grandma always slipped my mom some money and why my dad never went to my grandparent's house or to visit Vito. He didn't care and no one wanted anything to do with him. Every time there was a break-in or a robbery in the family or neighborhood we all suspected dad. Not to mention, he was a constant pest asking to borrow money from everyone. Like he'd ever pay it back?

I had to go to the store daily to buy whatever food mom could afford. My mom never became a saint but she should have. She carried the load for our family. I don't know how she kept the rent paid, the utilities on and us fed and clothed, but she did. We always had a meal, clothes on our backs and she was always there for us. **Always!**

* * *

I remember as a kid, my dad would send me to the drugstore to buy a money order for a dollar. Later, he would have me go to another store and cash it for $10. Tony became very proficient at forging checks and money orders around town and it didn't take long for all the shopkeepers to get wind of his schemes.

As I grew older, I heard from family members that my Uncle Johnny, Aunt Joan's first husband, was the reason my dad got hooked on drugs. He, too, was a junkie and he caused my Aunt Joan and my grandparents a lot of grief. But Aunt Joan was tough. She kicked his ass out and divorced him. Go figure, two sisters, two junkies for husbands, what are the odds on that? Needless to say, this broke my grandparents' hearts.

Another excuse for my dad turning to drugs was Vito. He couldn't handle it. Can you imagine that - my poor brother with all the shit in his life was even taking the blame for my dad's terrible deeds? I believe my dad used drugs because he was a player and a daredevil, someone who will try anything, do anything and for whom, enough was never enough. He liked the escape from reality. He liked getting high. No, he loved it, plain and simple. My dad didn't want to work and have a normal life. He liked to escape into the fog that the drugs provided for him. The only problem is, he dragged all of us down with him.

I wish I had a nickel for every time someone said, *"He'll grow up and be just like his father, a bum."* I don't think so! We should never judge a book by its cover or a child by its parents or surroundings. You can't measure heart, passion, grit or determination.

I used to think, *"why me?"* Why did my life have to turn out like this? Why couldn't I have been born to different parents? Why did my brother have to be handicapped? Why? Why? Why?

As I grew into a man, I learned to think, *"Why not me?"* Shit happens to everyone. Nobody is insulated from life, hardship and our surroundings. It's all in how you deal with things. It's all how you cope. It's all between your ears.

But as a kid, I wasn't dealing very well.

* * *

"Things turn our best, for the people who make the best of the way things turn out" - Abe Lincoln.

* * *

I remember watching a movie later in my life where one of my most profound questions was answered. The movie was "Oh God" with George Burns. In the movie, a little girl asks God something like this, *"God, I don't understand, why does there have to be so much pain and suffering in the world?"* God answers, *"I didn't know how to create up without down, happiness without sadness, good without bad."* Now those may not have been the exact words used but that's the meaning that I took away. It's funny, where and how you learn things in life. I guess education is education no matter how or where you find it.

I seemed to have learned more from movies, music lyrics, metaphors and clichés than from all the years I went to church and school put together. On that day, I learned the real meaning of the *Yin and Yang*. It all started to make sense to me.

* * *

Yin and Yang. You can't have one without the other.

Vito (left) and Me as toddlers.

My first Holy Communion and the dreaded white suit and shorts, yuk.

My Confirmation with my Godfather Benny Balsamo.

Home - 387 Clinton Street and our stoop.

Our block on Clinton Street.

**Our apartment windows facing the alley
(first one on left is my bedroom).**

Our rooftop and the view of the NY city skyline.

That's Franks Dept. Store on Union Street.

**Me and my famous mailboxes on the corner of
Clinton and Union Streets.**

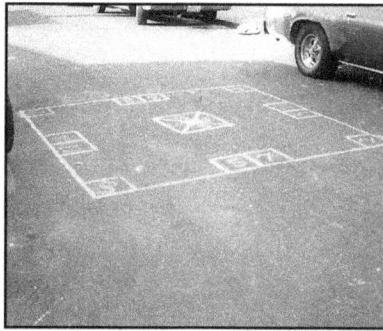

Skelizes game we played with bottle caps in the street.

Fire escapes leading to our back alley.

CHAPTER 3
DOUBLE DIGITS

By ten years old, I was sure that I knew everything and I was smarter than everybody. In fact, I'd even picked up a few nicknames of my own, mostly from my mom. Things like Smart Alec and Smart Ass. You see, I told you I was smart. She had a few other choice nicknames for me but she only used them when I was really bad and I guess I was really bad a lot. I don't know if it was that or just pure frustration but sometimes when I misbehaved she would go nuts.

I remember one time I was outside riding my bike. Mom always called me from the window. She would throw down money and a note so I could go to the store and get the groceries for the day. Well, this happened a lot and between going to get groceries or cigarettes for my dad, I guess I'd had it. So, when she told me I had to go to the store again, I got pissed and threw my bike down. I guess I embarrassed her in front of the neighbors, not smart. Well, she insisted I come upstairs *"this instant"* and I knew I was going to get it. The second I walked in the door, she went to town on me. It was one of the worst beatings I'd ever gotten and I'd had a few. Mom used to say I was too big to hit with her hands anymore. I'd hurt them, so she would use whatever weapon she could find. On this day, it was the heel of her shoe. That's gonna leave a bruise and it did, quite a few in fact.

I had a few beatings from time to time. I think it helped mom blow off some steam, some of the frustrations of her life. She had it brutally hard and I didn't mind so much. Mom would always be very sorry and really nice to me for days after that. I loved my mom and I tried to understand all she was going through. I wished I could have been a bigger help to her but I, too, was going through a lot.

By now, my life was really messed up. I had nowhere to turn and no one to turn to. I was in trouble in school and close to failing. I'd try to work hard to get passing grades so I wouldn't upset my mom. I always managed to pull off a C or a

D so that at least I passed, barely. She had enough on her mind and I never wanted to do anything else to cause her more problems. I mean, enough is enough. So, I took life on as a man or so I thought.

I needed a job so I could have lunch money and stuff without asking my mom. I remember riding the bus downtown to get a Social Security card and work papers; I think you had to be eleven at the time. Then I applied for the newspaper boy's job and I got it. I hated delivering those damn papers - especially with all the bullies, dark hallways and bums along the route - but I endured. I liked making the money. It felt great to help out and provide for some of my own needs.

From then on, I always had a job. In my final three years in Brooklyn, I worked at the butcher shop as a cleanup boy, the S & S grocery store as a delivery boy and another grocer as a stock boy. But my favorite job of all was in the winter when it snowed. The superintendent in our building would let me shovel the snow off our stoop and sidewalk and, as payment, he let me borrow the shovel for the day. I'd head up to Court Street and for 50 cents to a buck I'd go from store to store as fast as I could and shovel off their sidewalks and entryways. By the end of the day, I'd be busted but sometimes I'd make as much as $25 in a day. To give you an example, the grocer would pay me $10 for three hours a day, five days a week, so when it snowed, I was rich. I was pretty enterprising even as a kid and I bought my own shovel. Now if the super wanted the steps cleared, he either paid or did it himself. He always paid, 50 cents.

I'll never forget the old neighborhood or our building. Everywhere I looked we had relatives and friends. In our building alone was our apartment on the top floor; next door was my dad's cousin, Chiro, and his wife, Dolores. Right below them was my dad's Aunt Netty (Chiro's mom) and right next door to her was my Aunt Mary and Uncle Red.

Three blocks down was my Grandma Balsamo's house. Uncle Sally and Aunt Jeanie also lived in that apartment. My Uncle Dominick and Aunt Francie lived across the street from grandma as did Aunt Rosie and Uncle Sammy. My Aunt Joan lived about four blocks away on Union Street. I'm not sure where Uncle Joey lived but he hung out on President Street with the rest of the wise guys. Cousin Donny married his childhood sweetheart, Marylou, and they lived right around the corner on Sackett Street, next door to the lumber yard.

The reason I mention the lumber yard, which was more like a lumber garage, is I was infatuated with the place. I would go by there often when I had nothing else to do and just watch the men cut wood. They would always chase me away but I'd always come back. I liked watching them work and make things. I liked the smell of the lumber and the ring of the saws. Little did I know at the time but this would have much more meaning later in my life.

Grandma and Grandpa Hoffman lived about ten minutes away by car. They were always a big part of our lives and then one day to my surprise, they announced that they sold the bar. Sold the bar? Where the hell were we going to go on Sundays and holidays now? If you think that was bad it gets worse, much worse. Grandpa and grandma decided to move to California to be closer to Uncle Billy. Uncle Billy! I thought they didn't get along. I guess the cost of living and the great weather was a major attraction. I think getting away from my dad and all of us wasn't too bad either. I freaked out. How were we going to visit Vito on Sundays? And California's on the other side of the world. We'll never see them again. It might as well have been Mars.

My mom cried a lot the day they left Brooklyn. She was very close to my grandma. She cried often after that; she really felt alone now. They would write each other letters and I think grandma slipped a little money into the envelope from time to time. On Sundays, mom would have to take several buses to get to Vito but she went every Sunday, rain or shine. I went with her at first but as I got older, I tried to go as little as possible. I hated it, really hated it. My Aunt Joan would go with her once in a while but it was tough with kids and all. Mostly, it was just mom and my baby sister, Jackie.

As time went on, even mom started to go less often. It was a lot of effort with a young child and public transportation. Either way, it was very tough on her. If she went, it was very time-consuming and costly, both financially and emotionally. If she didn't go, it would eat at her for days and she would feel very guilty. Me, I'd just pretend I was someone and somewhere else.

I was out of the house more and more, working or with friends. I was home as little as possible. I'd use any reason to get out; I was just angry. Our lives sucked and the neighborhood was changing. Everyone was getting out of Brooklyn and leaving us behind. All of a sudden, our neighborhood was not good enough to live in. There were a lot more drug addicts and drunks around. The wise guys were making things very uncomfortable with all their antics and everyone complained that there were way too many Blacks and Puerto Ricans everywhere. I thought this was our home, our neighborhood. Well, sure enough we stayed and everyone else left. All the doctors, lawyers and dentists, the professionals that used to line the bottom floors on Clinton Street, were gone.

My relatives were pulling up stakes and leaving like it was a sinking ship. Uncle Dominick bought a home and moved his family to Long Island; he was the first to go. Aunt Rosie and her family bought a home and moved to Flatbush and so did Uncle Joey and his wife. Aunt Joan and her kids stayed in Brooklyn but moved up past Fifth Ave; so they were now no longer within walking distance. Mom had to take the bus to go see her. The real crusher to me was that my Aunt Mary and her family moved to Bensonhurst - some 20 minutes away by cab (who could afford that?) and much longer by subway and bus. Aunt Mary is one of my *Angels,* she helped me through a lot of rough times. I never really got to thank her properly so:

"Aunt Mary, wherever you are, I love you and I can't thank you enough for all you did for me. May God bless and keep your soul."

* * *

Angels. I believe we all get some angels in our lives, most of us just never notice. It's kind of like this fable I heard: This woman was trapped on a rooftop during a great big flood, maybe like the one Hurricane Katrina caused in New Orleans. Well, a rowboat came by and a man yelled to her, *"Jump down and swim to me,"* but she said, *"No."* She was too scared and trusted that God would save her. Another man came by in a motorboat and he yelled to her, *"Climb down and swim to me,"* and again, she said, *"No."* She was too scared and trusted that God would save her. Finally, a helicopter flew over her and dropped a line and a man yelled to her, *"Climb up the rope to me."* One more time, she refused, saying she was too afraid and that God would save her. She perished on that rooftop that day and when she got to Heaven she asked God why he didn't save her? God said, *"I sent you a rowboat, a motorboat and a helicopter."* **Angels.**

I guess the moral to the story is, *"God helps those who help themselves."* There are angels everywhere, sometimes you just have to open your eyes, ears and mind. This is a lesson I was beginning to learn.

* * *

Of all my aunts and uncles, my Aunt Mary was the only one who ever showed that she really loved me. I mean love where you could really feel it. She was the only adult person in my childhood who I could talk to and she actually listened to me. She had my back, she hurt for me and she was concerned and worried about me.

I was distraught when they moved away. My cousin Vito, her middle child, and I had become very close. We played together all the time. We didn't quite like the same toys and games but that didn't matter to me. I had someone to be with who liked me and accepted me for who I was. Vito always made up games where we dressed up like priests and played church. He preferred to play indoors and he really liked costumes and dress-up games.

Remember, I told you about Nina, my beautiful cousin who became my first wife? Well, one Saturday, when I was maybe 11 years old, Vito, our head priest, held a wedding and married Nina and me. It was beautiful. We had the music, the tux and wedding gown, guests, everything. All the neighbors were watching us perform this fake wedding out on our stoop as if it were the real thing. It was a blast.

Aunt Mary promised that I could come and stay at her house during summer breaks from school and she kept her word. My cousin Donny, whom I loved being around, would pick me up and we would take the train and bus to her house. I'd stay for the weekend and sometimes for as much as a week. Aunt Mary was always very good to me. She even bought me a used bike so I could fix it up and ride with Vito. Vito would take me to the movies, shopping and the Murray the K rock-and-roll shows at Radio City Music Hall. It's there that we saw big name acts like the Temptations, Jay and the Americans, The Four Tops, The Hollies and The Supremes. And who could forget Soupy Sales and that silly song, "The Mouse?" Now, I don't know where you were on Aug. 15, 1965 but I was with my cousins, Vito and Nina, and we were at Shea Stadium watching the Beatles perform in concert. Yes, I said Beatles: John, Paul, George and Ringo. I saw the Beatles. How many people do you know who can say that?

So for a while, it was great to visit Aunt Mary and cousin Vito, a safe haven. Now you just know something bad had to happen, right? If I didn't live my life, I'd say someone made up this story. There are just too many things that seemed to go wrong to be real, just a little too much bad luck. Well, as we both got older, my cousin Vito and I changed. I started to become girl crazy as if I wasn't enough already and my cousin Vito discovered that he liked boys. Starting with me! He was gay, *"Not that there's anything wrong with that."* A clever quote from "Seinfeld" (my all-time favorite TV show). But it became quite uncomfortable for me to spend time with him after a while.

Though I loved my cousin and learned so many great things from him, I just did not want to change teams. That made him angry a lot of the time. You see, we had to sleep in the same room and the same bed. I'll leave the rest up to your imagination. Let's just say, the pressure became more than I could handle and the trade-off was no longer worth the stress. Vito was still just a kid himself, maybe 14 years old, and he was just exploring his new-found world. I never held it against him. I just never went back and I never told anyone other than my wife until now. I was alone again.

* * *

Finally, I graduated from grade school. Of course, I had no idea where I would be going to high school. Most of the kids from Sacred Heart's were headed to St. Steven's Catholic high school but it was way more expensive than grade school and there was no way mom could afford that on welfare. Father Del Vecchio was long gone by now so no more freebies for me. But, hey I was 13! A teenager. Man, I'd waited a long time to say that. I had the Beatle-type long hair cut. I was buying myself some hip clothes and I had finally found a group of friends that didn't give a shit who I was, who my dad was or anything.

I became a *Third Place Boy* - that's what we called our gang. (Third, hmm). My best friend at the time was Sebastian Grasso. We called him Sibby, and he was one tough son of a gun. When we were together, no one messed with us. Sibby was a big, strong, good-looking Italian kid and all the guys respected him and the girls loved him. We did everything and went everywhere together.

As luck may have it, Sibby's folks couldn't afford the Catholic high school either so we both awaited word from the school system as to which public high would accept us. You see, we had to take tests to see if we qualified to attend the five or so public high schools in the area. Day after day, we both received rejection slip after rejection slip. It finally came down to the last two schools: Grady High School, the easier of the two to make, and Aviation High School, one of the tougher schools in all of New York. I prayed each night that we would both make Grady High. We didn't, we were rejected again. Now it looked like we would have to go to Jefferson High School in Brooklyn, a school so poor and in such a bad area that they would take any flunky from anywhere. Luck had it again; we both got accepted to Aviation High.

Until this day, I never could figure out how or why. Neither of us had very good grades. Our track records were checkered, to say the least, and the test seemed very hard. I think the good Lord took pity on us or they got us confused with someone else. Either way, we were ecstatic.

To get to school, we would walk to the subway and then take the train to Queens. After the train, we had to walk for a bit but we didn't mind. Another friend of ours made that school also, Nicky Valencia, so the three of us traveled in a pack. It was much safer that way. I'll never forget our first day. We listened to the Doors' song "Light my Fire" on Nicky's portable record player all the way to school. For the first time in our lives, we were going to school without a uniform. It was very exciting until we discovered it was an all-boys vocational school. Somehow, we missed that.

I knew it was too good to be true. My stinking bad luck followed me all the way out to Queens. We were bummed at first but we got over it. I especially liked the fact that no one in the school knew me or anything about my family. I could walk the halls with my head held up high and I did. Life wasn't so bad here after all; I was beginning to like it. Besides, there was an all-girls high school just up the street. So before and after school we could mingle.

One day at lunch in our giant cafeteria that looked more like a prison mess hall, I was sitting with my buddies. Along came a guy who decided to help himself to my dessert. I said, *"Hey asshole, that's mine!"* Oh noooo, wrong thing to say. He decided to grab me by my hair and slam my face into the table, busting my mouth and chipping my tooth. I jumped up and slugged him and the next thing I knew the whole cafeteria was up on chairs throwing food all over the place.

Once order was restored, we were escorted to the dean's office by a couple of the teachers. I was given a stern warning never to fight in this school again or I'd be suspended for a week. My new friend was a sophomore and had been in trouble before. So he was suspended for starting a riot. He swore to me that he would kill me after school when he got back. Right in front of the dean, I mean this guy had guts. He scared the crap out of me and I thought, *"I'm dead."*

Well, so much for walking the halls with a clear head. I was scared to death for two reasons: he was much bigger and tougher than me, and I could ill afford to get suspended from my new school. If I did, my mother would have a cow and finish the job if he didn't kill me. So for the only year I attended Aviation High, I treaded very carefully. It felt like I was back in Sacred Hearts all over again.

And now, I needed a trip to the dentist. I still think of that time whenever I look in the mirror and see the cap on my front tooth. I have two memories of the dentist from my childhood, bad and worse. The first was a free clinic (can you say public health care). There were about ten dentist's chairs all in a row. You had a number and when they called it, you filled the empty chair. Now, I think these quacks knew only two things: how to poke you with a great big needle and then jerk out what-ever tooth was causing you trouble. I don't think fillings were invented quite yet or they were too expensive. Actually, the way it worked was if your tooth was bad enough to need a root canal or a cap they pulled it because it was cheaper and that was all the government would pay for.

My second experience wasn't much better. This quack was a private dentist who my mom actually had to pay. He gave me some funny gas that almost made me sick and then he jerked my tooth out. I felt the whole thing and the gas made it worse because everything was spinning and the voices sounded slurred and weird. Nightmare city, both times for me. But hey, I've had my share of nightmares.

In fact, I was so scared at night that as a kid I could not go down the hall past the dreaded dumbwaiter to go to the bathroom. I would hold it as long as I could and when I couldn't hold it any longer I would just pee in the closet or behind my dresser. When I got busted I just started to pee out the window. Needless to say, every now and then I'd hit the neighbor's clean clothes that were hung out to dry. Need I say more? Ouch!

One time, I was walking home on Court Street and a car drove by and opened fire hitting some men inside the paint store. I panicked and ran home scared to death. Another time, we were out in front of my Aunt Joan's house on Union Street and a man walked by us. We all knew he was carrying a large butcher knife because he dropped it right in front of us. Mom and Aunt Joan made light of it so we didn't think much of it until about 20 minutes later when he was chasing a lady down the fire escape.

I was knocked out in a gang fight one time, and when I woke up I was under a car with my buddy who apparently pulled me to safety. We waited under that car for what seemed like hours until the streets were cleared of the gangs and police. We scampered home knowing we got off lucky. I had a few close calls along the way.

Brooklyn could be a scary place indeed, but it was my home. I was a Third Place Boy and this was our turf. I had a new girlfriend, Margaret, who was a blond cutie. I had a decent job, I was going to a good high school and most of all, I had finally found a group of friends that I could hang with for life. That big bully at school never bothered me again so my life was improving or so it seemed. Dad was in jail for one of his longest visits so things around the house were even a little peaceful for mom. School let out for summer soon and I couldn't wait. I could pick up more hours at the store and spend more time with my friends and girlfriend. I might even go with mom to visit Vito one of these Sundays, who knows.

* * *

You know, as a kid you hear things and you never pay much attention to them. Well, I did that often - still do. I have a joke with my wife and buddies that goes: *"I was listening, I just wasn't paying attention."* You get to where you only hear what you want to hear. The rest you just tune out or ignore completely. Well, what I was about to hear next was going to really rock my world and forever change my life.

Vito (left) and Me outside building #8 - Willowbrook State School.

**Grandma Balsamos apartment (2nd floor) and
my Dad's old restaurant (bottom floor) on Union Street.**

Me standing beside the lumber yard on Sacket Street.

**This is the corner of 3rd place where I hung out and a monument for
my Dad's uncle Tutty in his front yard.**

CHAPTER 4

GO WEST, YOUNG MAN

A pparently, mom had been talking with my grandparents about the great escape for some time. I'd heard this rubbish talk before, about mom leaving dad, but it never transpired. Then one day, mom said we were going to sell everything and move to California and live with grandma and grandpa. She seemed very serious this time and that troubled me a bit but I still didn't believe we'd ever leave Brooklyn or our apartment. We moved into that apartment when I was just a few months old and we'd been there ever since, it was home. I convinced myself that there was no way she could leave Vito, sell everything we own and raise the money and guts to go.

No way! *Way...*

* * *

Shortly after school let out for summer, grandma and grandpa appeared one day. They were driving a new, light blue, Volkswagen van. A camper van my grandpa called it. This van had everything: a bed, a toilet, drawers, stove and even a refrigerator. I'd never seen anything like it before. The talk was, they had traveled across country to pick us up and take us back to California with them. I was never so scared in my whole life. How could this be happening to me? I had friends, a girlfriend and a life, finally. I was going to Woodstock. And what about Vito and daddy? What was going to happen to them?

Well that was it! I decided I wasn't going. *"You can't make me."* I cried. *"Let me move in with Aunt Mary."* I begged. *"I'll be good."* I promised. *"I'll do anything you want."* I begged and pleaded for days to no avail. Meanwhile, mom and my grandma went about their business readying for the trip. They were selling everything or just giving it away.

Grandpa tried to buy me off with promises that we were gonna have a great time traveling. He was going to take us on a Cook's Tour, whatever the hell that was. It meant that we were going to zigzag our way across the United States stopping in each state and seeing the sights and camping out. Camping out? For crying out loud, the closest we'd ever come to camping out was sleeping with the window open. And what about Vito? No one seemed to have an answer to that question.

We went to visit Vito that Sunday in the blue van. No one talked much that day as we drove away from Willowbrook State School for the last time. Mom cried and cried. The next morning, we loaded up the van with all that we would take on our journey to California. It wasn't much, just a few bags of clothes and a few personal things. After all, there wasn't much room in the van with the five of us and the built-in house. Gone forever was my stamp collection, my coin collection, my fish tank, all my baseball cards, my chemistry set and my whole record collection with the exception of about ten albums. All my stuff, gone! I'd never see my friends again, my girlfriend, my cousins, my job. I was distraught, we didn't even get to say goodbye to most of the family. I prayed that this was just another horrible nightmare but it wasn't. California here we come...

We, too, were finally gone!

* * *

I cried and carried on all the way to California. Mom cried a lot also but for different reasons, I guess. I swore I'd run away as soon as I could and hitchhike back home. I told them I hated them all. I know I made the trip a living hell but I didn't care. I just wanted to go back home. This exciting little vacation trip, the Cook's Tour, turned out to be quite an adventure. I had never seen so many trees, mountains and lakes in my life but I didn't care. I wanted to go home! I cried more than I'd ever cried in my life. But deep down inside, I was a little curious and somewhat grateful. My grandpa went through an awful lot of work, planning and expense for us and I knew it. I just was not gonna let them know. Teenagers, what can I tell you?

Our first stop was in Florida. I had heard stories about Florida. That's where all the old folks go to die and from what I could see, that was the case. Everywhere you looked, everyone looked like someone's grandparents. At least until we hit Miami Beach. I guess grandma had some relatives in Miami just a few blocks up from the beach. This is where we were going to spend our first night on the road. While they all visited, I walked down to the beach; that's where the girls were. By the time I reached the sand, it started to pour. It rains hard in Florida, really hard. So I started walking back and before I could reach the house it stopped and was sunny again. That's life in Florida. We spent the evening in their backyard. I mean what's the big deal? I felt like we were animals in a big wooden cage. But to everyone else it was pretty special with the barbeque, fruit trees and all. I didn't get it.

The next morning, we were on our way again. We drove for hours and hours and our next stop was Jacksonville. I didn't care. I just wanted to go home. Mom threatened to kill me if I didn't straighten up. She said I was making it worse on her. Mom always knew how to reach me and I always tried to protect her. Grandpa pulled into this campsite, paid the man and we had our spot for the night. Grandpa made me help him pull out this thing he called a cabana which attached to the side of the van. It was just a big stupid tent with cots in it. Grandma, mom and my sister took the bed in the camper and grandpa and I got the cots in the tent.

That night *Walter Mitty* was at it again. I couldn't sleep so I was in the Army. Mom was a nurse and grandpa a patient. The van was a tank and we were in an old army tent out in the middle of a war zone with bombs going off all around us. Zzzzzzzzz…

By morning, we were all going nuts. In Florida, they have mosquitoes the size of small pigeons and we got bit everywhere. Mom and grandma bitched so much the whole next day that we never did use the cabana again and that was fine with me. I didn't care much for sleeping outdoors in the wilderness. From here on, we stayed in small motels along the way and ate fast food - maybe that was the cook's tour part. I kind of felt sorry for grandpa though, he really was trying his best to show us all a good time, to see this great country. Unfortunately, nobody was in the mood. But he kept on trying, nonetheless.

* * *

Remember I said that God gives us all *Angels* in our lives? Well, I think grandpa was one of my mom's. My dad hated him. He resented grandpa because he was always there to rescue mom whenever she fell. He also didn't like the fact that grandpa would never give him money. Grandpa was not a saint, don't get me wrong, but he was a good, honest, hard-working man who was always there for his family. I loved and respected my grandpa. He was smart. He could see right through my father's bullshit lies. He was none of the bad things my dad ever said about him. To be unkind to me, sometimes my dad would tell me that I was just like my grandfather. That was supposed to offend me but I always took it as a compliment. Unfortunately, I never really properly thanked my grandpa either but he gave me the blueprint on how to be a father, how to be a respectable man.

* * *

Now, I can't tell you all the other places we stopped along the way but I believe we visited New Orleans and the Grand Canyon. As for the rest, it was a blur. I didn't care and after a few days, the tour was over anyway. By now, all anyone wanted to do was get home, wherever that was. Grandpa drove eight to ten hours a day and that had to be tough on him. We were all hot and getting on each other's nerves. The air conditioner in the van sucked and some of the states were extremely hot. We were cramped and bored and the complaining never stopped.

Finally, after what seemed like weeks, we were crossing the border into California. I thought, *"Thank God, we're finally here."* Wrong! It seems California is a pretty big state and we still had many hours to go. We arrived in Huntington Beach, our new neighborhood, and I hated it immediately. We met Uncle Billy and Aunt Donna, which was a first for me, as far as I can remember. He seemed like a pretty good guy and I would never have admitted it, but I liked him instantly. He helped us up to our apartment and he lived in an apartment right across the street. Our apartment was a joke; it had two bedrooms, a bathroom, a really small kitchen, dinette and a living room. Mom, my sister and I had to share the small bedroom. I got the cot. Again, with the cot! I could just see this was going to be more of the same, like the trip in the van, cramped and uncomfortable. The next morning I couldn't wait to get out of the house and hit the streets.

It didn't take me long to meet the kid across the street. He was my age and he had no shoes. Shit, I thought, this kid must be really poor. Maybe I could give him a pair of my old shoes. Silly me, this was California, near the beach, and back in 1969, no one wore shoes. The outfit was just swim trunks and a T-shirt even if you weren't going swimming. I thought to myself, I can afford that. Daniel and I became good friends right away. In a matter of days, I met a few more guys and a couple of girls. And then, wham! There she was, Virginia, and she was a knockout. It didn't take me long to want to ask her to go steady but I had nothing to give her.

I wanted to get a job right away so I could buy her a chain or a ring, something. I mean, we always gave our girl something. Getting a job when you're 14 in California is not an easy task. Hell, there are no small grocery stores or butcher shops around here. And forget about delivery boys. There was nothing to deliver unless you had a car. There was nothing around the corner from us except a bowling alley, a mobile home sales lot and a liquor store. Imagine that, a store the sells nothing but booze? We didn't have those in Brooklyn.

Mom gave me an old ring of hers and saved the day. Virginia and I became an item; we were going steady. That mobile home lot came in handy, also. We'd go to the liquor store, get a couple of RC Cola's and then sneak into one of the mobile homes and hang out (and make out). And what's with RC Cola? Where I came from, Coke or Pepsi were the sodas of choice. But hey, I had friends and a chick. RC was fine with me.

At home, the latest talk was grandpa wanted to buy one of those liquor stores and maybe a house. Mom wanted to learn to drive and get a job and grandma just wanted some space. Me, I was making big plans, too. I was going to Huntington High in the fall and would maybe become a lifeguard. We had a house full of lifeguards on our street and they looked like they were having a blast. They all drove sports cars and had girls coming and going. Holy crap! These guys were living the life.

Virginia, Daniel and I went to the beach most days and hung out in the mobile homes when the weather was bad. Isn't it amazing? I wasn't there a month and I'd already forgotten about Brooklyn. All of a sudden, California and the apartment weren't so bad. Well, as always, things change and shit happens! Uncle Billy bought a house in Orange and he moved away. Grandpa and the family were always out business and house hunting and I was oblivious to it all. I was enjoying my new beach boy lifestyle. As I mentioned earlier, sometimes we hear things but we don't seem to comprehend what we're hearing. Either that or we just choose to ignore them.

We lived on Clinton Street for 14 years, my whole life. Now you'd think we could stay in one place a little longer than three months? Wrong! We were moving to Orange, thirty minutes away by car, right around the corner from Uncle Billy and there were no buses or trains. And I thought grandpa and he didn't like each other that much. If that's the case, why the hell were we following him all over the place? I was distraught all over again and I think by Uncle Billy's reaction, that he was not too happy about it either. I really think he wanted his space and still resented my grandpa. Years later, I got the feeling that Uncle Billy expected grandpa to put him into a business when he came to California and when he didn't, well you get the picture.

Virginia and I cried, we said our farewells and then that was that. We promised to call each other and keep in touch. We did for a week or two but that faded fast. Distance has a way of doing that.

* * *

Orange, Calif., here we come. To us New Yorkers, this was considered living in the country, a term we used to describe any place without tall buildings and with grass and trees. Mom thought I should be happy because at least I'd get my own room again, but who cared? The house grandpa bought was modest, with three bedrooms, two baths, a two-car garage and a decent-sized backyard. This one seemed like a prison because it had a block wall all the way around it and no trees. To me, Orange sucked! It was real hot and there were no kids around my block and no beach.

Now, my best friends were grandpa and my Uncle Billy. I'd go to his house on the weekends and he would teach me things. Like how to mow the lawn, pull weeds, dig holes, plant trees and work around the garage. He had lots of tools, a table saw and other cool stuff. He'd build things on weekends out of wood and I'd help. I had a weakness for saws, wood, tools, etc., so this was right up my alley. Uncle Billy was pretty cool and all that but I couldn't wait for school to begin. I mean I needed to be around people my own age and girls. Man, I really missed Virginia. Grandpa tried to help by playing cards and games with me most nights but truly, I was bored to death.

Well, September took its sweet time to arrive but it finally did. The high school was named El Modena High after this little ghetto town in Orange about three blocks away. They say that's where the Mexicans lived. Wetbacks and beaners were the terms locals used to describe them. I wasn't shocked to see that some things don't change. Even 3,500 miles across the country, if you're different we'll find names to call you. Up to that point, my only exposure to Mexicans was what I'd seen in cowboy movies. You know, the great big hats, riding horses, getting drunk and taking naps, pretty much harmless people. So that was okay with me.

In Orange, the Mexicans replaced the Black's and Puerto Ricans. I didn't mind much; those people scared the hell out of me. Shortly after we left Brooklyn, I got word that one of my best friends was on his way home one evening when he got jumped by three black guys and was stabbed in the stomach. Thank God he was okay but I just couldn't help thinking that if I would have been with him maybe it wouldn't have happened or maybe it would have been me. Scary!

* * *

Finally, it was my first day of school and I was so excited. I couldn't wait to get there and mingle. This was my first year in a high school that had girls so I was jazzed. They had a thing called homeroom, which was a class but not a class. I still to this day never figured out what its purpose was. I remembered back home at Sacred Hearts, in the eighth grade we had a new girl arrive in school and she was from California and everybody loved her. She was a blond with sparkling blue eyes, very different from our girls who had brown or black hair and brown eyes. And the accent and tan, wow! She was a knockout. She was an instant hit with everybody at our school. The guys drooled over her, and the girls wanted to be like her.

So I was thinking, *"Hey, I'm from New York. I'm cool and I have an accent. Hell, I'm Italian and I can dress so this should be a piece of cake for me."*

I had on my best bell-bottom slacks, a Paisley print shirt, Italian leather shoes and a Neru jacket. I had just bought that jacket in the Greenwich Village before my family kidnapped me and took me to California so it was brand new. As I entered the class, I could sense something was terribly wrong. Everyone turned to stare at me. If that wasn't bad enough, the homeroom teacher decided he wanted me to come up front so he could introduce me to the class. Oh noooo, I was dying. Can you say panic?

As I stood there in horror, I could see that this was not the right outfit for this school. All the guys had on something called Levi jeans (we called them work pants) and white T-shirts (undershirts). They all wore white socks and tennis shoes, which we called sneakers. How classless and out of style can you get? And why do they call them tennis shoes? Who plays tennis?

Well, it was a very long day, to say the least. You see, in California, which was about six months behind New York in style at that time, bell bottoms were only worn by girls, according to most of the boys I met that day. To make matters worse, long hair was not that hip for guys yet either. I guess they hadn't heard of a little band called the Rolling Stones. They were still listening to the Beach Boys of all things. Needless to say, this one day set the course for my next three years in this school. It was grade school all over again except worse because here, even the girls snubbed me.

That night, I rummaged through all my clothes. I needed to find something to wear. I was panicked. The white T-shirt was easy and I had a pair of gym sneakers. But the pants! What the hell was I going to do about the pants? I was not about to go back in time and wear straight leg pants for anybody. So mom saved me again, she took me out the next day to find some bell-bottom jeans. We searched all over Southern California, nothing. Finally, we found a small head shop in Newport Beach that had bell-bottom jeans for girls. I didn't care. They fit so we got two pairs. I wore those jeans day in and day out but the damage was already done. Needless to say, I never wore that shirt or jacket again.

High school was very weird. I couldn't believe how these slobs dressed. I couldn't see what the girls saw in them. After a few weeks of being tortured or worse, ignored, on my way to class one day faith intervened and I bumped into my first real friend in Orange. His name was Richard Boyd and he was a year or so older than me. I was climbing the stairs on my way to class when he ran by. I could see several guys were chasing him and not for fun. By now, I'd had it up to here and I wasn't scared of anybody so I blocked their path and he got away. Later that week in P.E., we finally met. Some big joker named John and one of his buddies were making my life miserable when Richard happened along. All of a sudden, the odds evened out and they lost interest.

Richard and I became best of friends from that day on. Richard was a really different sort of guy. He was short, drove an old red Jeep, wore a cowboy hat and boots and had a really bad attitude and a mustache. Leave it to me and my luck. I made friends with the most disliked guy in the whole school. No, check that, in all of Orange. I mean, no one liked this guy and I could understand why - he was a prick. But who was I to be picky at this point? I was desperate for a friend and he liked me so, from then on, we had each other's backs. Richard introduced me to quite a few new experiences in California and life in general.

There was the time his parents took us to the Colorado River and he and I were floating down the river on rafts. Richard-being Richard-was teasing the boaters and they were trying to run us over. I got scared and tired and decided to walk along the bank while he floated but, somehow, I ended up on a big hill and he was getting further and further away. I panicked knowing that if I went back down, he would be gone by the time I got there and I'd be lost. So I decided to throw my raft off the hill and dive onto it in the water. I missed! I landed in the brush. I didn't even know brush grew in water; I was scratched up from head to toe, bleeding everywhere.

Another time, we took his Jeep out to the desert. There was nothing but sand for miles and miles. Richard was driving and Bobby (another friend of Richard's) and I were riding on the back bumper. It was all fun and games until I flew off and landed face first in the sand. Richard got a real kick out of that and never stopped and once again, I panicked. I ran in those tire tracks for what seemed like miles. They all had a good laugh and said they would have come back for me. Yeah, real funny. Ha ha.

We had quite a few other misadventures. Richard loved to hunt, steal and have sex. Richard's parents were older because, unlike his sister and brother, he came along later in life for them. This may explain why he was a bit spoiled (rotten) and used to getting his own way. Richard's dad was a big time CPA and owned a lot of real estate in Orange; they were rich. His mom was a real society lady and belonged to all the clubs and did lots of charity work. Richard was a real handful for them.

I used to leave the laundry room door unlocked in our apartment complex so Richard could have a place to take his girlfriends. Richard had a steady girlfriend named Sherry and she got pregnant and out popped Richard Jr. He did the honorable thing and married Sherry when they were just 17.

We went hunting one time and Richard loved to play quick draw. Tris (a friend of mine) and I were walking up a hill while Richard was practicing his quick draw and shot himself in the leg. He was such a tough son of a bitch that all he said was, *"I shot myself in the leg, go get the car."* We laughed at him thinking he was joking until he got real serious, pointed the gun at us and threatened to shoot us if we didn't go get the car.

We rushed Richard to the nearest hospital and they dug that bullet out of his leg and stitched him up while we watched in shock. Tris had to leave the room - it made him sick. Richard, he just watched and never uttered a word. Afterward, Richard made us take him to a drugstore where he stole a cane and then made us take him back out hunting for the rest of the day. He sat in the back of Tris' dad's El Camino on a beach chair as Tris drove and he just shot at things from there. Now that was one crazy, tough son of a gun.

* * *

In Orange, getting a job was much easier. It seemed to me that most kids in California didn't need to work so there were plenty of opportunities for me. My first job was at The Pool Hall. I'd vacuum the carpet, brush the tables and clean the restrooms and pinball machines for three hours a day after school. For this, I'd get $10 per week cash and all the sodas and pool I could enjoy.

From there, I went to work at the donut shop, Mr. Donut. I didn't stay there for very long. The work wasn't bad and the pay was better than the pool hall, about

$20 a week. But it was right across the street from the practice fields for the high school and I just couldn't take it. I was out there mopping the floors and busing tables while all the other kids were playing football. I'd get really depressed. Sometimes, *Walter* would show up and I'd be running down the sidelines, just about to catch the winning touchdown pass when someone would yell, *"Hey... get back to work."*

After that, I went to work at the Hancock Gas Station on Chapman Ave. Richard was the evening manager there and he got me the job. The owner was never around. He'd show up on Fridays and pay us in cash but he would always hold back some of the money for taxes. This was my first real experience with my new lifelong partner, the Tax Man. I didn't like him very much then and come to think of it, I still don't 'til this day.

Richard and I would dream up different ways to make money. Customers would drive in and we'd give them full-service (whatever happened to that?). While I'd pump their gas, Richard would check their oil; it was always low by two quarts. We'd fill it up with empty cans of oil and then pocket the cash. When it was a female driver, Richard would let the air out of a tire while I pumped her gas and before she could leave the station we'd let her know she had a flat. Naturally, we'd repair the flat tire which meant more cash for us; sometimes, we'd even get a tip. We were making a killing. However, we never did get a W2 Form at the end of the year. I wonder why? What goes around, comes around.

With all that, it still wasn't enough for Richard. He figured out how to pull the cash out of the slot in the safe after the first shift would leave. You see, after each shift, you had to fill out a report and put the cash into the safe and we'd help ourselves to $10 or so each day. Funny thing, the first shift guys got fired often for being short.

I worked there until Richard and Mike, another crazy friend of his, started taking things to the next level and then I moved on. I worked in half the car washes, restaurants and gas stations in Orange. I liked to work; it got me out of the house and made me the money I needed for lunches, clothes and dates. Plus, I wanted to save up for my first car. Wheels equaled freedom.

* * *

One evening, the whole family was at home watching TV when we heard a knock at the door. As I swung the door open my heart jumped into my month. Standing before me in all his glory was my dad. I just turned and walked away. I didn't say a word. My kid sister jumped into his arms. *"Daddy!"* she screeched as everyone else just stood there with their mouths hanging open. I think we were all in a state of shock. Nobody knew quite what to say or do.

Thus began another chapter in our lives. My dad had gotten out of jail a few months back and he'd been living and working with his brothers in Brooklyn. He said he been searching for us and when he found out where we were he flew out to reclaim his family. Mind you, after he sowed his seeds for a few months, his brothers paid the expenses just to get him out of Brooklyn and out of their hair. Thanks a lot! He started all over with the bullshit promises. He was a *"changed man,"* all he wanted was to be with us, he'd get a job and he'd never use drugs again. Blah, blah, blah. I didn't believe a word he said. I can't speak for the rest of the family, but I can assure you that my grandfather didn't believe him either.

It wasn't long before we were moving out of my grandparent's house and into a small broken-down shack in El Modena. The house was the pits, very old and shabby, and we had nothing all over again. My uncle Billy lent us some old lawn furniture for the living room, a card table and folding chairs for the kitchen and an ice chest for our refrigerator. Somewhere, we scrounged up an old couch and some beds. At the time, mom was working at Zody's Department Store and I had just introduced my father to a man named Bobby Rallo.

Bobby was friends with Richard, and I used to wash his car for some extra cash. Bobby was an older guy from New York and I thought maybe he could help my dad find a job. He did but, like usual, it didn't last too long (jobs for Tony never did) although they became very good friends and hung out together from that point on.

Somehow, my dad was making a few bucks here and there, *"hustling,"* as he would call it. Hustling for my dad was always something illegal, like running numbers, collecting a debt for someone via gunpoint or selling stolen merchandise or drugs. His favorite was *"making a case,"* his terminology for suing someone. Dad had a habit of slipping in produce departments or getting hit by big department store doors. He'd quickly settle for whatever they offered so as not to get lawyers involved. He was also famous for collecting unemployment or disability though he rarely ever held a job. He could sell an Eskimo ice in the winter.

Dad managed to stay clean but he was already up to his old tricks: chasing women, hanging out at the pool hall and massage parlor, drinking and coming and going whenever he pleased. Somehow, he even managed to scrape together enough money to buy an old, tan Cadillac. Soon enough, mom and he began to argue a lot. Sounds like an old, broken record.

One night, we were invited over to my Uncle Billy's house for a party. By the time we were ready to leave, mom and dad both had had too much to drink. Now I'm not sure what she said at the party, apparently something that embarrassed or upset my dad, because as soon as we got in the car he started hitting her. My sister screamed and I yelled at him to stop but he didn't. When we got to the house, he beat her up like nothing I'd ever seen in my life. He punched her in the face, knocked her down and then he started kicking her in the head and face. I did my best to stop him but he was too strong for me. He pushed me away and kicked her again and again.

I was holding onto my baby sister who was screaming so she wouldn't see this incredible violence but she'd seen enough. She was horrified. Finally, he kicked mom so hard in the face that I think even he realized he had gone too far, finally he stopped. Mom was a mess after that. She was black and blue all over, her lip was busted open and her eyes were blackened. It's amazing he didn't kill her that night. My grandfather and uncle threatened to do something but never did. I think they all feared him and rightfully so.

Another night, we were driving home and my dad demanded that mom take him to George's house. You see, while my dad was still in New York, mom went on a few dates with a man named George. He was a house painter, a regular nice guy. Well, mom made the ultimate mistake and she confessed that to my father either because she was stupid or just to get his goat. The latter, I do believe. Dad was out of his mind. He had her drive by his block and then he demanded she show him which house was his. She refused and all hell broke loose.

Once again, my kid sister and I were in the back seat while they were duking it out in the front. Mom went nuts and was trying to stomp on the gas and drive the car off the road. Needless to say, we screamed in horror and begged them to stop but they didn't. It's amazing we weren't all killed that night. She finally did show him the house and he went to the door and talked to George, but nothing happened. Such a coward, he was only good at hitting defenseless woman.

I had school the next day. Try going to high school after something like that! By then, my backup, Richard, had gotten kicked out of El Modena and was sent to something called continuation school. I was alone again. I had no real friends to hang out with, no one to talk to. Believe it or not, now the jerks around school were giving me shit about my father. And to top it off, of all the crazy things in the world, they thought he was a *narc* (an undercover narcotics officer). Can you imagine that? My dad, a cop! They believed this because he didn't work and he was always around the pool hall and the massage parlor so he had to be a narc.

On that particular day, I wasn't in the mood for anybody's shit so the first jerk who bothered me I was to going to flatten. That jerk was named Chuck and sure enough, he said something and the next thing you know, we were going at it. We got pulled into the dean's office, Mr. Gunderson, and we each got three swats with this big wooden paddle on our asses. I couldn't sit for weeks. I had welts the size of the paddle on my ass. I couldn't tell anyone, it was so embarrassing. Not to mention, my mom would have been pissed. Some many years later, Mr. Gunderson reappeared in my life. He was my oldest daughter's principal in junior high. He didn't remember me, thank goodness, but I remembered him and my ass still stings whenever I think of him.

Through my new friend, Chuck, I met **Chester Arthur Farris III** (three, must be fate) but he went by Chester Bonner after his stepdad, Warren. Chet was nothing like Richard. He was funny, more of a class clown, and he had a pretty peaceful and cool demeanor. Chet didn't cause or want any trouble with anyone and that was okay with me. I liked Chester. We had much more in common. He was tall with long blond hair; he loved music, girls and black light posters. We were like two peas in a pod (or *"peas and carrots,"* according to Forrest Gump).

Chet came from a large family and I really liked them also. Chet had four sisters; Dee, Shea, Landa and Cheryl and a younger brother, Robbie. Chet's mom, Jan (Mrs. B,) gave me my first real nickname, *"Balls"* short for Balsamo, I guess. Or it could have been for ball breaker, you make the call. But I liked it and I loved her and her husband, Warren. They were always really nice to me. I started to hang out more and more with Chester and less and less with Richard. I guess I figured it was safer and better for my health. Chet and I did everything together. We became best of friends. We'd cut school and hitchhike to the beach, go to parties and drool over all the girls we couldn't get. We even worked for Chet's dad, running cable for his TV store so we could make a few extra bucks and help him out. Okay, to make the extra bucks, but it sounded good.

The first time I'd ever gotten in trouble with the law, Chester, Richard and I were in Newport Beach and Richard wanted to get some beer. You just knew Richard would have to be involved, didn't you? Well, Richard had a phony I.D. so he bought a couple of six packs and we parked the car and started to drink. Beer, of all things! Both Chet and I hated beer and we still do to this day but we were cool so we drank it. Now comes the really stupid part. We were tossing the empty beer cans out the window onto the street when a cop car pulled up. Off we went to the Newport Beach City Jail. They threw us in a large holding cell and called our parents. We were all under age. Chester and I were scared to death, we just knew that we were going to get killed (or worse put on restriction) and now we'd have a criminal record and everything.

Richard, on the other hand, didn't seem bothered by all this. In fact, he was trying to dismantle everything in the cell. We all took turns peeing in the toilet but not Richard; he had to pee on the wall. Richard was scaring us to death. Our parents finally came and collected us and we were free once again. You'd never guess but the very next night we got busted again, for curfew of all things. Ouch…

Another time, we all went to Disneyland and were on the submarine ride when Richard decided he was going to use the screwdriver on his pocket knife to unscrew one of the port holes in the sub while under water. Needless to say, we got busted by security. Richard went to jail again and Chet and I got thrown out of Disneyland, *"The happiest place on earth."* Hanging with Richard was getting to be troublesome and sometimes dangerous. He was such a daredevil and a trouble-maker. He really was harmless but he just loved to be mischievous, maybe to get attention, who knows?

Richard's in his mid-fifties now and I hear that he lives somewhere in the Ozark Mountains. I can just picture him now, with a cowboy hat, boots and a gun raising hell as usual. He's probably cruising around in some four-wheel-drive vehicle with some gal wreaking havoc. Some things don't change. I hope he's doing well…

* * *

After a short time passed, my family moved into the apartment complex right around the corner from Chet's house and a few blocks from my grandparents. This apartment was a major step up from the old house in El Modena. It was a two-bedroom and my sister and I shared a room. Mom helped me put up a tapestry to split the room down the middle and give us each some privacy. I had black light posters everywhere; it looked like a real hippie's den. This place was newer and had a pool, it's also where I found my new girlfriend, Terry (Twinkle). Twinkle was a little cutie who also lived in the apartments and we hit it off right away. A little kissing, cuddling and hand holding but not much else.

Like most teenage loves, it didn't last long. Her parents went and bought a house (damn them) and she moved about a half a mile away, just far enough to end the relationship. I was still hanging out with Richard from time to time but I spent most of my spare time with Chester, who now lived just up the street.

I'll never forget the night my new girlfriend Debbie's best friend showed up at our apartment door. She said Debbie was waiting in the alley to talk to me. I threw on a shirt and out the door I ran. Well, as I approached the car I was surprised to find no Debbie but her older brother, Mike, instead. As I approached him with my hand out to shake his, he punched me in the nose so hard that I was dizzy and bleeding. My first reaction was to run and grab something to defend myself. As I got a few yards away he yelled out for me to stay the hell away from his sister and her friends.

I was confused and freaking out. I had no idea what had just happened. I was covered in blood and needed someplace to clean up so I ran to Chester's house. Chet snuck me in the back door and I washed up and he gave me a clean T-shirt to wear. Luckily, my nose wasn't broken, just my ego. Days later, we found out that Debbie's best friend told her that I tried to rape her. Rape her! Are you kidding me? She was short, fat, ugly, had frizzy red hair and a bad complexion. I wouldn't give her the time of day. Problem is, the day Mike appeared at my house I had given her a ride home from school. Big mistake.

On days when I could take dad's car, I'd pick up Debbie and her girlfriends from school and give them a ride home. This particular day, Debbie had to stay after school and I made the mistake of giving her friend a ride home. She tried to sit next to me and I told her not to so I guess I hurt her feelings. She made up the story to get even and she did. I never did see Debbie again and I swore that one day, I'd get even with her older brother for sucker-punching me but as time passed, I let it go. But if I ever run into him…

* * *

It wasn't long before we were moving back into my grandparent's house again. Seems my Aunt Joan had some health problems so my grandparents were moving back to New York to live with her and help out with her six children. Somehow, my parents convinced them to let us rent the house and live there until they came back. Grandpa even left the camper van for my dad to use. He must be getting soft in his old age, I thought.

Well, we moved back in and in no time at all, my parents had fixed up the place. They bought some new furniture and carpet and made it their home. They even seemed happy for a while. Things seemed to be somewhat normal. As normal as they could get for our family, that is. I finally had my own room again and dad and mom seemed to be doing much better. I was beginning to think, *"Well, maybe he is changing."*

"Fool me once, shame on you. Fool me twice, shame on me."

* * *

In my life, good things never seem to last. It wasn't long before my dad started losing weight again. That's the first sign and I knew them all too well. He was using drugs again, my worst fear. He and mom started arguing and the fights were just around the corner. I had it; I would only come home to sleep. If I wasn't at school, I was at work and if not there, I was either out with Chet or at his house.

Chet's house is where I met what would become one of my best friends for life, *Tristrum Arthur Mumford (Tris).* At first, we didn't like each other very much. Tris was a pretty common guy with long brown hair, Levi blue jeans, white T-shirt and black motorcycle boots. Why the boots, I thought? He didn't have a motorcycle. I think I was a little jealous that he was friends with Chet so I treated him like shit. I even nicknamed him *"Scro"* short for scrotum. How's that for being a jerk? Sorry Tris.

But as time went by, we all became very close. I finally had a couple of really good (peaceful) friends and that was great. But at home things weren't much better. I hated my life, my parents, my school, everything. All teenagers go through that I guess, some worse than others. I was barely passing in school. School was where I'd go to sleepwalk through the day and get some rest. It's amazing I ever learned anything. All I could think about was buying my own car, getting a full-time job and moving the hell out.

As time passed, dad went on another of his little trips. Jail in Norco, Calif., I believe. Meanwhile, mom, my sister and I were finally living in peace when grandma and grandpa showed up one day to reclaim their home and belongings. Well, we had nowhere to go so mom moved into Jackie's room and my grandparents moved back into their bedroom. I got to keep my room because mom felt I was too old to be sharing with my kid sister. I wanted to buy a car in the worst way and grandpa had two. He made me a deal that if I stayed in school and paid him $20 a month, I could buy his 1961 Pontiac Bonneville. It was a big, red, four-door sedan and I paid a total of $200 for it. I paid it off in no time at all. Grandpa was pretty cool; the day I paid off the car, he took me down and bought me four brand new tires.

So, I had a car by my 16th birthday. That's driving age in California. In New York, I would've had to wait until I was 18 before I could drive and most people don't ever own a car there. I took driver's education at school and amazingly enough, I aced that class but I was barely passing the rest, including physical education. Now, how in the hell do you struggle with PE? I mean all you have to do is show up, I don't know but I managed to find a way.

With my own set of wheels I was finally free. I could venture off further from home for jobs that would pay more and have a social life. Everything was about the job for me - who would pay the most or give me the most hours. On Saturday and Sunday mornings, I'd get up early and go wait in line at Metro Car Wash on Tustin Ave. If I was lucky enough to get picked, I would wash car windows all day and then go to my evening job at La Marguerita Mexican Restaurant, where I'd bus tables until ten. From there, it was out with my friends looking for parties and girls.

* * *

Dad got out of jail and was snooping around mom again. But mom had had it with him and there was no way grandpa was going to ever let him back into the house. Dad started hanging out with Bobby again and they moved the party up to a restaurant/club in Anaheim named Anthony's Red Vest. Dad was running around with different women at the time - this was his pattern. Whenever he would just get out of jail and be on probation, he'd stay clean for a while and then go back to his old wise guy ways. He'd drink, gamble, chase women and just have a ball. This time, though, he had no home to go to so he hooked up with a woman named Heidi and moved in with her. I met her a few times and I thought she was very nice but nuts for wanting him around. Still, I was glad he was out of my mom's hair for the time being.

Mom, on the other hand, was doing okay. She got a good job at an insurance company and bought her own car. She was still fighting off my dad from time to time as he was always begging her to come back. Mom and my grandparents did not always see eye to eye on things either. One night, they got into it pretty good and she wanted to go out. Now, I don't know where her car was but she needed to borrow mine. I didn't want to give it to her because it was raining really hard and I had just gotten new wheels and a paint job but I didn't have a choice. About an hour later, she had gotten a ride home from the police. She totaled my car. She was making a left turn and accidentally drove over an island divider and a car slammed into her. She was lucky; my car was not.

I walked and bummed rides for a short while and Uncle Billy let me use his car to go to work until I could save up enough for another piece of junk. By the way, as the saying goes, *"no good deed goes unpunished."* I totaled my uncle's car; an old Datsun, on the way to work one day as a guy pulled out in front of me in an intersection. Sorry about that Uncle Bill but thanks for the help. After that, my next few cars (Ford Falcon, Chevy Corvair and a Fiat Spider) were junkers and barely ran but they got me to school, work and out so they did their job.

Dad called me one day and told me that he could get me a job as a busboy at Anthony's Red Vest. I jumped at it because it paid better and I could make tips. The only drawbacks were that I had to see him most nights and drive much further to work. Dad was doing okay; he still had the weight on and the wise guy act going pretty strong. He was still on probation and he had to go in for drug testing biweekly or go back to jail. If anything in the world would keep my dad clean for a while it was the fear of going to jail. But for me, the money was pretty good so I put up with seeing him and the drive.

As a busboy, the waitresses liked me and tipped me well because I was good and fast. When you're a waitress, you want a fast busboy so you can turn your tables quicker and make more tips. I also got to eat two meals a day there, which saved me a lot of money. I think the owner was a little intimidated by my dad and his group so he treated me pretty well also.

Dad was back hanging with Bobby and a few other Italians from back east. There was Sal (who thought he was Frankie Valli), Tony and Johnny *"o-bazzo"* - slang for crazy or having big balls in Italian. Now understand, my dad was famous for making up words in English so it wouldn't be a stretch for him to make up o-bazzo in Italian. Either way, you won't find it in any dictionary. They all acted like wise guys but these guys were all just a bunch of big windbags. Real wise guys don't hold jobs and go home to their wives. Bobby worked at a bakery, Sal owned a hair salon across the street from the restaurant, Tony drove a lunch truck and Johnny was in some sort of sales. The only one with any real balls was my father and he was the biggest actor of them all.

But it was actually kind of cool to see him straight for a change and hanging out with some regular people instead of junkies. So, I just went along with the program. All in all, it wasn't a bad gig. I had a car that ran, a decent job, I'd be graduating school in about a year and I was dating a few different girls. Truth be known, I'd date just about anyone who would have me but she had to be cute.

CHAPTER 5
LOVE

A h, love. Now, I'm no expert on love but I have learned a few things over the years. At 16, I fell in love with my high school sweetheart and love was so brand new. Sounds like lyrics to a song but it's kind of true. Really, I didn't know what love was all about. I mean, I loved my parents. I loved my sister and my brother because let's face it, you have to. They're your family. But is that really true love?

I was the kind of kid who rejected affection from my family. I hated when mom would try to kiss and hug me even at a very early age. I was always so angry and full of rage. Most of the time I was too busy hating and blaming my family for just about everything. My dad for the way he was, mom for putting up with him, my brother for being born handicapped and even my kid sister for just being a pain in the ass.

So, I could honestly say at this point, I didn't really know what love was at all. To me, it was just something we all had to do because we were related. As far as other relatives and friends go, I was never around anyone long enough to get that attached. But in time, that would all change for me and it all started with my first love. She's what taught me what love is and how to give and receive love freely. She also taught me how painful love can be. Sometimes, it's very painful to be in love (take my mom, for instance) and for most people, they're miserable when they're not in love. I've had it both ways in my life and I can assure you that having someone to love who loves you back is definitely the better of the two options.

Oh, and one other thing that I learned about love. Remember the movie "Love Story" with Ryan O Neil and Ali McGraw? In that movie there is a scene where Ali tells Ryan that *"Love means never having to say you're sorry."* That's bullshit! When you're in love, you better know how to say you're sorry because you will screw up from time and time and if you want a relationship to work and last, you better know how to apologize and how to accept an apology for that matter. Trust me I know.

I guess I owe some credit for my first love to my dad for getting me the job at Anthony's Red Vest. On the way to work one day, I met another of my *Angels* and my first true love. Her name was Carrie. We met while we were both stopped at a traffic light. She was with her best friend, Carla, and I invited them to the Red Vest for a cup of coffee. To my surprise, they actually showed up, barefoot. I snuck them in and it was love at first sight for me. I just didn't know which one I loved until I heard Carla say that she had a boyfriend.

Carrie was 16, she had long, straight, light brown hair, brown eyes and was a five-foot-six beauty at a 112 pounds. She had a nice personality and a knockout body. Now you know why it was love at first sight? Her friend, Carla, was a carbon copy of her only with a darker complexion, dark brown hair and smaller boobs. I asked Carrie out on a date and, to my surprise and delight, she accepted.

Carrie lived in Brea long before the Brea Mall and the 57 freeway crossed over Imperial Highway. In fact, no one had ever heard of Brea. It was a long way from Orange, where I lived. Today, it's a pretty big city in Orange County and it's just a 20 minute drive on the 57 freeway from Orange, with no traffic. Carrie came from a pretty big family. She had an older sister named Janette and an older brother, Mick. He was a jerk and we disliked each other right from the start. Next came Carrie and then the two youngest, the twins, Mac and Mavis. Her mom, Doris, worked for the school district and her dad, Frank, well, I can't remember what he did but he made an honest living. They were an all-American family.

Carrie and I got along great for the longest time. In fact, we stayed together for almost two years. I was thrilled to finally have someone to love and someone who loved me. Life was good! I'd go to school, rush to work and then off to Carrie's so we could spend the rest of the evening together. We'd go to eat and maybe the movies, anything just as long as we were together. We did this everyday for the longest time. We were in love. We even started talking about getting an apartment together and maybe marriage. But how? We were still way too young. We were both still in high school and I wasn't making much money with all those part-time jobs. I needed a plan. So I thought if I could graduate early I could get a full-time job and save while she finished school. I was a senior and she was a junior so she had two years left to go but I knew that I could get us a jump-start.

I needed to get out of high school now; I needed a full-time job. I had to make more money to support my car, an old Ford Falcon that over-heated two or three times a week just for the hell of it, and for our social life and to save for an apartment. Dating, as you know, can be very expensive with movies, dinners, gifts and clothes and now I was thinking about an apartment all the time. Besides, Carrie's old boyfriend had already graduated, had his own *pad* (as we called it back then) and a good job so I was a little intimidated living in his shadow, to say the least. He was real good friends with Carrie's older brother Mick, the jerk, and Carrie's best friend, Carla, was going steady with his brother.

So, the three of them were real good friends and hung out together. They tried their best to make my life in Brea as uncomfortable as possible but I didn't care. Nothing was going to stop me from seeing my girlfriend. One evening, Carrie's brother and I got into a fist fight in her driveway. Her dad came running out in his underwear and broke us up but things were never quite the same for us after that. I'd like to tell you what the fight was about but I promised her I'd never tell anyone and I never will. A promise is a promise and a man is only as good as his word but her brother was the cause of it. The rest I'll leave up to your imagination.

* * *

I marched into my counselor's office and told him I needed to get out of school. His name was Mr. Anderson and he would not hear of it. He insisted that I graduate high school first (thank you, Mr. Anderson, wherever you are). I told him I needed to get a full-time job and I couldn't do both any longer and that if he didn't help me graduate at the end of the semester I'd have to quit school. I was bluffing, of course. I never would've done that to my mom, and I had promised my grandfather I'd graduate. But I had heard of kids graduating early and I wanted a piece of that action. Mr. Anderson finally agreed to help me but said first I had to pass three tests (three again). I already had enough units to graduate because I had taken so many classes my first year in high school in New York. Still, my grade point average was below par so I needed to pass these tests to qualify for an early pardon.

I guess I did okay on the first two but I failed the math test. I was bummed out but Mr. Anderson took me in his office and taught me how to do five of the questions on the test that I had missed. He worked with me until I got them and then retested me the next day. I PASSED! I was elated. I couldn't wait to tell Carrie the great news. I had just turned 17 on Dec. 20, 1970 and I graduated Jan. 15, 1971.

I got a full-time job right away at a roofing company, Armstrong Roofing. I got out of work much earlier and I could spend much more time with Carrie. We went to Magic Mountain, Disneyland, Knott's Berry Farm, the movies, the beach - you name it and we did it. Our weekends were full and we were having a blast. I wasn't saving all that much but who cared? I was in love and really happy for maybe the first time in my life.

In June, I went back to school and graduated with my class. I'll never forget the cap and gown, the excitement and all of my guests: mom, Jackie and Carrie. Yeah, I noticed the big crowds everyone else had but I didn't care (wink, wink). Carrie and my mom were there and that was enough for me. Deep down inside it killed me that my dad didn't bother to show up but what else is new? He'd been a no-show most of my life so I figured why start now? I just sucked it up, pretended it didn't bother me and moved on like I always did.

Armstrong Roofing was an interesting job and my first in the construction field or should I say destruction? I was hired as a laborer back in the day when teenagers were the laborers. My job was to clear off the old rock roofs (remember them?) and haul all of the debris to the dump so the real roofers could come in and re-roof the house. Now picture this long haired, shirtless, music-blaring teenager on top of your roof with a shovel and a wheelbarrow, my tools of the trade. First, I'd shovel off all of the old rock and then pull up all the old roofing tar paper. I fell through a few old roofs and off a few also; it was hard and very dangerous work. (But, hey, I was making about $1.85 per hour). It's pretty hard to manage a wheelbarrow full of rock on a roof top and get it to the edge of the roof to dump into the dump truck without slipping and falling. Most people don't put a new roof on until the old one is so rotten and bad that it makes it extra dangerous. Trust me, I still have a few scars to show for it.

I did like driving the big old (and I mean old) dump truck to the dump. However, brakes were optional in those days and when the truck was full, stopping became optional also. And this dump truck looked nothing like you'd think a dump truck should look like. It was just a long, flatbed, rusty, old truck with bulging wood stake sides that didn't match anything and the debris would leave a trail as you drove down the street.

One fine day, I was barreling down Katella Ave. with a full load when traffic began to merge into one lane because of some road construction. Sunglasses on, music pounding, sun blaring - I guess I was a little distracted. All of a sudden, I noticed that the traffic had stopped. I realized there was no way I could stop that truck before plowing into the cars in front of me so I veered off the road through a sign and into a field. After a 50 yard wild ride the truck came to an abrupt halt. The only problem was, it was now on its side, engine screaming, wheels spinning and the load, well, let's just say it was spread out all over the place. As I crawled out of the window, a little battered and bruised (no seat belts back then), I was so proud of myself that I didn't hit anyone.

After I explained to my boss back at the yard how some crazy lady cut in front of me and jammed on her brakes, I was fired. I guess he didn't share in my pride or my story. Come to think of it, he never even asked if I was okay. I guess that was of little concern to him.

My next job was at another roofing company. Seeing how I was now experienced, I was moved up to what they called the Hot Crew. Some promotion. I was the laborer to a five-man crew and I did all the dirty, hard, dangerous work. Stuff like carrying 50 pound rolls of tarpaper up a ladder to load the roof or running and loading the kettle. The kettle is the small black trailer that roofers haul behind their trucks and it's heated to about five million degrees. I had to drop these 50 pound blocks of tar into it so it could melt them for the roofers. Hot tar would splash out, burning the shit out of a bare-chested, brainless kid. For crying out loud, put a shirt on!

The experienced older guys would wear leather jackets, gloves and masks to handle the hot tar but not me; I was too cool and too busy working on that never-ending tan. Another of my duties was to fill big buckets of the hot tar and connect them to a rope and pulley so they could be pulled up to the roofers two stories above me. Very dangerous. The splashing never stopped and cleaning the hot kettle at the end of a long ten-hour day just became too much for me after a few months, so I was on to another career change.

Well, as time passed, I guess Carrie and I grew apart. Finally, one day we broke up. There was always lots of pressure on Carrie to get rid of me. Her old boyfriend was still hanging around and calling her. Carrie missed hanging out with her best friend, Carla, and vice-versa. Her brother, besides the fact that he couldn't stand me, looked for any reason to make me look bad and after our little fist fight in the driveway, things just seemed to deteriorate.

Besides, I don't think her mom and dad were too happy that we were getting so serious at such a young age. I mean, who could blame them? We were just kids, way too young to be talking marriage. So maybe we weren't meant to be. It sure seemed like everything was against it. At first, I thought, great! I'm free again! I can go back to chasing girls with my buddy, Chester. Who needs this shit? Well, that lasted about 24 hours and then I called her, I already missed her. She said it was over and she didn't want me around anymore and for me not to call her.

She even gave me back the poodle, FeFe, that I gave her for her birthday and our pre-engagement ring. I kept the dog and pitched the ring out the window on the freeway.

At this point, I was getting sick to my stomach. Could this really be happening to me? I mean we were in love just two days ago or so I thought, and suddenly it was over? Over? Just like that. Love can't end so easily, can it? The next day I went to her house and I was informed again that it *"was over"* and that her parents didn't want me coming around there anymore. They said we were too young and there was talk that *"I'd never amount to anything anyway."* They wanted more for their daughter. Hmm, I'd heard that before.

Looking back, I can understand where they were coming from. I guess Carrie had seen too much with my family and I told her too many things about our history. Maybe Carrie driving my mom to Heidi's house to serve my dad with divorce papers and seeing him chase them down the street was the final straw. That might have been a mistake since she probably shared the story with her mom and that may have had something to do with it. Who knows? But the bottom line, is we were way too young. Things change, people change.

But not me, *"**When I love, it's forever.**"*

* * *

So, you see, Carrie really was an *"Angel"* for me. Through her, I learned about love. The hard way but I did learn. Some Angels are only with us a short time but they leave us better and richer for having made their acquaintance. I learned how to love and how to be loved through Carrie. I learned how it really hurts deep inside when you lose love and how lonely life can be without it. I learned that I wanted so badly to love and be loved. I even understood for the first time just a little of what my mom was going through with my dad. I was determined to find true love in my life sooner or later.

But not now. Not for a while. I was still too angry and upset over what happened. I was scorned. I wanted her back and the more she refused, the madder I became and the more I hurt. I got to a point where I swore that I would never love another girl again. From then on, it was *"use them and lose them,"* our new slogan.

My poor buddy, Chester, was also going through a really bad breakup with his first love. Her name was Betsy and she tore his heart out and stepped on it. They broke up around the same time as Carrie and me so now we were both miserable as hell. Misery loves company. Finally, I said, *"Screw them, let's move out and get a place of our own.* " After all, I was saving a bit and I already had most of the necessities; a waterbed, dresser, TV and a stereo. I had bought a bean bag couch for Carrie and I had a few other items, so we were ready.

Chester's parents were none too happy with me and my plan but they couldn't stop us. I think Chester's parents wanted to see if Chet could really make it on his own. Up to that point, Chet never held a job for very long. The beach and the girls won out every time so I think they thought he'd be back in no time. But we were gonna show them and we did. Our parents gave us some of the other miscellaneous things that we needed like towels, pots, silverware and sheets. We had no idea what we were doing, but we didn't care. We were on our own and it felt great (and it was).

We rented a two-bedroom apartment in Orange, on Glassell Street, just down the block from where I worked at California Campers. The two bedrooms were upstairs with a bathroom in between. And downstairs, we had a kitchen, living room and another bathroom. Chester was working odd jobs on and off but he could never really focus on work or money. He would report for a while and then he'd just stop going and report to the beach instead. If you could make money going to the beach and checking out girls, Chester would spit on Bill Gates today. I'd bitch at him all the time because we had rent to pay and I never wanted to go back home again. I even got him a job at my company so I could keep an eye on him. After about a week or so, he left for lunch one day and never came back. Do I have to say it? The beach!

After that, I got in tight with the manager of our apartment and he agreed to let us paint a vacant apartment every month for our rent. So I was working Monday through Friday at my job and we were painting apartments on the weekends. Chet and I would go over to the apartment and start painting around eight in the morning on Saturday. By nine-thirty or so, Chet would go for some food and never come back. I'd end up painting the whole apartment by myself but hey, the rent was always paid.

Chester was always sorry and I could never stay mad at him long. He just had a way about him and I loved him. He was truly my best friend and I would do most anything for him. When we first moved into the apartment we made one house rule, no parties. Yeah, right! That lasted until the second weekend. We were already getting lonely and we wanted to show off our new place so we invited every girl we knew and three of our best buddies, Tris, Mike Hill, and Henry, the druggy pot head from next door.

It was an outrageous party with about 20 girls and five guys. We had a blast. We thought, *"Now, this is the way to party"* so we tried it again the next weekend. I guess when you have a good party the first time, word travels. We had about 100 kids show up for the next party and we didn't know two-thirds of them. The next morning, our apartment manager was at our door bright and early. He asked us to step outside for a minute. When we did, he pointed to the complex and our street and said we better clean it up, now!

You should have seen the mess. There were beer and wine bottles, cans, cigarette packs and food wrappers all over the neighborhood. I guess when the party got too crowded inside people just started partying all over the block. We spent a few hours picking up the trash and cleaning up the neighborhood. After a stern warning from the landlord, that was the last big party we ever had. However, we still had plenty of small ones almost every weekend after that.

We were really living it up partying, dating, going to the beach and just hanging out at the apartment with friends. The music was loud and on all the time - Led Zeppelin, Ten Years After, the Cream, Blind Faith, just to name a few. The girls were coming and going constantly; we were like real playboys (or so *Walter* thought). Heck, we had girls who would come in and clean up for us and other girls who would buy us groceries and then different girls who would sleep over. We were living large; we were dating and having sex at an alarming rate. Surprise, surprise!

It's amazing and lucky we didn't get AIDS or some other life-threatening disease. We smoked tons of cigarettes, drank booze and even smoked a little pot from time to time. One of the things I liked best about Chet and Tris is that neither of them were much into drugs or violence. After all of my experiences with drugs and my dad, I was not into getting high at all. Yeah, I'd take a hit off a joint or drink some to be cool but I was always in control and I would never allow anything heavier than that in our place. Okay, a few *whites* (speed) might have slipped in but that was it. Alright already, maybe a few *reds* (downers) also but that was it, I swear! I was always very careful; I never wanted to get addicted to anything. Cigarettes did get me for a while but that was it and I quit them at 30 and never smoked again.

Today, I'll have a drink or two with a nice dinner but not much more than that. I'm still afraid of getting addicted to something, anything. Booze, gambling, food, work, exercise, sex, even money, you name it. They all can be addicting and dangerous.

* * *

My motto is, *"Everything in moderation."* Another *Stevism.*

* * *

I'd have to say the year we spent at that apartment was the finest year of my young life. But even with all the friends, girls and parties I still missed Carrie. I drove by her house in Brea from time to time. I'd never stop, I'd just drive by hoping maybe I'd run into her or over her brother. I just missed the relationship we had. I missed her and I missed having someone to love. It's funny how you can be surrounded by lots of people and still feel so very alone.

* * *

Another *Stevism:* **Three people can be at a party and come away with three different points of view. One will tell you it was a terrible party and they had a lousy time. Another will say it was just okay, they had a decent time but nothing special. The third will say it was outstanding, great, maybe the best party ever.**
As I said before, *"it's all between your ears."* Only you are in control of what you think.
You have a choice, choose wisely.

* * *

After about a year of fun and games we all got a real scare, the draft! We'd turned 18 and the Vietnam War was still going on. My draft number was thirty-nine, Tris' was much higher and Chet's was much lower. The talk at the time was that they were going to take up to number 40 that year. Chet was freaking out and wanted me to join the Navy with him. Now remember how I said I'd do anything for him? Well…I lied - this I would not do. I told him, *"If they draft me, I'll go. I'll do my two years and serve my country but I'm not going to sign up for a four-year stint."* He thought that joining the Navy might keep us out of Vietnam so he joined and he never did go to 'Nam. I stayed home and took my chances. The government cut off the draft at number 35 that year and Tris and I never did have to serve.

* * *

To Chet and all of those who did serve and who serve today, *"I salute you and thank you for protecting us and this great country we live in. You're all heroes to me."*

* * *

So, here I was without a roommate and I had to give up the apartment soon, bummer. My buddy, Tris, and I had been hanging out together for quite some time by then but he couldn't afford to move out yet. While he'd been a permanent fixture at our apartment since we moved in, he worked as a dishwasher and lived at home with his parents, Mort and Phyllis. Tris had an older sister, Candy, and a younger brother named Drew. I think our apartment was an escape for Tris because he was kind of intimidated by his dad - a pretty straight, strict and to-the-point kind of man.

So, with Chester going to the Navy, Tris and I became best friends. We did everything together. One night we were having coffee at the Parasol Restaurant in the Orange Mall when we met **Warren Dennis Cranford (Denny)**. Dennis was with his girlfriend, Lindy, and his buddy, Al, minding their own business. I, being the pain in the ass I can be, decided to bust their chops. I sent a note over to Lindy telling her to dump the loser she was with and join us. Our friend the waitress, Brandy, delivered the note and said Dennis was furious. Remember the song "Brandy" by the Looking Glass, I still think of her and that night every time I hear it.

As Dennis tells the story, Al saved my life that night because he wanted to kill me and Al talked him out of it. Me? I was just having some fun. I was just bored and looking for a little trouble, I guess. After all, my nickname was *"Balls"* and by then I was a real ball-breaker and afraid of no one (on the outside but still scared on the inside). I had grown up some and was bigger and stronger. I grew a goatee on a dare by Chet and my hair was long. A lot of people said I looked like the devil (I didn't like that much) but I looked a little intimidating and I used that to my advantage. I really didn't like fighting but if you looked at me the wrong way I'd be in your face.

Another lesson I learned from my dad was that if you strike first, the other guy will usually back down. He was 100% correct on that. I never looked for trouble but somehow it would always find me. Some guys would just want to see if I was all that and challenge me. But if I acted crazy they would back down most of the time. Thank goodness, it probably saved me from getting my ass kicked many times.

You know, as much as I resented my dad, I loved him very much. Looking back on my younger years, I realize I wanted to be just like him (before the drugs had taken over) a wise guy. I dressed well, and I was always clean and well manicured. I learned to talk and bullshit with the best of them. I was a thief, wore jewelry and I was damn proud to be a Balsamo and an Italian. I was a young, smarter Tony or so I thought.

About a week later, we ran into Dennis in the same restaurant. He was alone so I invited him to have a cup of coffee with us. At first, he was a bit unsure and standoffish but he quickly warmed up to us. Dennis was a pretty cool guy and we quickly became best friends. Dennis came from a nice family. Both his mom and dad were teachers and they demanded a lot out of him. He had a younger sister and brother, Carol and Dave. Dennis, who liked to be called *"Kansas"* because that's where he was born, was a few years older than Tris and me. Dennis had a good job, credit cards and a new car. He was a pretty snappy dresser and always had money in his pocket.

Dennis shared an apartment with **James Halle Jr. (Jim)** who would also become one of my best friends for life. Jim also came from a nice family. His dad was teacher and his mom a homemaker. He had three younger siblings - two sisters, Nadine and Lynette and a brother, Mark.

Dennis and Jim were already going to nightclubs because they were 21. After they told us the stories of all the girls in the nightclubs, I just had to get in on that. I went to the DMV and told them I lost my license so they had to issue me a new one. I took the temporary and doctored the date of birth well enough to pass. Before I knew it, I was on the inside. I guess I had mastered the art of criminal activity from watching my dad and Richard so forging a driver's license was not a reach for me. I was still up to some of the old tricks I'd picked up along the way. Shoplifting was my specialty. I felt I could steal anything from anywhere and get away with it. I would go into a jewelry store and if the shopkeeper showed me three rings I would leave with one. One time, I took the TV set right out of the waiting room at a car dealership. Can you say crazy? I was getting very bold and carried away with stealing. I'd go into a clothing store and leave with two or three pairs of pants.

But somehow, I would always make the excuse for myself that I would only take from the rich and give to the poor - me. I thought I was Robin Hood. I felt, like many thieves, that what I was doing was harmless. After all, I only stole from stores and companies, not individuals. Besides, they had insurance for stuff like that so I figured what's the harm? I would never steal from a person; I just never considered the store owner's people - very convenient.

A few years later, I stole a 14K gold chain from a small jewelry store near home and I was scared to death. I thought for sure they would figure it out and I'd get caught. I knew the owner from going in the store from time to time and I knew in my heart that I stole that chain from him. I ran home and pulled up the rug in the master bedroom and hid it under the carpet for weeks. As time passed, I realized I had gotten away with it but that fear began to seep in and my conscience caught up with me, I started to feel guilty about taking from someone without earning it. I didn't get caught but that was the last time I stole anything. I still wear that gold chain today to remind me of my past and what might have been.

* * *

At this point, I was hitting the nightclubs regularly with Dennis and the guys - drinking, dressing, dancing and picking up girls. Now this was what life was all about! It took me a little while to convince Tris to join us and, by then, Dennis and I were getting much closer. We became very well known at our club, The Santa Ana Clubhouse. The bouncers all knew Dennis, Jim and I so when Tris flashed my fake ID for the first time they just looked the other way. The first night Tris came, he was so nervous about getting busted that I had to take him home. After a while, that passed and he became good friends with Ray, the manager of the club, of all things. We didn't have to pay or show ID anymore. We were the cool guys and this was our club.

We would frequent other clubs on the off nights like St. George and the Dragon on Thursdays (ladies night and the wet T-shirt contest) or Big Daddies on Monday nights (when the Clubhouse was closed). But for the most part, we lived at the Santa Ana Clubhouse. I don't know how we did it. We'd work all day, club all night, pick up a girl and then meet up later at the coffee shop and tell our tales until the wee hours of the morning. Some mornings I'd go home, shower, change and go straight to work. At this point, Carrie was a fond memory and I couldn't imagine I'd ever want a full-time girlfriend again. This was just too much fun and I was having a blast.

I'd given up my apartment with Chester, and Dennis and I were going to get a place together. I was camping out temporarily back at my grandparents house with my mom and sister. Mom had taken over my old room and there was no place inside for me so I set up shop in garage. My grandparents were not too happy with me being there but it was just for a month. Grandma almost had a heart attack when she walked into the garage to do laundry and found me naked with a girl. After that, they wanted me out of there as soon as possible. Dennis and I had already rented a place but he still had to move out of his old place and there was a month's wait on the new apartment. It couldn't come soon enough. Everything I did caused a riff at my grandparents house and put more pressure on my mom, so I was pleased to get the hell out of there and I'm sure they were all glad to see me go.

Dad was up to his old tricks by then. He was using drugs and bothering my mom every chance he got. He'd even show up at her workplace asking her to take him back or give him money. He was still living with Heidi but that relationship was fading fast. Drugs will do that. You see, Tony had a way of draining the life and money out of everyone. He could wear out his welcome faster than anyone I've ever met. I hardly talked to him at all those days. I was still ashamed to be seen with him. He knew it and kept his distance although I was also careful not to let him know where I lived, worked or played. It was safer that way. Dad was smart and he knew that if he caught you off guard he could embarrass you so you would give in just to get rid of him. His famous saying was, *"Do me this one last favor."*

* * *

Dennis and I finally got our place in Santa Ana and Tris was around all the time. After a few weeks, I convinced Dennis to let Tris move in with us and split the rent (the splitting the rent part got him to go for it). It was only a two-bedroom place but we didn't need a dinette area so we made that Tris' room. So here we were, the lady killers, living a few blocks from our club and enjoying life. We all had jobs and we spent every penny on clothes, cars and entertainment. Heck, we didn't even date anymore. We would simply go hang out at the clubhouse and pick up girls there. Life was good and I was beginning to build my own family with people I chose to love - Dennis, Tris, Jim and a guy I'd just met named Clint. We were thick as thieves.

Roy Clint Sunderland. *Clint* was a cool guy; just ask him if you don't believe me. Clint lived with his mom, Moo, as he called her, and she was a special lady. Clint's pop died of a heart attack when Clint was 13 and he had no siblings. Clint was a little different than the rest of us as he was going steady with Lisa, a real no-no around us bachelor types, but we loved him and accepted his faults, Lisa and all.

As time passes, things change. Most friendships and relationships seem to fade but not for us. Despite our differences - wives, jobs, locations and families - we are all still best friends to this day. We have been each other's best men, attended family funerals together, raised our kids together and watched wives come and go. Despite it all, we have been together through the toughest of times and the best of times. It's rare that a group of teenagers go on to spend the rest of their lives together but we did.

It's easy to have a family and keep in touch with them because you're related, you have to. But when your friends become your family that's very special because you have a choice. We all could have walked away at any time, especially when things didn't go so well, but we stuck with each other through thick and thin. I guess we all needed someone in our lives and I am blessed that I had Chester, Tris, Dennis, Jim and Clint as a part of mine. I'm richer and better off for it. And finally, luck stopped escaping me. I've been truly blessed.

* * *

You know, time is a funny thing. When we're kids, a day is like a week, a week is like a month and a month is like a year. As a kid, one semester of school was like an eternity. The years went by slowly and if you were lonely or scared it was even slower; days would just drag on and on. As I look back over my life, I can't believe how many things would happen and change over the course of a couple of months. As we grow older and settle down, we get so busy with our families and careers that the days just blow by. We never seem to have time for anything or anyone anymore. We get too busy working, taking care of the house and family, paying bills, going to school functions, etc. We get to a point where we stop making time for ourselves, let alone our friends. And fun, what's that?

When we were young, we lived for fun and everything else was secondary. Our friends were the most important thing and we only worked so we could make money to go out, shop and have fun. Sex was fun and we did it often and wherever. We lived life to enjoy, be happy and party. We skied, played ball, went to the beach, had parties and went dancing - you name it and we did it. The guys and I played poker, darts, backgammon and casino regularly. We loved to gamble; we'd bet on anything.

Everything we did was for the next good time. All of our plans were about the next weekend, the next Dodger game, concert or date. We listened to music all the time and we really listened. We enjoyed learning the words and they were meaningful to us (especially me). When was the last time you did that? TV was of little importance unless there was a big game or fight on. Now TV has become our entertainment. We live vicariously through the celebrities we see on the boob tube. We used to exercise for the fun and community of it all. We liked to run and climb and swim and ride a bike. Do you remember? I do, but then we grew up. Now, we never have time for anything - we're either too busy or too tired. In another of my favorite movies, "The Shawshank Redemption," Morgan Freeman says, *"It's time to get busy living or get busy dying."* Don't you just love when Morgan narrates a movie? I sure do.

* * *

Let's do something just for fun. Say you're 55 years old. Now for me, that's 20,075 days old or 481,800 hours or something like 29 million minutes. Do you see where I'm going with this? How much do we really remember? I'm writing a book about my life and I have a great memory, but really, I only remember snippets of things, the very best or worst of times. I remember that I lived in my grandparents garage for a month but only remember an hour or two of that time. The rest is a blur.

We spend our lives racing through moments but how many sunsets do you remember? When was the last time you kissed your spouse and really meant it? Not making love and not that peck on the cheek as you run out the door. I mean just kissed that person because you really love and appreciate them? When was the last time you really listened to the wind or to a friend in need? We're all so preoccupied with ourselves that we forget our lives, spouses and kids. We forget to smell the fresh air or just gaze at the clouds or stars. When the hell did we all grow up? And why?

I guess that's just part of life but who planned this thing called life anyway? If I been in charge, we would work weekends and have the other five days off. There would be plenty of everything to go around. We would never fall out of love and hurt other people. Friendships would last forever. Dads would be good, never leave and take care of their families. There would be no wars, hate, crime, hunger or prejudice.

Ok, wake me up, I'm dreaming again. Dang you, *Walter Mitty*.

* * *

If you like someone, tell them.
If you love someone, show them.
People only get flowers when they can't smell them..."

Sadie Hopkins dance (left to right) Tris, Me, Mike and Chester.
(We're all about 17 here.)

Me and the boys (left to right) Clint, Jim, Me and Tris.
(We're in our mid 40s' here)

CHAPTER 6
I LOVE CHOCOLATE

I know that sounds like a funny title for a chapter but as we move along, it will make more sense to you, I promise. But speaking about chocolate I do love it; I'm almost addicted to it. I'm always five to ten pounds overweight because of it. Like the number three, *chocolate* is a big part of my life. I mean who doesn't like chocolate? I love it all: chocolate brownies, chocolate chip cookies, chocolate cake, candy, ice cream, malts and lately, Java Chip Frappuccinos or Cafe Mochas at Starbucks. I can't drive by a Starbucks without getting the craving. Now there's a company we should have all bought stock in.

And forget about having any chocolate goodies in the house. I'll consume them in no time at all. Give me a giant glass of milk and some brownies or chocolate chip cookies and I could die a happy man. I've been known to consume a half gallon of milk and a big bag of Famous Amos cookies in one evening. I also put away large quantities of chocolate chip ice cream at a time. But that was when I was young and really active. Now I drink nonfat milk and I limit myself to a few cookies per night, if that. I hate getting older, I just look at food now and I gain weight. Name me one good thing about growing old other than the fact that you're still alive? See, I knew you couldn't.

Let's get to the real reason I named this chapter chocolate before I get going on a rant about age and weight. I had just turned 19 and I was living my life to the fullest. Well, as full as possible considering I was working at a going nowhere job, making shit for money and driving a used junker for a car. But hey, we were having fun and that was all that mattered. We didn't need much.

By then, Chet was in the Navy and he was getting a taste of working for a living - 24/7, 365 days a year. Ouch, that's not too much fun but hey, it was a great life lesson and he lived at the beach all of the time. The guys and I were out almost every night and meeting all kinds of people, mostly girls. I used to have a silly saying that I'm not too proud of, *"I hate all men and ugly woman."* What can I tell you? I was young and dumb but having fun. Clint was working at a tux shop and he was very much in love with Lisa and planning on getting married so he wasn't around us all that much. Dennis was in sales by day and stocking drugstore shelves in the evenings. Tris was delivering newspapers for a living - filling the actual newsstands. Jim was breaking into sales but was unemployed a good portion of the time. As for me, I was toiling at Overland Industries building motor homes and learning all kinds of things that would come in handy in years to come.

As for my family, things don't change that much at the Balsamos. Mom got into a spat with my grandmother one day over the use of toilet paper, if you can believe that. Mom may have mentioned that grandma was cheap and grandpa overheard it and told her *"that was it,"* she had to *"get out."* Mom and Jackie moved out of my grandparents house shortly thereafter. Like the days back in the camper, there were just too many people in one small place. I guess someone had to go. They moved into a small, one-bedroom upstairs apartment right down the street from the Orange Mall.

Back when I was living at my grandparents house, I upset my grandparents with everything I did. I ate too much, I opened and closed the front door too often, I used too much water when I showered and I dirtied way too many towels. I mean, come on! I was a teenager and if that's the worst thing a teenager does, most people would jump for joy. But then my kid sister was growing up and I don't think they wanted to have another teenager in the house. Let's face it, they were getting older and wanted some peace and quiet. Frankly, they deserved it.

Jackie was a good kid, though. She got really good grades in school, never got in trouble and was quiet, polite and respectful. She was also my mom's best friend but she was still just a pain in the ass to me. She would call me *"pimple face"* and *"four eyes"* of all things and that would piss me off but that's what kid sisters are for. Maybe, just maybe, I resented her a little bit for being mom's favorite. After all, she was the baby and the baby gets most of the attention. Me, I was pretty much the invisible man. As for my dad, I didn't see him too much anymore and I liked it that way - the less the better. Don't get me wrong, he was still around and always after my mother to take him back. I just avoided him as much as possible; it was better for me that way.

* * *

The date Jan. 19, 1973, stands out for two reasons; One, I had a rare date that night, her name was Jody. She was a cute little blond I'd met recently and the big spender I was, I took her to where else? The Santa Ana Clubhouse. As we were walking in, my buddy Jim was out front and he introduced me to a few new people. But I didn't pay much attention at the time because I was on a date. We went inside and got a table and, as usual, the best club band in the world was playing - Emperor.

These guys were so good that when they played songs by Steely Dan or The Doobie Brothers you would swear it was the original artist. I can remember them playing "Stairway to Heaven" by Led Zeppelin, a personal favorite of mine, like it was yesterday. We knew the band pretty well and we'd follow them wherever they played. Jody, it seems, had a crush on Randy, the drummer and lead singer. It didn't take long for me to figure out that she was flirting with him so I got pissed off at her and said, *"See ya later"* and I split. I just left her sitting there, I didn't care. I was moving on.

As I was heading out, I ran into one of the girls that Jim introduced me to earlier that evening, the second and real reason I remember that date. She was sitting on this small back stage by herself and I walked over and sat down. I reintroduced myself to her and she told me her name was *"Chocolate."* I remember thinking, that's a funny name but I liked it and thought she was really cute. She had black hair, brown eyes and a cute shape. She was about five feet tall and 105 pounds, soaking wet. She was this little firecracker but looked nothing like the girls I was normally attracted to. We danced some and had a few drinks but mostly, we just sat and talked together for the longest time. I was really enjoying her company. Jody who?

As the night went on, my buddy, Tris, and Chocolate's best friend, Teri, joined us and later we all went out for breakfast. We hung out together all night and ended up watching the sunrise at the beach the next morning. We spent the whole next day and evening together. Our buddies, Tris and Teri, hit it off quickly and were already getting hot and heavy. But not us, we spent most of the time walking, talking and hanging out. I really liked this girl right from the start. I'd never met someone who seemed so interested in me. Not the playboy Mr. Cool me but the real me. It was like she could see through my facade. We started dating immediately. Me, dating, can you believe that? Most of the time it was pick up a girl, have sex and then it was over but we were beginning to see each other almost daily.

Choc (my nickname for her) had just turned 26 in November and I was just nineteen in December so we were seven years apart. I never told her my age and she never asked. She just assumed I was in my mid-20s and I let her believe it. Chocolate also had a four-year-old baby girl named Michael, after her dad, Chocolate's ex-husband. As time went on, we were seeing each other more and more. My roommate, Dennis, was beginning to have a fit because she was cutting in on our boy time together. Tris didn't seem to mind because he and Teri were having too much fun. They liked smoking pot and hanging out with each other and I'm sure Tris didn't mind the steady sex either.

As for Choc and I, we were both a bit conflicted. We really liked each other and liked spending time together but neither of us really wanted to get involved. She had recently broken up with her ex-husband and was finally free. She wasn't looking for a new man in her life. I, on the other hand, had sworn never to get close to another woman. You know, that broken heart stuff, a guy has to be careful. So we were both trying to play it as cool as possible. We were still going out with our friends and having a good time but we couldn't help but wind up together all of the time.

As for sex, well that was not in the cards yet but I liked her a lot and respected her wishes. I figured, I'd just have to get satisfaction when I wasn't with her. This, needless to say, caused quite few problems down the road. The more she held out the more attracted I became. A good lesson for all of you gals - Chocolate said she hooked me and she did. By the time she relented months later, I had already fallen in love with her. Now I was really confused, because that was the last thing in the world I wanted. I mean come on, I was 19, I was having a blast, and I had great friends and a nice pad. The last thing I needed was a woman in my life to screw things up and an older woman with a young child no less.

* * *

Marie Christine Vesentine. *Chocolate* was born in Los Angeles. Her dad built their first home in Fontana when she was just a baby and that's where she grew up. When I say built, I mean he got out there with hammer and nails and built the house. Chocolate had it pretty rough as a child. She was the baby of four children born to Raymond and Ruth Vesentine.

Ray Vesentine was Italian which may explain his tough temperament or maybe it was because he was on his own as a very young boy. Ray's parents both died early and he bounced around with uncles until his early teens so he had very little guidance or love as a child. Ray was a good-looking guy and a bit of a player as a youngster, a real ladies' man.

Ruth Cordova was Mexican and had a calm, peaceful demeanor. Ruth was diagnosed with epilepsy at a young age, which may have caused her to be a little off center. Ruth's mom ran around with many men and Ruth never knew her real father. By the time she was in her early teens, Ruth's mother was running a prostitution business out of their home. There was talk that she even put her daughters to work. Ray, who lived across the street, rescued Ruth and married her.

Ray and Ruth married at a very young age and they were a good-looking couple. So, my girl was half Italian and half Mexican, which made for one beautiful gal who could lose her temper from time to time and I certainly helped. Although Ray always worked hard, they were still a very poor family. Ray worked all day while Ruth took care of the house and family. On evenings and weekends, they raised goats, chickens and grew their own food. All of the kids had to work - there was no such thing as play. If they ever said they were bored or looked like they had nothing to do, they'd find themselves outside weeding the property or milking a goat.

Her brother, Raymond Jr., was the oldest. He, too, was epileptic like his mom and a little slow. Ray was not retarded but he was slow to say the least and maybe a little crazy. As a child and young man he could be very mean and would bully and hit his siblings. Ray never got along with his dad at all. Back in the day, if you were slow you were kind of an outcast.

Next in line was her sister, Esther, who was the lone wolf of the family. Being the eldest girl, Esther, was stuck with most of the household chores and caring for the little ones. Esther was always Ray's favorite. He would tell the others how they were not as good, smart or as pretty as Esther. Esther grew up to resent both her parents but her mom especially, maybe because she was unable to protect them from Ray.

Esther was followed by Chocolate's favorite, her brother, Johnny, the black sheep of the family. Johnny was in and out of trouble his whole life. He was truly Ray's whipping boy. At 17, he joined the army and went to Vietnam just to get away from his father. For him, this was the safer life choice, which is really sad.

Like most families back in the forties, this family was dysfunctional at best. Raymond worked long hours and when he'd get home he worked on the house he was building for his family. Ray always drank way too much *vino*, as he would call it, and had no patience for his children. Ray was the type of man who really believed that children *"should be seen and never heard."* He ruled with an iron fist and a long leather belt which he used freely and often on his kids. Ray was downright cruel! But we'll blame it on the booze, the stress, the depression, his childhood. Yeah, right!

Ruth was as sweet as the day is long but back in the 1940s and '50s, women had to mind their place in the home. She really couldn't do anything about Ray and his bad habits. Ruth would just have to watch and cry as he beat their children. Her job was to cook, keep house, raise the kids and help Ray with whatever he needed. I don't think Ray ever raised a hand to Ruth. He loved her very much but I'm sure he was verbally tough on her, too. I think Ruth had a good heart and loved her children dearly - especially her baby, Chocolate. She would always tell everyone to take care of her baby. She told me that the first time we met and every time thereafter, *"Take care of my baby."* I promised her that I would. A promise is a promise.

* * *

When Chocolate was a child, her brother Johnny nicknamed her Chocolate because she was so little and so dark. I've seen photos of her as a kid and she was this little ragamuffin with long ragged dresses and no shoes on her feet. She always looked dirty but it was just because she was so dark. She tells the story of how when she grew out of her shoes, her dad would cut off the fronts so her toes would stick out and she could wear them a while longer.

Chocolate and Johnny were very close as kids. He was her big brother and her protector. Everything Johnny did she would do. She went everywhere with him. She loved and idolized him. Choc was the biggest (or should I say smallest) tomboy around and she still has a few scars to show for it. Whenever Ray would hit the kids, Johnny would get in front of Chocolate and beg that he hit him and not his baby sister. Johnny would always stand up for Chocolate and he would even take the blame for her when she did something wrong.

The Vesentines were not a very religious family as Ray would not allow it; in fact, he would burn Ruth's bibles. However, that didn't slow down Ruth or Chocolate. They both managed to keep the faith. Chocolate would go to the Catholic Church on Sundays because she wanted a relationship with God, even at a young age. She even considered becoming a nun for a while. Funny, I wanted to be an altar boy. It's a lucky thing for me that she took a different path, a path that led her to me.

At nine years old, Chocolate was kidnapped by some freak of nature who had a thing for little girls. He gave her some cock-and-bull story about his car breaking down and being late to pick up his kid from school. He managed to talk her into the car and the second they drove off together she knew she screwed up. She could hear her mom telling her, *"Never talk to strangers."* She began to scream and cry; as he exposed himself, begging him to let her go home. She kept pleading and crying so much that maybe this nut job had a change of heart and pulled over on the freeway. He instructed her to get out and stand in front of his car. Why? Who knows? But as soon as he reached over and opened the door, she jumped out and started running and screaming. Being a relentless fighter, she still had the guts to look back and flip him off as she ran. She got away safely, thank God! She was the lucky one. I sometimes wonder how many others who came into contact with that bastard were so lucky.

Chocolate went to school and worked until she was old enough to leave home. So she, too, was on her own at 17. One of my favorite stories is how, as a young girl, she worked at a chicken ranch and had to cut the chicken beaks. The woman can't kill a bug - she'll make me take a spider outside - but she de-beaked those chickens, because it was her job. At 17, she was waiting tables and living with her brother Johnny and her sister-in-law, Teri, her best girlfriend from school.

Not long after, she met Michael Lemmon while working in the restaurant and they started dating. They married and had a baby girl, **Michael Marie Lemmon,** nicknamed *Tisby* by Grandpa Ray. Chocolate and Michael separated after a few years of marriage but she always stayed in touch with him and his wonderful family. I remember when I first met Mom and Pop, as everyone called them, they were so nice to me. They always made me feel welcome and like part of their family. At that time, Chocolate was full of piss and vinegar and she wanted much more out of life than a nice husband, family and a home with a white picket fence. She wanted to make her mark and she had a lot to prove; she was definitely a modern day woman. She had gone to beauty school and learned to style hair while she was married to Michael.

Chocolate also tried her hand working as a traffic girl for a radio station in Fresno. When that didn't work out, she and her daughter, *Mikee* (for short), moved to Garden Grove. Here they lived with Teri (her brother Johnny's ex-wife) and her two daughters, Tina and Cathy, and Teri's brother, Stan, and his wife, Lorraine. Lorraine, whose nickname is *Sam,* and Chocolate went on to become the best of friends for life. It was one, big, happy family and that's where I came into the picture.

* * *

As I was saying, the last thing I needed in my life was a woman to screw things up for me. Well, so much for self control. Chocolate and I were seeing each other pretty steadily by then and she had just moved down the street from my apartment with Teri, Sam and a new girl named Kim. Tris and Teri had cooled off by then and he was now chasing Kim around. Dennis and Jim were still going out every night and Dennis was still none too happy with me seeing Chocolate as much as I was. Chocolate started spending more and more time at the apartment with me and Dennis was losing his cool over this. He didn't want a woman and a child hanging out in his bachelor pad and really, who could blame him? Needless to say, we got into a few heated arguments over this and almost came to blows when he called her a *"bitch."*

So much for the bachelor apartment! We all decided it would be best to go our separate ways for a while. Tris caught a cold of some sort, got real sick and moved back in with his parents. Dennis moved into a house with Clint and a couple of other guys. Teri and Sam, who was in the middle of a breakup with her husband Stan, got an apartment of their own in Orange. Chocolate, Mikee and I stayed in the apartment in Santa Ana and played house for a while. We were having a good time together but the hard part was that neither of us were very committed to the relationship. We would still go our separate ways, clubbing with our friends on weekends, and I was always getting into trouble. I was just 19 for crying out loud but of course, she didn't know that, *yet.*

* * *

I remember the first time I met Choc's parents. They were coming into town to visit her and to spend the night and Chocolate had somehow failed to mention that we lived together. She was such a rebel (and still is), she felt it was none of their business and that she didn't have to report to them or anyone. When they arrived at the apartment, we had dinner and a nice visit. Chocolate introduced me as her boyfriend and later that evening, they began to wonder when I was going to go home. When Chocolate informed them that I lived there, they were a little taken back. Her dad looked perplexed but *Nonna* (Ruth's nickname) loved me from the very first minute we met. Needless to say, it was a little uncomfortable for all of us that evening but we got over it. Things were going pretty good for a while but we were still torn between our freedom and our relationship. I guess freedom won out!

After several indiscretions on my part, we were barely holding it together. Chocolate had left me once already but I convinced her to come back. I really loved this girl but I had such a hard time showing it and giving up the playboy lifestyle at the same time. Believe me, it wasn't sex that drove me, it was the game - the flirting and seeing if I could get the girl. The winning! Most of the time I didn't even have sex once I knew I could, I'd just go home to Chocolate. I was completely addicted to the chase, finding a target and seeing if I could land it. I know it sounds disgraceful now but as I mentioned earlier, addictions come in all sorts of forms.

I never wanted to hurt anyone, least of all Chocolate, the love of my life. But I did, too many times, and I'm still sorry about that to this day.

One night, Choc and I were out shopping innocently enough when we each purchased something at the same clothing store. This was back in the day when you wrote a check for everything and they checked your identification. Well, this extremely sharp sales lady thought it was so cute that we were a couple despite our age difference. Chocolate really didn't hear or register what she said but I thought she did and my guilty conscience took over. When we reached the car, I confessed to the age difference and told her I was just 19. Well, she was floored: disgusted, upset, mad, disappointed and any other emotion you could imagine but mostly, she was sad. She felt she had wasted all this time falling in love with me. All I could do was apologize and beg her forgiveness.

Things seemed okay for a little while but she moved out shortly thereafter. She and a girlfriend of ours, Nancy Keester, got a small apartment together in Orange. It wasn't just the lie about the age, it was more about trust and the fact that she believed I was too young and immature to ever be faithful and maintain a long-term relationship. I was broken-hearted again but I regressed to the screw her mode just like I did after Carrie.

So, I needed to find a new place to live. I'd run out of roommates and I could not afford a place of my own on the money I made. Overland Industries was a steady job but didn't pay much. Mom had upgraded her apartment to a two bedroom and guess who was back? My dear old dad! Somehow, he had weaseled his way back into her life. He used the typical, *"I'm going to change, I'll get a job, I love you, I missed you"* lines, and the winner, *"I have nowhere else to go."* Mom fell for that one. She felt sorry for him and she let him move back in. My mom always loved my dad dearly; she just hated everything he did.

I ended up crashing on their couch for a few weeks until I could save a few bucks to get a new place. Things were pretty much the same as I remembered them except not as violent. They still argued often but not as bad. Dad was on parole again and committed to the methadone program. Methadone was a drug provided free from the state to help keep him normal and it was required by his parole officer.

I took him to get his meds one day and asked the doctor about the drug and why he needed to take it. He informed me that my dad had used heroin for so long and at such high doses that he would never be able to live without some form of drugs again. He was doomed to live on this type of program for the rest of his life or the pain and cravings he would suffer would be more than he could handle. He also told me that he was receiving the highest possible dosage allowed by law and that if I took it I would overdose and possibly die.

All in all, things were fairly calm for my family but I couldn't wait to get out of there and they were happy to see me go. Let's face it, it was a pretty small place and I was one too many.

* * *

Like father like son, somehow I convinced Chocolate to please, please give me another chance. Meanwhile, my buddy, Tris, got an apartment with Kim in Tustin. I could never understand what he saw in her; she was such a bitch to him all the time. Kim and I didn't get along at all. In fact, I think she hated me. Chocolate and I were spending the night at their apartment one night when Choc finally conceded and agreed to give us one more chance. It only took me begging and being rushed to the hospital with an asthma attack to win her back. You see, Kim had a cat and I found out the hard way that I'm very allergic to cats. I had such a bad attack that the next morning, we all thought I was going to die. I didn't and I was relieved and elated.

Chocolate and I moved out and got an apartment together right away. We moved into the Walnut East Apartments, an all adults and no pets complex, right down the street from Tris and Kim. I don't know how we pulled that off because we had Mikee and later, my dog, *"Bo,"* an Irish Setter, as well as an aquarium full of tropical fish. Playing by the rules was never my strong suit so I guess I lied and just snuck Mikee in. We didn't want to live in an apartment complex that allowed kids because they were all older, messy and who wanted to put up with the racket?

I was keeping my nose clean when it came to women but like father like son, I was up to some old tricks of my own. I was shoplifting everything and anything I could get my hands on. I think I just needed the rush and I couldn't get it from chasing girls. When I look back, I think that the chasing girls, the stealing and the gambling all had one common denominator, *winning*. When you grow up as a so-called *loser*, you need to win at something and these were three things I was good at. I guess I needed to prove to myself that I was worthy of something, even if it's wrong or bad.

The stealing got so bad that if Chocolate was with me she would nearly strip search me before we left a store. She pleaded with me to stop but I didn't. She warned me that I was going to end up in jail but I knew every trick of the trade. I was too good to ever get caught or so I thought.

My second time going to jail I went alone and had no one else to blame but myself. You see, every year around Thanksgiving, Overland Industries, the wonderful company I toiled for, would lay me off and then rehire me around the second week of January. They did this so they could save on the holiday pay for Thanksgiving, Christmas and New Years Day. I worked for these cheap bastards for seven years and I never completed a full year so they never once paid me for a vacation. They really worked the system well and back then, we were too dumb and scared to know our legal rights. They always rehired me because I was a really good worker. I could out-work anyone in the place but I always had a bad attitude because I knew what they were doing. Still, I needed the job so I always came back.

It was bad enough to be out of work around the holidays when you're single but now I had a family and that made it really terrible for me. I would panic and race around town trying to get any work I could find. This one particular year, there was a strike at the Alpha Beta Super Markets and we heard the warehouse was hiring scab labor (workers who were willing to cross the picket lines). Hey, I needed work and money for the rent, and Chocolate's birthday and the holidays were right around the corner. Tris was out of work also so he went with me and we got hired. I didn't give a shit about crossing the picket lines; I wasn't afraid of the strikers. I thought that if these greedy bastards were willing to walk off a union job that paid $15 an hour plus benefits then screw them. At the time, I was making about $3.50 an hour with no bennies at all. So, here we were driving a forklift for four times my normal pay, I thought this was too good to be true.

As I was heading home after my shift one day, I noticed a large black lunch pail that someone had left behind. I couldn't help myself; I picked it up and marched out with it. As I reached the guard gate I was asked to open the lunch box. I did so and to my surprise there were two cartons of cigarettes in there, Virginia Slims of all things. I tried to explain to everyone that it was not my lunch box but I just got the yeah, sure, okay, look as they hauled me off to jail.

Now, I have two questions. First, who the hell would want to steal Virginia Slims? And second, how could I get away with stealing TVs, jewelry, clothing and then get busted for a used lunch box? Shit luck, I guess. I called Chocolate and she bailed me out a few hours later. She had to take up a collection to raise the money. I had to hire a lawyer and he got the charges dropped down to misdemeanor trespassing. That experience cost me about $800, which was a lot of money back then. But hey, look at the bright side, I did get to keep the lunch box.

My third visit to the pokey is the one that finally scared me straight. I had a Pontiac Firebird and I had lost the little emblem off the front hood so I went to the dealer where I bought the car and always had it serviced. I knew the service manager pretty well, and we were friends. He told me to get a spare from the parts department and then take the car around back and have another friend of ours (the mechanic) put it on for me, *"no charge."*

That Friday evening, I had just come in from the pool and Chocolate was down the way visiting Dennis and his new girlfriend (and future wife), Pam, who just moved into our apartment complex. As I was drying off, these two plain clothes detectives knocked at the door and asked for, you guessed it, Steve Balsamo. I said, *"That's me"* and they said, *"Oh goodie"* as they spun me around, handcuffed me and read me my rights. I asked *"What did I do?"* and they said they didn't know or care, they were just picking me up because they had a warrant for my arrest.

Mikee, who was with me at the time, went running down to Denny's apartment to tell her mom what was happening. These bastards wouldn't even let me put my clothes or shoes on; they took me away in a wet bathing suit. I was taken to the Orange County jail and stuck in a big holding tank with a load of Friday night drunks. They were all fighting and acting crazy and here I was, barefoot in a pair of swim trunks. I was scared to death.

It gets worse. As they called each prisoner, the guards would slap them around if they didn't obey their every command. They called this one big Hispanic guy who was so screwed up he could hardly stand, let alone answer their questions. Well, three guards went to town on him. One held his arms through the bars while the other two beat him with their clubs. Once he was limp, they grabbed him by his feet and dragged him off somewhere, out cold and bleeding.

I was up next, and this big, burly, bald-headed cop called me out of the cage. I obeyed his every command and *"yes sired"* him to death. When he was all through fingerprinting and booking me he stuck a pair of ugly, old, black boots in my chest and said *"Here's your shoes."* I made the mistake of saying they weren't mine and then he hit me in the chest so hard with those boots that they almost stuck. He said, *"I said, HERE'S YOUR SHOES!"* I said, *"Thank you."* I spent about eight hours in a cell holding onto those boots like they were a bag of gold until Chocolate bailed me out. As I walked out to meet her, I was still in my trunks, barefoot and holding onto those boots. I tossed them into the trash right outside the door and we went home.

It was a long ride home with a lot of *"I told you so's"* followed by a longer weekend wondering why I had gotten busted. Every crime I'd ever committed ran through my head like a bad dream. I had to wait until Monday morning at court to find out what the charges were - petty theft. To my surprise, the kid in the parts department at the Pontiac dealership thought I stole the emblem and he called the cops. Needless to say, my buddy the service manager dropped the charges and told the court it was an honest mistake. By the way, the emblem cost about $5 back then.

So between going to jail, having to hear *"I told you so"* from Chocolate and owing the bail money for months, I swore I'd never break the law and go back again. Three's a charm for me. I never have gone back and I don't plan on it anytime soon. But, I still didn't completely learn my lesson at that point.

* * *

So now that I was too scared to steal, what was I going to do for excitement? Well, one night, I went to the Clubhouse with Tris and the guys. By now, the love affair between Tris and Kim had run its course so he was on his own again. You know they say, *"You can't teach an old dog, new tricks?"* So what did I do? I picked up on some blond chick and left with her. What I didn't know was that Tris' sister, Candy, was at the club, too. She saw me, called Chocolate and told her all about it. Why? That's a good question. I guess I'll never know the answer.

When I got home, Chocolate was waiting up for me, and she was furious. She told me that she was there and saw me with her own eyes leaving the club with the blond. I tried to lie my way out of it but when she started to describe the girl and what she was wearing I knew that I was screwed. So I confessed and Chocolate moved out that next day. Only this time it was different for me, I really was sorry. I could finally see that I had someone who really loved me and all I could do was hurt her. I was crushed; she was crushed. I was so disappointed and disgusted with myself. I felt I had turned into my dad. I told myself that if she ever gave me another chance I would never hurt her again, not for anybody or anything.

Tris moved back into the apartment with me while I tried everything I could to win her back. After a couple of months of begging, pleading and being on my best behavior, somehow I managed to convince her to give me one final chance. I promised her that if I ever screwed up again I would let her go and never bother her again. And you know how I feel about a promise. She moved back in and poor Tris was out on his own again. Tris got a place close by with another friend of ours, Bob, a real chick magnet, so he was in good hands.

Finally, I was really committed to Chocolate and our future. I got a new job making better money at a produce market called Bumper Crop Produce, my first and only union job. After a while, Chocolate and Tris also came to work there. The work wasn't bad and the pay was really good; union pay and rules heavily favor the employee.

A few months into the job, I hurt my knee unloading a truck but that didn't slow me down. I continued to work for weeks until my knee blew up three times the size of the other and I landed flat on my back at Kaiser Permanente. Now I hadn't been in the hospital since I was born so it was a little scary to say the least. After a few days and a few dozen doctors trying to figure out what was wrong with me, I was really getting nervous. Chocolate was by my side every moment that she wasn't at work. By that point, whatever I had was spreading to all my joints. My ankles, elbows, knees, wrists and jaw were all swollen and hurt like hell. The doctors kept coming in and draining them with these great big needles. Ouch! After about a week of tests, the doctors finally came up with *"Writers Arthritis,"* whatever that is. They treated the condition with large doses of antibiotics and rest and it seemed to subside so they said I could go home a few days later.

One day while still in the hospital, I wanted a hamburger so bad I could taste it. Chocolate and Nancy had come to visit and I convinced them to sneak me out a back door in a wheelchair with the IV bottle still hooked up to my arm. We went to the first hamburger joint we could find. We thought that was really funny but the nurses were none too happy with us when we returned; I guess that was a real no-no. After about two weeks, they finally let me go home. I was relieved but I was told that I'd have to be out of work for a few months. *"Like hell,"* I thought.

When I got out of the hospital I could barely walk. My knees and ankles were so sore and my muscles had atrophied so much I had to actually rebuild them. I got fired from the produce market because they couldn't hold the job for me any longer or so they said (where was the so-called union?). I think it was because their insurance company had to pay the doctor and hospital bills and that pissed them off. So, now I was out of a job and I couldn't work; I had to collect disability. What a disgrace, I thought. I hated it and I could barely survive on the mere pittance that they provided.

* * *

Meanwhile, my buddy, Chester, had just gotten out of the Navy and he was a changed man. He got a real good job right away and for once, he kept it. We introduced him to our friend, Nancy, and they started dating. One night we went to his apartment for his birthday party and all was going well when Chester went to walk Nancy to her car. A few minutes later, he came rushing in looking for help. I limped out to the parking lot on my crutches to find him arguing with these three guys. Just when it looked like it would blow over, Chocolate came out to get me and one of the guys started making rude comments about how much he liked Chocolate.

The next thing I knew, I was slamming his head on the hood of Chocolate's car. Well, needless to say, the three of them started to go to work on me pretty good when Chet's sister, Dee, and her boyfriend, Bobby, came to my rescue. Now it was three on three and they lost. Bobby was body slamming them while Dee was kicking them. It got really ugly. So much for taking it easy on my legs. What can I say? Young with no brains.

After about a month or so I couldn't take it any longer, I was finally strong enough to get around so I went back to work at Overland Industries. They would always find a place for me and were always my fallback position. Hey, it was a job. Besides that, over the years I learned a lot working there. We built motor homes, which were just small houses on wheels, so I gained a lot of construction and cabinet-making skills along the way.

Shortly thereafter, Chester and Nancy split up and Chet met another girl named Nancy at his work. They hit it off right away. They married and bought a house in a little town called Pedley which was in Riverside County, about an hour away. A house, a real house! Well, this we had to see. Choc and I went out to visit one weekend and we were blown away. He paid something like $48,000 for it and it had three bedrooms, two baths, a living room, dining room, kitchen and a two-car garage. Wow. They also had a half acre of horse property which meant they could have animals. Chet didn't need a down payment because he had the GI bill so they got in with virtually nothing out of pocket. I guess going into the Navy really paid off for him. Chet learned how to settle down. He got a really good job, a wife and now a house all at 22 years old. Not bad for a kid. I was really proud of Chet and still am.

Well, after seeing Chet's place, Chocolate and I had our first real goal as a team. We wanted our own house and we were going to do anything to get it. Over the years, I'd worked hard to establish my credit and it was pretty good. I had a wallet full of credit cards and purchased a few cars on credit but nothing like a house. Chocolate and I started house shopping on weekends and we soon realized that the only chance of us ever buying a home was to do what Chester did and move out to Pedley.

The price difference between Orange County and Riverside County was considerable even back then; Riverside was about half as much. I also thought this would be a good way for us to be together without the distraction of friends, family and the nightclubs. We had just one major problem - we had no money for a down payment and no GI bill so we had to think outside of the box.

We found a new housing tract that was being built about a quarter of a mile from Chet's house. These were new homes and that really excited us. We picked a model that we liked: a four-bedroom, two-bath, with a big kitchen, a dinette and a large living room. This, too, was horse property on a half acre of land. We had to put down a $1,000 non-refundable deposit and the house would be built and ready in a year. This was our only chance to buy a home so we jumped at it. We borrowed the money on our credit cards and signed our lives away.

Next came the drama of coming up with the rest of the down payment that was due when the house was ready. Chocolate and I agreed that we would find second jobs so we could start saving right away. We needed about $10,000 plus money for the upgrades and furniture. I quickly got a job (at a factory) just down the street from Overland cleaning machinery on the swing shift at minimum wage. I would go to work at 7 o'clock in the morning at Overland, get off at 3:30 p.m. and race up the street to start my next job at 3:45 and work until midnight. From there, I'd go home, eat dinner, visit with Choc and do it again. I was also working half-days on Saturdays at Overland whenever I could get the overtime.

Chocolate, on the other hand, was working days at Sunwest Bank and at night, she did people's hair in our apartment because she had to be home with Mikee. She cut and colored more people's hair at night and on weekends than Carter had liver pills.

After about three months of doing this, we weren't getting very far and we were beat all the time. I could barely keep my eyes open at either job. Something had to give. I was always making something at work for our apartment and, one day, I made a hanging wall planter for Chocolate and everyone who saw it liked it.

I quit the night job and used the time to make these planters on our apartment patio. We sold small ones for $12 and the large ones for $20. Chocolate was still cutting hair on evenings and weekends as much as she could but she was also trying to help me sell the planters.

To tell you the truth, I don't know how in the world the neighbors put up with all the noise from the saws and routers but I worked every afternoon until dark and all day on weekends. Our next door neighbors, Danny and Sherry, were a big help also. Sherry worked at Quickset Lock and they had over 200 employees there, mostly women. Sherry would take the planters to work with her and hang them in the restrooms and sell them for us. She sold a lot of planters. Thanks Sherry, wherever you are.

We were possessed. We sold Chocolate's car, a nice 240Z and bought her a used Volkswagen bug so we didn't have to make payments and could save more money. We never went out or bought anything. We lived on hamburger meat and rice and man, did we learn to love rice. A big treat for us was a drive-in movie. Chocolate would make popcorn and *"shit in the oven,"* her version of stuffed bell peppers with more rice, cheese and hamburger meat than bell peppers, and we'd eat it in the car.

Most nights, after working all day, we'd pile into the car and drive out to the new house to see how much progress they had made that day. That became our entertainment. Mikee and Bo would run around the lot and play and Choc and I would daydream about our new home. I would bring tools and a flashlight and sometimes, I would add little things to the house like extra outlets, speaker wire or more TV and phone jacks. No one seemed to notice or care. Chocolate and I were growing closer and closer. We were finally learning to lean on and trust each other completely. This was an exciting and challenging time for both of us and we loved and treasured it.

* * *

Meanwhile, dad got off probation and it wasn't long before he was up to his old tricks, heroin. He started driving my mom crazy so she kicked him out, again. Mom didn't want him around the house with my sister and who could blame her? Sure enough, he appeared one night at my door with nowhere to go. Chocolate gave me the, *"He's your father, you can't leave him out in the street"* speech so we let him stay on our couch for a few days but I really didn't want to. I knew in my heart this would not work out well. The reason it only lasted a few days was because one day after work, I went to get my tools and guess what? They were gone! All of them.

I'll be damned if he didn't take and sell my power tools for drugs. He didn't come back that night. I guess he knew better, because I wanted to kill him. When Chocolate got home from work we noticed a few other things missing: a pearl ring that was a gift to her, some change we were saving and some $2 bills we were collecting along with some old coins.

He did it to me again. **Shame on ME!**

* * *

So, I had to spend some of our savings on new tools. What a waste, I thought as I kicked myself. I should have known better, I should have used my head. Why did I ever let him into my house? Over the years, my dad has broken my heart over and over again. The more he did things like this to me the more distance was created. Distance that no time, apologies, or love could erase.

But, as I said before, nothing was going to stop Chocolate and me. We were more determined than ever. We were going to get that house if it killed us and believe me, it almost did.

Chocolate and her brother Johnny with Santa.

Chocolate as a young teen.

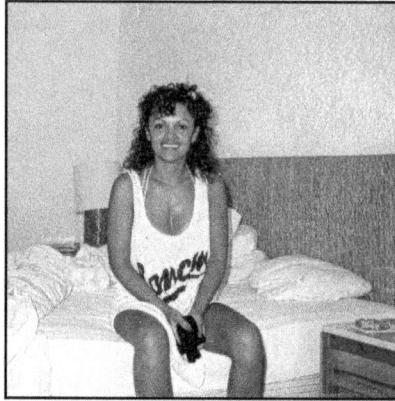

Chocolate - Our family vacation in Cancun.

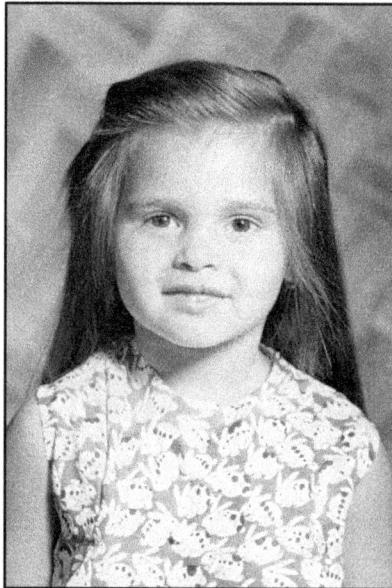

Mikee - 4 years old.

CHAPTER 7
HOME SWEET HOME

It was early December, 1975. I was just 22 turning 23 in a few weeks and our house was finally ready. We had saved most of the money but we did add a few upgrades to the house so we needed about $13,000 in total which put us a few thousand short. We ended up borrowing the remaining amount on our credit cards, so now we were up to our eyeballs in debt. We didn't care though; we just figured we'd pay off the credit cards the same way we saved for the house. It was pretty rough for a while but I quickly learned a surefire way to get out of credit card debt.

What we did was pay the minimum on all of the credit cards but one, the one with the lowest balance. That one, we'd *attack* with everything we could until it was paid off. Two good things would result: first, we felt a sense of accomplishment that we paid something off and second, we had one less bill so we could now attack the next lowest one. It took a while but once we paid off all of the credit cards, I swore that I would never charge anything again on a card that I couldn't pay in-full when the bill came due that next month.

It's a good rule to live by. No, check that, it's a great rule to live by and I still do to 'til this day. I've also taught that *"get out of debt plan"* to many others over the years. It really works. The only part they never seem to get is the part about never charging more than you can pay when the next bill arrives. People always seem to fall back into the same old traps and habits. They make excuses for themselves; they want something now so they charge it. But credit card debt is one of the worst things you can do to yourself financially and it's a tough habit to quit. We Americans tend to live way beyond our means and credit is to blame for it. If you can't afford to pay for it, *"don't buy it."* It's that simple.

* * *

I'll never forget the Saturday we moved. My buddy, Tris, was coming over to help us but he got sick and canceled. I had already rented a large U-Haul truck so we said, *"To hell with it"* and we did it ourselves. Between Chocolate, Mikee and I, we loaded everything, cleaned up the old apartment and were on our way to our new home. Once we arrived, we worked our butts off until everything was unloaded and put away. Even the pictures were hung on the wall and perfectly leveled at that!

At about 1 o'clock in the morning, we finished putting up the aquarium and were ready to call it a night. We were lying on the floor in our new living room watching TV and having a snack when we heard this loud crack. We all looked at each other and then, all of a sudden, the bottom of the aquarium let loose. Fifty-five gallons of water, fish and gravel were all over our new carpet. We were so bummed out. It took us hours to clean up the mess and dry the carpet. My poor fish had to make due in a large trash can with a makeshift filter for the night. But the next day, I bought a new aquarium and we were back in business.

For the longest time, I blamed my buddy, Tris, for not being there to help me but I never made a big deal of it. I just moved on. The aquarium was just too heavy for the girls to handle and we must have tweaked it, causing it to break. But I learned a very valuable lesson from this: *Don't ask people for favors.*

Asking for favors puts people in an uncomfortable position and sometimes they say *"yes"* when they really want to say *"no."* I made a commitment to myself right then and there to never ask anyone for a favor again and I don't. If I can't afford help, I just do it myself or we do without. This, too, has served me well over the years; I've never been in debt to anyone for anything. Now, don't get me wrong, I'm not bitter. I do favors for people, friends and family all the time. In fact, I offer up my services freely. I like to help others.

* * *

Now, I hope you realize that aside from the normal trials and tribulations we all go through in life, I was happy. Really truly happy for maybe the first time in my life. We were having a blast in our new home. We'd work on decorating and furnishing the inside and landscaping the half-acre outside every chance we got. When I wasn't at work, I was working in my garage or around the house and Chocolate was never too far from my side. I always made sure she was close by. I liked it that way. Still do.

All of that experience I got from working with my Uncle Billy around his house and at Overland Industries finally came in handy. We did everything ourselves, just the three of us. Mikee had always wanted animals and a horse so we decided to get some. We got her a horse named Tonapah and Mikee was in heaven. She rode him every day after school for hours on end. It was nice to see her happy again after being stuck in an apartment with us for so long. I built her a barn and corrals to house the horse and his supplies but we didn't stop there.

We already had a tank full of tropical fish (with my big black shark) and my dog, Bo. Bo mated with our neighbor's Irish Setter and we ended up with two of the pups, Sadie and Dallas. Dallas was named after my favorite football team, the *Dallas Cowboys*. Why Dallas you may ask? I fell in love with them when I was just 14. When I first arrived in California, I needed a new team the Jets were miles away. The Cowboys were on TV a lot and they had the Dallas Cowboy Cheerleaders. Need I say more? We also added two cockatoos, a litter of kittens (that had to live outdoors), a prize-winning goat named Peaches and if that wasn't enough, I brought home a baby rooster and some little chickens. Chocolate was asleep one Sunday morning and I put them in bed with her to wake her. It was Green Acres all over again, Chocolate was the country girl and I was the city boy playing farmer. We were madly in-love and life was good.

All of the neighbors had animals, too. The people behind us had a prize-winning giant turkey which was really beautiful, as turkeys go. My dogs loved to chase the birds and animals around the yard. Bo would run right into the chain link fence while looking up and running after a bird.

One evening, when we got home from work, I noticed that the dogs were playing with something big out in the backyard. When I went out to see what it was, to my surprise I noticed that it was my neighbor's prize turkey. It was dead and the feathers were all over our yard. I panicked. I ran inside and grabbed Mikee and Chocolate and some trash bags and we went out and cleaned up the mess as quickly as possible. I took the bags around the corner and dumped them into a trash dumpster. We never spoke another word of it around the house. To this day, our old neighbors must still be wondering what the hell happened to their turkey.

Another time, I came home to find Bo all beaten up. I couldn't figure out for the life of me what could have caused this so I started watching the big German Sheppard next door more closely. I mean, this dog was the size of a lion. I let Bo out into the yard one day and I watched in horror as this great big dog leaped over the 5 foot fence like it was nothing and attacked my dog. I had a nice talk with the neighbor but he didn't seem to take it too seriously. After it happened again, I told him that the next time his dog jumped over the fence it would be dead before it hit the ground. From that point on, his dog was on a chain whenever it was outdoors. Needless to say, that neighbor and I didn't speak much anymore.

One last animal story. I found a beautiful black Doberman who must have gotten lost in our neighborhood. Naturally, I brought him home and fed him and took care of him until we located his owners. One day, we were all out in the backyard when he and Bo started fighting. I, like a fool, got in between them and Bo was biting my knee while the Doberman was biting my hand. Chocolate decided to help; it seems she heard somewhere that if two dogs are fighting you should soak them with a hose. Well, she tried, however the only one who got soaked was me. She somehow missed both dogs completely. So here I was standing in a foot of mud, soaking wet, bleeding from my knee and my hand while both dogs were just fine. We laughed about that one often.

* * *

Mikee was just eight years old when tragedy hit her young life. Her dad was on his way home from work one night on his motorcycle when a drunk driver ran a red light and hit him. Michael died before he could make it to the hospital. When we got the news, Chocolate was very distraught and Mikee was at the babysitter's. I had Chocolate stay at home with a friend. I didn't want her driving in that condition, and I picked Mikee up and broke the news to her. We just sat in my van and talked and cried together for the longest time. We stopped by a church and said some prayers and then we went home. It was probably the toughest thing I ever had to do in my young life. To tell a child her dad was gone and that he was in Heaven. It hurt, still does!

Clearly, I had big shoes to fill. Somehow, I had to take the place of Mikee's dad and, to be perfectly honest, I didn't do a very good job of it. I was just too young to really know how to be a father but I did the best I knew how. For me, it was providing a good, safe, solid home with the bills always paid and plenty of food in the cupboards. In short, all of the things I lacked growing up. I went to every school function, no matter how big or small. I guess I did the best I could but I never had much of a dad for an example.

I was always easily moved and very emotional, even as a kid. I remember, at the tender age of ten, I heard of another ten-year-old boy in the neighborhood who had gotten hit by a car and died. I was so touched by this that I went to the funeral by myself to say a prayer for him. I just couldn't believe a boy my age wouldn't have the chance to grow up, kiss a girl and get married. It was so unfair. I wept over his casket and prayed. I'm sure his family members were asking themselves who this kid was at their child's funeral? Well, it was me. That's just the way I am. I cry when a dog dies in a movie so you can just imagine how emotional I can be in real-life situations.

I must have picked this up from my mom at a very early age. You see, she would confide in me and I would listen intently and feel her pain. So I started to tune into others and I could relate to most people's pain as a child and now as an adult. I find that compassion to be a good thing but not so much for a child. To tell you the truth, the most painful part of my childhood wasn't the beatings or the bullies, it was the knowing, the knowledge of what went on around me.

* * *

My brother Vito was still in New York wasting away in Willowbrook State School. I had told Chocolate about him and Willowbrook and we both wished we could move him to a better place in California, closer to family. I spoke with my parents about it a few times but they were reluctant. They always said there was no place that would accept him out here. I think they feared the inevitable reality of dealing with him again, which was very painful for them. It was for all of us.

One day, we heard on the news that the great state of New York finally came to its senses and was going to close Willowbrook down for good and everyone there would have to be transferred somewhere else. Thank God, I thought. Willowbrook was a horrible place, worse than any prison could ever be.

I would be remiss if I didn't elaborate on this. The residents there, young and old, boys and girls, were herded into large gymnasium-type rooms and just left to do whatever came naturally with very little care or guidance. In the winter, it was cold and damp on those hard floors and they were never dressed appropriately. In the summer, it was hot and muggy, not much temperature control. There might be three or four attendants to care for 40 or more of these mentally, and in most cases, physically handicapped people at a time. That would be a challenge for the most highly trained but these were regular folks who just needed a job.

Whenever I would go there it was insane - the screaming and crying and the foul smells of who knows what with people sick. It really was helter-skelter and I hated it. It scared me to death for my brother and saddened me for everyone who lived there. Vito was always so glad to see us when we went but somehow he had always just fallen and busted his lip, nose or head. Mysteriously, no one ever knew how, why or when. The cuts and bruises were endless and the scars and broken bones began to mount even when we were still back east. The poor guy already had enough problems with losing his sight. He was sick so often and now he had to put up with abuse. We always suspected that some of the residents would fight and also that the attendants would beat them but couldn't prove it. My mom and Aunt Joan got into more than a few shouting matches with the staff, all to no avail.

* * *

After grandma and grandpa left for California, the visits to see Vito became less and less frequent. Without a car, mom would have to take several buses, which took hours with my baby sister, just to visit for an hour or two. Once there, they would have to sit in this large loud cafeteria with a hundred other families visiting their loved ones - there was nowhere else to go. As for Vito, all he ever asked was to go home; he never complained. He just wanted to *go home.*

Instead, he got a rotten cheeseburger, some fries, a coke and hour or so visit before he went back to the dungeon and my mom embarked on the long journey home. Whenever Vito disappeared behind that big door my heart would sink and I'd get knots in my stomach fearing for his safety. I went with her several times but as I got older, I just couldn't do it anymore. I just couldn't take it. Even *Walter* couldn't help me with this problem.

When mom was notified about Willowbrook's closing, she found a small place called CLIMB in Pasadena, Calif. that would take him and made the arrangements. Within a few months, Vito was there and we went for a visit. It was heart-breaking to say the least. Vito was about five feet tall but could barely walk upright without pain. He was balding, blind and looked like a really bad boxer who had lost every fight he'd ever been in. His nose had been broken so many times that he could hardly breathe through it. He had cataracts in his eyes so large that they looked like white caps covering his eyeballs. Horrifying! I could hardly look at him. I was so full of guilt, rage and pain, call it what you want. I, somehow, thought I was at fault for not doing something sooner. I will live with that guilt until the day I die but what could I have done? I was just a kid when we left New York and I'd been trying to survive on my own ever since. Still, I believed it was my duty to somehow rescue him and I failed. I failed him badly, we all did.

I try not to blame myself; there was nothing I could do. I tried not to blame anyone for Vito; it was just part of God's plan. The old *yin and yang.* I guess he was the yin and I was the yang. I guess one of us had to get lucky. I just wished things could have been different for both of us.

Vito, God bless him, was just happy to see us all. It was like time stood still for him. The second he heard our mom's voice he smiled and he was happy. He remembered all of us like it was yesterday and it had been over ten years since he'd last seen any of us. Jackie was a baby back then but he was thrilled to see his baby sister as a young girl. He got a real kick out of my afro hair cut and beard and moustache. He liked Chocolate the second he met her - she just has that way about her - and he also got a kick out of Mikee.

So he was here, finally close enough so we could visit him from time to time. We could keep an eye on him and get him the medical attention he needed. The ball was rolling. The new place, CLIMB, was much smaller and the staff was nicer, younger and much more considerate and understanding of Vito's needs. We all felt pretty good about that but the minute we'd go to leave, Vito would cry and ask to come home. Here's a person who spent most of his life just wanting to go home, the same home I spent most of my life trying to get away from. Go figure…when it comes down to it, I guess neither of us will ever really go home again. He can't and I won't.

* * *

Getting back to our friends, Tris and I grew apart just a bit because of the geographic distance between us but Dennis and I grew closer again. He would come out and spend Friday nights eating *"shit in the oven"* (his favorite) with us and we'd play Monopoly until we couldn't keep our eyes open. Then he'd spend the next day helping me dig holes for trees or fence posts. By evening, he'd be gone, off to the clubs again searching for his next mate.

Jim bought a house just up the road with his first bride, Fran. A while back, Jim and Dennis were both drafted into the Army for not attending their reserve meetings but that finally paid off for them. Jim got to use the GI bill for his down payment and also got paid to go to school when he wasn't working. He wanted to be a teacher someday and not just because he thought teaching was such a noble occupation, which it is, but because he would get lots of time off, decent pay and a good retirement plan. He knew this because everyone in his family besides his mom and younger sister was a teacher.

Clint was married and living in Anaheim with Lisa and his dumb dog, Spot. Clint was working for a tux shop that he would eventually own in Buena Park. Chet and Nancy were both still working in South Orange County and enjoying their life and home together in Pedley.

So we were starting to have a nice group of friends and family around us again; all married, happy and safe, for a while at least. With all of that said, Chocolate and I were always deemed the couple least likely to succeed so we were bucking long odds. Still, we kept plugging away. We believed in us even if no one else did.

* * *

We were both still working in Orange County and living in Pedley. It was a long drive. We would spend an hour-and-a-half to two hours a day on the road without much traffic. Even worse, we had to take different cars because we worked different hours and went in different directions. Mikee was going to school and she was your stereotypical *latchkey* kid. Choc would get her off to school in the mornings and then she would go to work. When Mikee would get home after school, she would call Chocolate to check in. This was tough on them both but we did what we had to do.

As time went by, we both decided that we needed to get jobs closer to home. The drive was tough and Chocolate was nervous all the time about us being so far from Mikee. Chocolate got lucky, Sunwest Bank, where she working in Tustin, opened a small, satellite loan office in Riverside about ten minutes from our house. She quickly transferred there and was now much closer to home.

I continued my trek down the 91 Freeway each day until one morning I saw a sign that said that Winnebago was now hiring managers. Winnebago was opening a plant just down the road from us and they were looking to fill management positions. As I drove to work, I got up the nerve to call and see if I could get an interview. I was connected to a man named Dan Gust. He was the manager of the engineering department and he told me that all of the jobs were filled except one, a quality control supervisor, and that he had his man sitting right in front of him. I begged him to at least meet me before he made his final decision. He agreed and told me to be there within the hour. I called Overland and reported in sick, a rarity for me. I raced home and changed into my best clothes when there was a knock at the front door.

To my surprise, it was my buddy, Chester, and he told me a story about being at an interview this morning and while discussing the salary the man got a phone call and decided to wait another day before he made his final decision. He said he saw the guy write my name on a piece of paper. I told Chester, *"I won't go."* I couldn't do that to him. He said, *"I've already got a good job. I just wanted to see if I could get something closer to home. Besides, you have way more experience with motor homes than I do so you go talk to him and try to get the job. May the best man win."*

I may have won the job that day but he truly was the best man. I had the experience and I also came much cheaper than he did. Chester stayed on with his company for many years and grew into a top management position. He went on to make a lot of money working for that company, in spite of the long drive.

* * *

While we're on the subject of Chester, I feel it necessary to tell you that if you're reading these words right now he's partly responsible. About two years ago, Chet and I were talking and reminiscing about the past and he said to me, *"You should write a book."* I said, *"It's funny that you should say that because over the years I've kidded with Chocolate about writing a book."* I then went on to tell him, *"I even have a title, "Through My Eyes."* To which he replied *"You should do it, you have an interesting story to tell with your childhood and all."* We laughed about it some and I said, *"Who knows? Maybe someday."* Six months went by and I didn't give it much thought until one morning I woke up at 6 A.M. and went down to my computer with a cup of coffee to check my email. After doing so, I opened a Word file and typed three words *"Through my Eyes."*

About sixteen hours later, I had written the first twenty pages or so of this book. This went on for four straight days. I only stopped to eat at my desk and sleep a few hours a night. I was like a man possessed but then that is how I am with most things. After about sixty pages, I had to limit my writing to just a few hours a day because I screwed up my back and neck almost to the point where I couldn't sit or write at all. Overzealous, I guess but then again, I have always had a lot to say. So if you love this book I take all the credit, lol. If you hate it, blame Chester for planting the seed. It's funny how things get started.

* * *

So, where were we? Oh yeah, I gave notice and quit my job at Overland to start my new adventure as a Q.C. supervisor at Winnebago. I had my own office, well cubical to be exact, but a desk nonetheless. I was so nervous that Chocolate had to come down and show me how to set up a desk and how to use the basic equipment - phone, calculator, etc. I was really green and had never stepped foot into a front office other than to ask for a raise or voice a complaint. I had worked as a lead man with people reporting to me for years at Overland but this was different. I was now considered upper management. I had no idea what I was getting into but the pay was good and it was a mile from home so I was ready to try anything.

Dan turned out to be my direct manager and he piled a bunch of different state code books on me to learn. Now, as you may remember, I suck at reading and studying so this was a problem for me. I knew my way around a motor home, since I'd been building them for the past seven years of my life, but all of this code stuff was scary. We would have inspectors from all of the western United States come to the plant and it was my job to show them through and ensure we passed their inspections.

At first, I didn't have a clue what I was going to do but I learned how to get the inspectors to like and respect me very quickly. It seems, if you tell someone the truth, offer up that you need help and share that you respect them and their knowledge, most people will go out of their way to help you. I ended up making friends with all of these older guys and they thought I was this great respectful kid. We never had one write-up the whole time I was there. I learned a lot from these fine men including the fact that it's okay to ask for help.

Overall, the job turned out to be a pain in the ass. My people and I had to inspect all these motor homes and mine was the final word on whether or not they were good enough to ship. Needless to say, none of the employees liked the fact that I took my job so seriously. They always wanted me to let things go but I wouldn't hear of it. The plant manager and I argued often. I think he hated me but I was just doing my job. I liked working there, but the pressure was tough. But things didn't last long, they never do. I had just received my first-year review and a raise when they decided to close the plant.

Dan called me into his office and explained that the gas shortage had slowed the industry down. Winnebago wanted to protect their plant in Forest City, Iowa, their home base, so this plant had to go. He offered me two options: stay on until the end and get a month's severance pay plus vacation or leave immediately and get two weeks of severance pay plus vacation. Dan and I got along well and I think he thought highly of me so he recommended that I take the money and run. He felt that I, being the youngest and most inexperienced manager in the plant, would have a harder time finding work with everyone else out there looking at the same time. I thought this was a good tip and I respected him so I took his advice and handed in my resignation that day.

By the way, did I mention that we were having a baby? Yep, we had tried for a while and Choc miscarried once but this time it stuck. I was going to be a dad in about six months and we were overjoyed. That was until I had to go tell my girl I was out of work again. By the way, all of my buddies stayed on at Winnebago until the very end and I heard through the grapevine that they never did get any severance pay, bummer for them.

On my way home that day, I noticed a new building just down the street from Winnebago, a company called Flexsteel Industries. Flexsteel, as it turned out, was a furniture manufacturing plant that made sofas and chairs. They were already closed for the day but I could see some men still inside so I knocked on the door. A man named Tom answered and I asked if they were hiring. He said they needed a shipping manager and that I should come in Monday morning and talk to the plant manager. I did just that and got the job. It was for less than I was making at Winnebago but with the promise that I would be raised to that level after my first review six months later. A job is a job, so I took it.

I started a week later so I was way ahead of the game with the severance pay and all. The new job was easy actually, too easy to the point of being boring. I couldn't keep myself busy enough and the production manager was a total jerk. He was always looking over my shoulder just waiting for me to screw up but I never gave him the satisfaction - my work was always done.

I did make a few mistakes, though. The first was hiring my buddy, Jim, to drive the truck and make local deliveries for us. Jim always had a hard time keeping a job and timeliness was a constant issue. Like Chester when he was young, Jim and work just didn't agree with each other. Jim got the job done but he was always five or ten minutes late for work in the mornings. The production manager would wait by the door for him to arrive and then escort him into my office and ball me out because he was late.

He wanted me to fire Jim. My buddy? I don't think so. I would plead with Jim to get there on time and he would for a few days but he was still late all too often. Jim ended up quitting the job before I had to fire him (thank God) to save us both from the embarrassment but it was the beginning of the end for me also.

* * *

On July 15, 1979 A Star was Born.

Nicole Marie Balsamo was bestowed upon us from the heavens. We were planning on naming her Stevie but under pressure from my family and others we changed it to Nicole. Nicole was a chubby, dark, big baby, bald as a cucumber and she caused us much anxiety on the wonderful day she entered the world. I rushed Chocolate to the hospital late in the afternoon and she was in labor until after midnight. The doctor (a total jackass) should have known that this big baby was never going to pass naturally through such a tiny woman after all the tests he ran and the hours that had passed. He also knew Chocolate's history: Mikee wasn't an easy delivery and she was much smaller than Nicole when she was born.

When the situation got ugly, the doctor decided to do an emergency "C" section. I got kicked out into the hall and had to wait alone until Jim showed up. He stayed with me until Nicole was born. Afterward, he left and I stayed at that window all night watching my baby to make sure she would be okay. It seems the doctor gave my wife too much anesthesia and the nurses had to keep the baby awake for fear that if she fell asleep she would die. I was in a state of panic; even one of the happiest days of my life had turned into a nightmare. I paced and watched as they walked and rocked and pinched to keep my baby awake all night. I was scared and alone, as usual.

My family said they would come the following day and Mikee was at Jim's house with Fran. Obviously, we all made it out of there okay and I wanted to sue the doctor, but noooo! Miss Chocolate wouldn't hear of it, she didn't want to cause him any trouble. That butcher hacked up my wife at the last moment, almost overdosed my baby and made a happy day hell for me and my family and she didn't want to cause him any trouble. ***That's my girl.***

* * *

The next five months crawled by for me. It got to the point where I hated working at Flexsteel. It was the most boring job I'd ever had. We had a manager's meeting every Wednesday. All of the managers but Joe and I were from Iowa. Our shift would end at 3:30 and we would all report to the conference room by 4:00 and wait for the plant manager. He would always be an hour or so late and then he would want to share stories about Fred back home on the potato farm. Our meetings would run well into the evenings because of this. One night, I offered a polite suggestion, my second mistake. I suggested we start the meeting on time and take care of the business end first. After that, everyone who wanted to could stick around and talk about potatoes while the rest of us went home to be with our families. Needless to say that didn't go over to good.

I had my review with the big boss shortly thereafter and he told me how tough things were and how even though I was doing a good job all he could give me was 25 cents more an hour. That was $10 a week; he had promised me $60 when he hired me. The fat bastard lied to me and now he was promising me more in another six months. I told him not to insult me with that raise. I told him not to bother putting it in my check, I didn't want it. I also promised him that I wouldn't be there six months later for his next review.

Several months after that, I got to work early one morning and was getting a cup of coffee off the lunch truck. Mr. Production Manager was outside and told me to bring in two rolls of fabric. I said, *"Sure I'll send one of my guys up to get them right away."* He said *"No, I want you to do it."* I said, *"Okay, just let me go put my coffee and briefcase in my office."* He said, *"No, I want you to do it NOW!"* Without much thought I said, *"Go F—k yourself and shove the two rolls of fabric up your ass, I QUIT!"* I went back to my office as he followed closely behind, cleared out my desk and left. It was just under a year and I had kept my promise. I never made it to the next review.

Shortly after I left, one of my buddies at the plant told me that they would say I was a loser and would never amount to anything. Talk like that always made me more determined. Screw them, I thought, they're nothing but a bunch of backward potato farmers from Iowa. I'll show them.

My final mistake at Flexsteel was a blessing in disguise. Up to that point, I had over 40 jobs in my life and I worked at one, Overland Industries, for some seven years on and off. I started out delivering newspapers at 11 and from that point on, it was a series of jobs from meat stores to grocery stores to restaurants, where I toiled as a dishwasher, busboy and assistant cook. After that, I did my time at fast food joints like Mr. Donut and Ozark Fried Chicken. From there, it was onto pool halls, gas stations, car washes and a few car dealerships, washing cars. Always the low man on the totem pole, I labored at several roofing companies and a few construction companies along the way. Throw in four motor home companies and a portable housing company and I think you get the picture.

I was 26 years old and I was going nowhere fast. I was beginning to feel like the loser everyone predicted I would be. I was a jack of all trades but an ace at none. I always said that I could do everything well but nothing great. So I decided to become self-employed. I'd tried everything else, so why not?

The only person in the world who really believed in me was Chocolate. I used to tell her back when we were first dating to stick with me because *"Someday I'm going to be a millionaire."* The scary thing is I really believed it *(Walter)* and I think maybe she did also.

But time was slipping away and I wasn't getting any younger or going anywhere fast with all those low-paying jobs. I had to make a change. So, I knew I had to make it happen on my own. I started working out of my garage, which I transformed into a wood shop. Remember the lumber yard from when I was a kid? I now had my own shop. I was doing odds and ends for everybody and anybody. I would install garage door openers, panel a room, build a patio cover, hang closet doors, run a little electric, you name it and I did it. I went back to building furniture in my garage when I had no work. Anything we'd see in a store that we wanted and couldn't afford I'd figure out how to build myself. Then I made more of the same for other people.

With Christmas right around the corner I needed to make something happen soon. I built this really nice butcher block gourmet kitchen cart as a present for Chocolate. She had seen it in a magazine, clipped the page and asked me to make her one. It turned out really good so I decided to build a few more and go peddle them. My first stop was Al's Woodcraft (my first real customer), an unfinished furniture store in Tustin. I used to go in there all of the time to get ideas and buy supplies so I thought they might be interested in my work. I met the owner's daughter, Donna, who was the buyer for the store at the time and she ordered ten carts from me. She also said that if I made a larger one she would take five of them but she needed them well before Christmas. I was stoked; I couldn't wait to get home and tell Chocolate and get started. I made the 15 carts and delivered them on time as requested. After that, I would make her some more every couple of months or so.

Another unfinished store, Mr. Bare, was in Anaheim and we eventually got a similar deal working. Between the butcher block carts and my side jobs I was knocking out over a $150 a day and for me, that was good money. I was my own boss, working out of my garage and I was home a lot more. This was really working out great for our family, since I also could keep an eye on Mikee.

For a little added security, I landed a large apartment complex in San Bernardino that I could work for whenever I needed some extra money. All I had to do was show up and the maintenance manager would pay me $100 a day to do whatever he needed done. This was a really large complex so there was always an apartment that needed painting or laundry room doors to hang. As quick as I would hang them the crazy people that lived in the complex would break them so there was always plenty of work.

Once I did a job for a guy up in the mountains, in Big Bear. It was a little old cabin that needed to be completely remodeled. I spent about eight weeks up there doing the work and I fell in love with Big Bear. I would go up for two or three days at a time but I would get so lonely I'd have to drive home even if it was for just the night. I told Chocolate that I wished we could buy a home and live up there but there was no work at that time. I would buy things like snowshoes, old skis and odds and ends and save them because I swore that someday, I would buy a cabin in Big Bear. What can I say? *Walter,* always the dreamer.

I was really putting together quite a nice package for myself or so I thought. I was self-employed, I finally had a boss who wasn't smarter than me and who I liked and respected. I was feeling pretty good about myself and the road I was on. Things were starting to look up. Chocolate recovered well after Nicole was born and she was back to work within a few months. Shortly thereafter, she was offered a great job at a new mortgage company in Orange called Precision Mortgage. But it was an hour away back down the dreaded 91 freeway. I didn't want her to take it but a friend of hers, John, convinced her to join his company.

I, personally, loved the fact that we were all home early and together every day and I didn't want her driving the freeways again. But as I mentioned earlier, Chocolate had goals and desires of her own. She was full of get-up-and-go and she wanted to push herself to new heights so she got up and went. It was very important for her to become successful on her own. I guess she had a lot to prove to herself after growing up with Ray and his demeaning ways. So like the good guy I am, I said *"If that's what you want to do then go for it, I'll support you all the way."* She did and the job turned out to be great for her.

It didn't take long before she was running the office, working long hours, making decent money and loving it. To be honest with you (and myself), I think I was a little jealous. Here was my girl going to a nice clean office, dressed well, with all of these guys wearing suits and making lots of money. And here I was doing lowly handyman jobs, always in work clothes and the money I was making paled by comparison. They were all educated professionals, driving nice new cars and living high on the hog. I felt like a chump. Chocolate always tried to reassure me and build me up but I knew that I couldn't compete with these guys.

Shortly after Chocolate joined Precision Mortgage, I started doing work for her two bosses, John Nixon and George Ryder. They were great guys, the work was fine and the money was good but now I really felt like I was just a handyman. I was doing stuff that was beneath them, taking care of their grunt work so they could work and make the real money. It was all in between my ears but I was having a tough time dealing with it. I believed I was a second-class citizen. Chocolate was growing and I was staying the same. I wondered and worried if sooner or later, she would meet some nice suit and dump me.

Chocolate hired our friends, Nancy and Sam, which was great for her. She could work and be with her buddies at the same time. It all looked like something I'd never achieve and the happier she was the more I felt like a failure. But I sucked it up and pushed forward. What else could I do?

With Chocolate working back in Orange County again, we were having my mom babysit Nicole because she lived just a few blocks away from Precision Mortgage. It worked out well for everybody. Chocolate could drop her off on the way to work in the morning and pick her up each evening. Mom and dad got to spend time with their only grandchild and mom made a few bucks for her trouble. For me, it was a relief just knowing she was with my mom and that she was safe. Dad was getting a little older now and he was actually beginning to slow down and act almost normal. He was still on the methadone program and as long as he was, he was okay.

My dad loved Nicole to death and he was always on his best behavior around her, thank God. And Nicole loved her grandparents. She would often cry when Chocolate picked her up to take her home. I guess it's quite confusing for a child to be bounced around as an infant, all day long with grandma and grandpa and then all night with mom and dad.

By then, we'd been in our wonderful home about three years. Chocolate was doing well at her job but the travel was a bit much and she would come home late and tired often. Her company bought her a new car so that made things a little better - at least it was safe and sound. Our kids were growing also. Nicole was a toddler and a lot of work to keep up with, and Mikee was becoming a dreaded teen and a bit of a slob with a habit of lying. Mikee was always a pretty good kid, she got straight As and Bs in school and she joined everything that was ever offered. My biggest issues with her were that she would never clean up after herself and if you asked her anything she would lie just for the sake of lying. She couldn't help herself and this would cause some of our biggest arguments.

One afternoon, I came home from a job early and she was supposed to be at school. When I got in the house I could tell someone was there. I found her hiding in her closet and when I opened the door I asked her if she had ditched school and she gave me some cock-and-bull story that I knew was a lie. I asked her again and she swore she was telling the truth. I was so pissed off that she would lie to me and ditch school that I slapped her in the face. That was the first and last time I ever hit Mikee and I don't know who felt worse, her or me. Kids have a way of forgiving and forgetting and moving on quickly but I never did forget. I felt I had no right to raise a hand to her. I didn't believe in hitting - kids, wives or anybody for that matter. I didn't like hurting anyone, ever. It never happened again.

* * *

As always in life, nothing stays the same for long. Jim and Fran were breaking up, mostly because of jobs, booze and money. They sold their house and went their separate ways back in Orange County. Jim was drinking too much and working too little. Dennis and Pam divorced and remarried for the second time and they bought a house in Placentia. Tris was still living with Bob and they were doing their very best to satisfy as many women as they could. Clint was the proud owner of the tux shop that he toiled at for years and he and Lisa were renting a house in Anaheim. Chet and Nancy were still in their house in Pedley and they were busy working and having two baby girls to go along with Nancy's son, Steven.

* * *

My dad called me one day and told me that he had a rich friend who wanted to meet me. *"Why does he want to meet me?"* I asked, skeptical as hell. My dad, though he was not a very good husband or father, really did love us all. He was very proud of me and always sang my praises. He was always bragging about *"My son this, my son that."* As for me, I was always very suspicious about anything to do with my father, naturally. So when he told me that his friend wanted me to build him an oak birdcage I agreed to check it out, cautiously. A job is a job.

My dad invited him out to my house one day and he proceeded to show me some pictures of oak birdcages and told me the story behind them. It seemed he once owned a small company making these birdcages and somehow lost his partner, the guy who ran the shop and built them. He said they were doing very well together and he was looking to start up again. He wanted me to make a sample unit for him to see and then he'd consider a partnership. He said he would run the sales and marketing and I would run the shop. We'd be 50-50 partners.

Needless to say, I was very excited and anxious to get started. I built the sample birdcage and brought it to his home for his approval. He lived in Peralta Hills, an exclusive neighborhood in Anaheim Hills. When I got to his home, I was very impressed. It was the biggest and nicest home I'd ever seen. We sat and talked for quite a while and then we made the deal. He wanted me to go rent a shop close to his home. He asked if I had any money and I told him that we had about $15,000 saved but that was all we had in the world. He said, *"No problem, use the money for the rent, tools and whatever else to get started and bring me the receipts for reimbursement."* We shook hands, *a deal's a deal*. I couldn't wait to tell Chocolate, she'd be so excited for me.

I immediately went to work on the project. I found a shop in Anaheim, about an hour from my house but just 15 minutes from his. It was a 1,000-square-foot shop with a small office, bathroom and a small showroom. I signed a two-year lease on my own, which was pretty scary. My home mortgage was $350 a month and I'd just signed a lease for $550 a month. I didn't care, though. After all, he was going to handle the business side of things, which included the rent.

Next, I needed to get insurance for the shop, which is how I met Tom Christie, my friend and insurance agent for life. Unfortunately, Tom passed away in his early 60s after fighting cancer for many years. Tom was a lovely man and a good friend and he is sorely missed. In addition to insurance, I had to get all of the utilities turned on and pay the deposits. I went out and bought a bunch of new tools and equipment and moved everything into the new shop. I ordered some oak lumber from a company called Peterman's Lumber and supplies from Louis and Company, two of my very first suppliers. I was just about set. All I had left to do was cut off all of my old jobs and check in with my new partner about what to do next.

I was so excited I could hardly sleep nights. I had always wanted a business of my own, my own shop, to be my own boss. Working out of my garage and doing all of the odd jobs was okay but it was never quite good enough for me. It never felt real enough either, it was like I was just playing at business. Even though I was making decent money I would always panic whenever I was between jobs. That's why I always had the apartment complex and the butcher block carts to fall back on. I needed that security, something that I could depend on; you know, kind of like a full-time job.

I couldn't wait to tell everyone that I was through with all of the handyman stuff. I called everyone who would listen, including all my friends. I drove out to the apartment complex for one last time to thank them and let them know that I wouldn't be coming back. I cut all of the ties that bound me and I was now ready for my new business venture. I was going to be a real businessman, with a real shop. I'd dreamt about this day my whole life and now it was a reality. I was feeling great about my new future.

There was a quote in movie that I just love and have adopted as another *Stevism*. It's from a very good movie called "Fallen" with Denzel Washington and

John Goodman. I learned a lot from this movie. It helped answer a question I've always asked which is: *"What makes some people do such evil, terrible things?"* You'll have to see the movie to answer that question for yourself but in the movie, Denzel says…

* * *

"There are moments which mark your life. Moments when you realize nothing will ever be the same. When time is divided into two parts, before this and after this."

* * *

This was one of the most profound statements I've ever heard. It may be my favorite of all time. And I believed that deal, that business, was going to be one of those moments in my life. Kind of like the day my daughter, Nicole, was born; yesterday she didn't exist and today she does and nothing will ever be the same.

We all shared a very rare moment like that on Sept. 11, 2001. It was a moment when our nation's innocence was forever taken from us. This horrific tragedy filled all of us with fear, insecurity and anger, leaving us all to ponder our futures. Indeed, it was a moment that *marked* every American's life all at once and things will never be the same after that day. It was truly a time when all mankind was divided into two parts. I, for one, will never forget that day and I never want to. It reminds me of how lucky we are to be Americans (and to be free).

It also reminds me that freedom has a price.

* * *

May God bless all of the souls that were lost that dreadful day and all the souls that have followed fighting for our freedom since. Amen.

* * *

I'd like to end this chapter with the lyrics from a song by Five for Fighting / John Ondrasik the title of the song is, "Freedom Never Cries":

I saw a man on the TV in a mask with a gun
A man on the TV he had a ten-year old son
I saw a man on the TV his son had a gun
He says that he's coming for me…

I never loved the solider until there was a war
Or thought about tomorrow 'til my baby hit the floor
I only talk to God when somebody's about to die
I never cherished freedom, Freedom never cries...

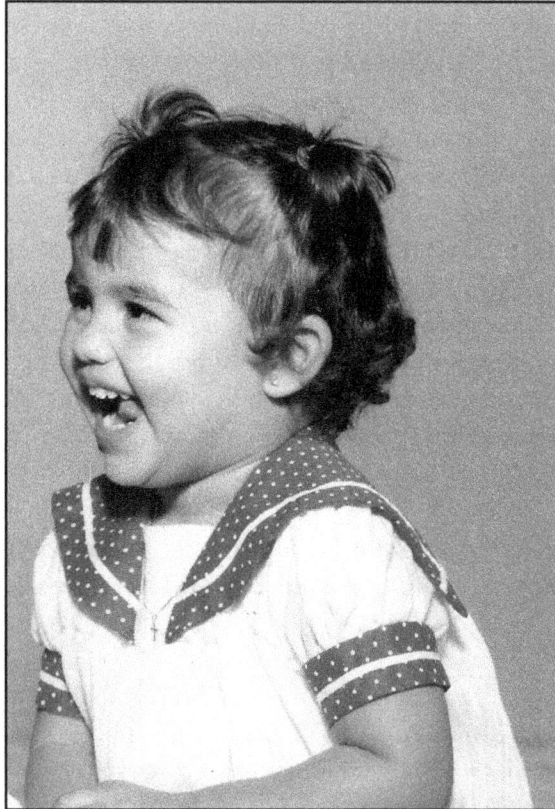

Nicole - Terrible two's (my favorite picture of her all time).

CHAPTER 8
THE POWER

As I mentioned, there are moments that change your life forever and for me, this was another one of them. George was one of two partners at Precision Mortgage where Chocolate worked. He was a very nice man and I was doing a lot of work for him around his house and at the office. George was the kind of man who always wanted to see everyone around him succeed and he was willing to share his knowledge.

One afternoon, George gave Chocolate a book and recommended that we both read it. And we did, numerous times over the years. This book changed our lives and our way of thinking for good from that day on. The book was titled "The Power of your Subconscious Mind" by Dr. Joseph Murphy. This book enlightened us and made us think, act and live differently. I'd highly recommend it to anyone who would like to improve their life in any way, shape or form.

George was one of those *Angels* who pass through our lives for just a brief moment and leave us better for having known them. I am both lucky and blessed to have met him. Thanks, George, for the wonderful life lesson.

This book covers many topics but the main one is the power your subconscious mind has over your being. I learned to be really careful what I say, do and think as my subconscious doesn't know when I'm kidding. In other words, if you tell yourself that you're a loser or a bum, your subconscious will ensure you achieve that goal. I could see that clearly now. If you convince yourself that you're going to be successful and rich, the chances are good because you will work towards that goal, consciously and subconsciously.

This knowledge is a great asset to have working in your favor. It taught us both to never say anything negative and to immediately turn a negative thought around into something positive. This is no easy task as we all know but Chocolate and I were up for the challenge. We figured, what do we have to lose? As Tom Lasorda, the manager of my favorite baseball team, the *Los Angeles Dodgers*, always says, ***"You gotta believe."***

We started to believe and to practice what we read in The Power of your Subconscious Mind; it became our religion. We became addicted to positive thinking and why not? It really does work, it's been proven time and time again over the years. Our lives were forever changed by reading this book and others on the same subject.

I found one of my best mentors - Anthony Robbins - because of this book. I've read most of Tony's books, listened to his programs ("Personal Power" and "Get the Edge" to mention a few), watched his videos and even went to a few of his seminars. He, too, has been very instrumental in my life.

Over the years, I have lent out or given many of these books and programs to those I think would listen and benefit from them and like me, most have. I'd highly recommend them to anyone interested in improving their lives.

By the way, years later I named my boat, *"You Gotta Believe."* Positive thinking…it works!

* * *

By now, it was just after Christmas and I'd just spent our entire life savings on the new shop, equipment and supplies along with Christmas presents. I was supposed to meet with my new partner one night to go over all of the dirty little details. It was time for me to turn in all of the receipts and get reimbursed for all of the things I'd purchased on behalf of our new company. It was a long drive down to his house from Pedley but I was so excited to tell him about everything that I really didn't notice. As I pulled into his long driveway, I couldn't help but imagine someday owning a big home and property like this. I noticed the fine cars that he had in his garage and all I could think was if this business worked out, I too could afford cars like that one day. I had to do my best to temper the *Walter Mitty* from within; he was beginning to run wild.

My new partner's wife met me at the front door and showed me into the den where he greeted me. After a few pleasantries, we got down to the business at hand. I told him about the shop, the insurance, the utilities and all of the equipment and supplies. I presented him with a copy of the lease and keys, all of the receipts and a laundry list of other things that added up to about $15,000. I was very anxious to get that money back into our savings account and to get the business started. I also couldn't wait for my next set of marching orders. I was thinking and talking a mile a minute. I was just so excited and thankful for this great opportunity that I could barely contain myself. He, on the other hand, seemed very quiet and reserved. I couldn't help but notice his discomfort and I was a little confused.

When I finally shut up long enough for him to speak, he laid it on the line for me. He told me that times were getting tougher and money was getting tighter. He felt that this wasn't the best time to invest in a new business. He said *"Our country's heading into a recession"* and he had decided not to go forward with this new endeavor because he was afraid of losing his money. I think I must have gone into a state of shock. I really don't remember exactly what I said or did next. I know I must have put up some protest and maybe even got angry, but to tell you the truth, I really don't remember anything after that.

I found myself back in his driveway getting into my van for the long drive home. As I pulled out onto the road I started to cry. The reality of it all was more than I could take. The whole drive home I rehashed his words about recession and hard times. I thought about losing our money and the bad timing. I was distraught. I just gave up all of my work, spent most of our life savings on the business and here I was with a shop in Anaheim and a monthly bill that was almost double my house payment. I drove very slow all the way home - thinking, worrying, crying, trying to figure out what I was going to do. I couldn't believe this was happening to me.

"Why would someone do such a thing like this to anyone?" I wondered out loud. How could I be so stupid, foolish and naive to do all of this without a signed contract? Why did I trust this man? Just because he happened to be rich? I should have known better than to get involved with anyone my father ever recommended. The closer I got to home, the more panicked I was becoming and the slower I drove. How in the hell was I going to tell Chocolate and the kids what just happened?

As I pulled into the driveway, I could see my family through the dining room window, which made me break down and cry again. I felt like I had just ruined all we had worked for these past few years. When Chocolate noticed the lights through the window she came running to the front door. As soon as she opened the door she could see I was upset. I asked her to take a ride with me and she instructed Mikee to watch Nicole. We got into the van and I started to pour my heart out to her. I told her all that had happened and I asked her *"what we were going to do now."* I bitched and complained. I told her how I couldn't believe what this bastard did to me. *"How could he be so cruel and callous?"* I asked. We cried together and consoled each other for a while.

But my girl is such the trooper. As we pulled back into the driveway and parked she said to me, *"Well, you always said you wanted to start your own business so here's your chance. Get in there on Monday and make it work. You can do it, I believe in you."* I responded, *"But what the hell am I going to do? I don't know anything about running a business and what am I going to build?"* Chocolate said, *"You'll figure it out as you go. Why don't you make the butcher block carts and find more dealers for them?"* Ah, a plan!

Chocolate would always say things like that to me; *"You can do it"* or *"I believe in you."* She was always building me up and giving me something I'd never had before, support and confidence. How could I fail? If she said I could do it, it must be so.

Tony Robbins has a saying that we both love, another *Stevism:*

"If someone tells me I can't, then I must."

Believe me, we live and die by this rule and now it was time for me to prove it.

* * *

Monday came all too soon. I was nervous, scared and excited all at the same time. As I drove to work, my mind raced constantly; so many questions but no real answers. But somehow, as I pulled up to my new shop I gained confidence and a sense of pride. I started to believe that maybe, just maybe I could do this, and I could pull it off. I went in and decided this was now my shop and I was going to do everything humanly possible to keep it and make it work.

I immediately went out back and began to draw up new designs and other sizes of the butcher block gourmet carts. I also came up with racks that would sit on top of the carts with shelves and hooks to hold pots and pans. This would give me more items to sell. Each day, I would make a set or two of samples and start to put them into the lobby area of my shop. Within a week or so, the lobby was filling up; it looked like a small butcher block store. Chocolate and I went out and purchased some inexpensive props and accessories to decorate the furniture. It looked really nice and I was feeling very proud.

When I wasn't building prototypes, I was making work tables and running electric and air lines for the shop. By the end of the first two weeks, the whole place was just about finished. The lobby and all of the samples were done and looked great. The office was set up and I had built a credenza and some drawers for the desk. It was so small in that office that all I could fit was a chair between the desk and the back credenza but hey, I didn't care…it was mine. The back area also was set up the way I wanted. I even went out and bought posters of Farrah Fawcett, Cheryl Ladd, Jacqueline Smith and others to decorate all the back walls but no nudity - this was a business after all.

The place looked great; it was a nice shop and great place for me to work. I was putting in ten to twelve hours a day, six days a week and the time just flew by. But I made sure I was still home every night to be with Chocolate and the kids. Next came the real challenge, sales. I worked on pricing the products and giving them names, model numbers and descriptions, which is much harder than it sounds. I met a lady through a friend who helped me with a price list and made up some line drawings of the products. I was all ready to go but where?

My buddy, Dennis, was a salesman for a company called Kelly Clark. He had quite a bit of free time so he would pop in to see me a several times a week. Most days, he would just hangout and watch me work or we'd have lunch together. One day, the topic of the business came up. I mentioned how I used most of our savings to get it started and how I wished I had someone to help with the sales and marketing. Dennis loved the shop and the idea of owning a business was intriguing to him. He asked if he could buy into my company and become a partner. I told him I'd speak to Chocolate about it and get back to him.

Somehow, we all agreed. Dennis put up $5,000 and would get 10% of the gross sales. Now, as you can plainly see, we had no idea what we were doing. I mean who gets a percentage of gross sales? That's just downright silly but we did it. I got the five grand to put back into our savings and Dennis got a piece of the action. Dennis was going to take on the sales and marketing for our company which was a big relief to me. He had a company car through his job, a station wagon (remember them?), so we loaded a sample set in the back and he called on all of the furniture stores in Southern California. I stayed back at the shop and started building the furniture and making the deliveries. This sounded like a great plan and the beginning of a great partnership.

After the first 30 days we were having some problems. I was building up some stock but Dennis wasn't closing many sales. He would come by daily and tell me how no one wanted to buy the gourmet carts and that he was running out of places to go. I could not believe this. I told him to keep trying, to keep going back; we needed sales. Well 60 days into our venture and with very little business, Dennis and I went to lunch to discuss our future. He thought we were doomed. He felt that we would lose our money and be stuck with the shop and rent. He was sorry he made this investment and wished he could get out. I listened to what he had to say and I felt bad because I brought him in and didn't want to see him get hurt or lose his money.

That night, I discussed it with Chocolate. I told her that I didn't want to see Dennis lose his money if we failed. I also didn't want the business to affect our friendship and that his attitude about the company was starting to wear me down. I needed all the positive input I could get if I was going to pull this off. She understood and agreed. We decided to give him his money back and call off the partnership. The next day, Dennis and I met and I gave him a check for $5,000 and told him his friendship was more important to me then the business. He was delighted and told me he would still help me in any way he could, and he did.

I was on my own again. We were broke and the bills were piling up at the shop. Thank God, Chocolate was doing fairly well at her job and we had very few bills at home. One of the smart things we did was pay off all of our bills before we started this venture. Choc was covering everything at home: the mortgage, utilities, food and kids. Everything, but just barely. She refused to give up on my dream and she would not let me give up either. She gave me the freedom to just go to the shop and try like hell to make it work. I refused to quit, to let either of us down. I had to go get some sales, now! I never had any experience in selling so I was very nervous. I loaded up my van with as many samples as I could carry, stuck a motivational cassette in the tape player and took off.

My first stops were to my two original customers, Al's Woodcraft and Mr. Bare. I think I went to them first so I could gain some confidence and a couple of quick sales. I had already sold them before so I felt confident talking with them and asking their advice. I needed all the confidence I could gather. After that, I hit every store from San Diego to Orange County and up to Los Angeles. I'd get a few sales here and there, mostly from the unfinished furniture stores which, thank God, back then there were quite a few. As quickly as I would sell them I'd be back within a week or two making their deliveries. The problem was, I could make and deliver them faster than they could sell and reorder them. I couldn't wait three and four weeks for a reorder and payment. I needed more customers and sales now so I expanded my travels into Riverside and San Bernardino counties.

I also had no choice but to expand the days and hours I was working. I'd go in early, work until ten when the stores opened, and then I'd hit the road with deliveries and solicitations. At the end of the day, I'd come back to the shop and work late into the evening. I was working six and seven days a week and wearing myself out. Some nights, I'd work so late that I'd just nap in my office and then go back to work in the morning. But still, it was not enough. I needed more customers and I had exhausted all of my leads in Southern California.

After a few months, I decided I would make a trip up north to find new business. I knew that if I wasn't successful on this trip I'd probably have to either give up the shop or get a job to help cover the bills. Needless to say, I was frantic. My van was too expensive to drive and I needed tires so my buddy, Dennis, let me take his company car and gas card to help me out. I worked through the weekend, kissed my family goodbye and took off early Monday morning.

My first stop was a phone booth in Ventura. Once there, I pulled out all the pages on furniture stores and started calling on each of them. Most were either too small or not interested and some stores were already out of business but I just kept on going. For every *"yes,"* I got 20 rejections. But each yes made me more determined to carry on. It never dawned on me to call first, it would have saved me a lot of time, gas and work but I was just too determined. I wanted to call on them in person; I wanted to give myself every chance to make that sale.

This went on for six straight days and I wore out a lot of phone books up and down the state. I hit every town and store from Ventura to Fresno and well past Sacramento. From there, I crossed over to the coast and started up in Santa Rosa, working my way down through San Francisco, San Jose and so on until I found myself back in Los Angeles. I slept in the cheapest motels or the wagon when I slept, which wasn't often. For the most part, I drove during the off hours when stores were closed. I ate fast food and bags of sunflower seeds to stay awake while I drove.

By the way, I learned that if you're eating it's very difficult to fall asleep, hence the sunflower seeds. All of the smoking, coffee, loud music and open windows did nothing for me; I would dose off often. I sold, begged and pleaded for sales on that first trip. I made up stuff as I went along - specials, free freight and 30-day terms. Whatever it took. This went on to become our company motto:

"Whatever it Takes."

* * *

I sold a lot of butcher block carts on that road trip. I got home late Saturday night and visited with my family. I told Chocolate about everything. We talked for many hours. I was stoked. Then I went to bed and slept until Monday morning. On Monday, I started the cycle all over again. I was getting a little tired from all of the hours at the shop and now I had to drive up north every few weeks to make deliveries. I desperately needed some help. I had some steady customers but not enough hours in the day to build the furniture, order materials, pay bills, type invoices, keep the books, make the deliveries and sell. There is a saying that *"What doesn't kill you makes you stronger."* Well, I should have looked like Arnold Schwarzenegger by then.

I finally hired a helper. His name was Randy and he was a nice enough fellow but he was lazy. At this point though, anything was better than nothing. Randy could keep the shop open while I was out selling and answer the phone and take messages. Sometimes, he even got a little work done. The key was that he came cheap. The orders were finally coming in a little steadier and the bills were getting paid but there was never anything left for me.

I decided to make another long sales trip up north but this time my buddy, Clint, offered to come with me. Clint was looking to get away for a while since he and Lisa had just split up and he needed some time to clear his head and heart. I welcomed the company and the help driving. We spent about six days on the road together and had a blast for the first few days. By the third day, however, we were both getting tired and beginning to get on each other's nerves. Clint wanted to fool around, sleep in and stop way too often. I just wanted to sell, get new customers and go home. I missed my family whenever I was out of town but if this is what I had to do to make the business work then I did it.

I've got a couple of funny stories from our travels. Understand that Clint and I were a couple of jokesters, class clowns, so we'd do almost anything for a laugh. The first night, we stayed in a small motel in Ventura. We had each worked that day and then drove for several hours so we were busted. The last thing I remember was watching TV fully dressed in our twin motel beds. When I awoke the next morning, Clint was on his bed asleep in a pair of red Speedo underwear and nothing else. I was in my bed with my pants pulled down around my ankles. I looked at him, I looked at me and I yelled at him *"Did you violate me last night?"* We each got a couple of yuks out of that one.

When we pulled into San Francisco days later, Clint was so over being in the car that he was bitching like crazy. He said, *"Just pull over, I want to get out of this car and get a beer."* so I did. We parked on Columbia Street, in kind of a shady part of town. Clint started walking down the street and like a fool, I followed. As he approached a topless bar, a guy outside lured us in. We sat down and had the two drink minimum. He had two small glasses of watered down beer and I had two watered down Cokes. We got to watch some big fat woman strip and it only cost us

$25. Each! Now understand $25 was a tank of gas or food for a few days, maybe even a motel for a night. I was pissed; at least they could have had a nice-looking stripper.

But the best story of all happened on the way back home as we passed a bus load of female prisoners. Clint was driving and I was in the passenger seat. As the bus passed, the women were all at the windows whooping and hollering. I decided to blow Clint and the women away so I dropped my drawers and flashed them. Clint almost wet his pants he was laughing so hard. After a few minutes he started to panic thinking that maybe the guards would call the police on us, but they didn't.

Six days and nights with one person, even one of your best friends, is a long time. Trapped in a car, it's an eternity. By the time we finally got home we were so over each other we weren't even talking. But that only lasted about 24 hours. We could never stay mad at each other for very long.

From then on, I would go up north every couple of weeks for the weekend. I would rotate inland one trip and coastal the next. I had some steady customers so all I needed to do was deliver their product and write new orders. I would load up my van and a rental trailer on Friday and take off at about midnight. I would drive all night to my furthest destination and be on their doorstep when they opened in the morning. From there, I would work my way back down selling and delivering along the way. On each trip, I would try to fit in a few new sales calls. By Saturday evening I was done making calls and deliveries so I would drive straight home.

Most nights, I got in at about two or three in the morning after dropping off the trailer and unloading so I'd sleep all day on Sundays. It was hard work filled with long hours. Every dime that I made went back into inventory, new tools or expenses. I had no idea that my customers would pay their own freight so I spent a lot of my money and time on unnecessary deliveries. But I learned, like everything else in life, that the hard way.

As time went by, we got a little busier and Randy wasn't getting any better. After my long trips up north I would always treat myself to a car wash. One day, I was sitting there watching this Mexican kid wash my van and I couldn't believe how hard he worked and how seriously he took his job. As I was leaving, I asked him how much he made an hour. I think he said $3.50. I gave him a tip and my card and told him I'd pay him a dollar more per hour if he wanted to come work for me.

He showed up on Monday morning and never left. His name was Alberto Perez and he was the best man I ever hired. Al and I would joke about Randy and how lazy he was. Al called him *"the Hippie."* It didn't take long before I hired Al's brother, Francisco (Pancho), and fired the hippie. Now we were cooking. Pancho ran the mill, Al handled the assembly and I did the finishing and deliveries. We had a nice little system going and the business was beginning to grow.

The first year was really tough, though; it was hit and miss most of the time. We did $75,000 in gross sales. Not bad for a startup company in 1980 during a recession but still not enough for me to make a paycheck yet, let alone a living.

* * *

Over the years, I've learned that there are a few things you really need to build a business and I had all of them going for me. First, a partner who believes in you and is willing to do whatever it takes to help you succeed. I had this 100% in Chocolate. Second, you need a happy, tranquil home life so you can put all your energy and efforts into what you're trying to achieve. I was in love with my wife and kids, I loved my home and our life and we were all healthy so I had no distractions there. Third, having some money saved is a big help. Here, we lacked desperately but at least we had no debt and were lucky enough to be able to live off Chocolate's income. And I had an uncanny knack for being able to handle and stretch a buck so that helped also. You can't build a business unless you know how to handle money; I was the best at that.

Finally, there's blind faith; you have to believe. You can't take no (or failure) for an answer. Here, we had our belief system that came from within. If you keep telling yourself things like *"We can do it," "If God brings you to it, he'll bring you through it," "No pain, no gain"* and one of my absolute favorites, something my dad used to preach to me: **"When life gives you lemons, add sugar and water, mix it up and make lemonade."** The man had a way with words.

* * *

Needless to say, I became a very good lemonade maker. I would always tell people that if there were five doors and only one led to success I would go through nine before I got to the right one. But, I'd always get to the right one eventually. I just had to do it the hard way, with hard work and determination.

Lucky, I was not. I once heard a quote (so what else is new), *"The harder I work, the luckier I get."* I always hated people telling me how lucky I was - walk a mile in my shoes.

The bottom line is, you need to be able to believe in yourself and whatever it is you want to accomplish. You have to be inspired. I think the thing we had going for us that really helped us succeed is I was too stupid and naive to fail. I refused to listen to reason. Despite all the odds, I truly believed we could do it. A wealthy colleague of Chocolate's had warned us that the hardest business in the world was manufacturing (he was correct). People told us that five companies out of a hundred are still in business five years after they start and then the odds drop drastically from there. I didn't care; I just thought I would work harder, longer and smarter than everyone else. I would say that when my competition was sleeping, I'd be working. When they were vacationing, I'd be planning, and when they were relaxing, I'd be thinking. I'd never rest or take a day off. It wasn't the best plan but it was my plan and it worked pretty well.

* * *

As we were moving into our second year in business, our little company was growing. I added a third employee, a brash kid named Jeff Hughes. I liked him from the start. He walked in one day and said, *"I need a job. I'll do anything, mop floors, clean bathrooms, any hours, for whatever you can pay."* I hired him on the spot and I never regretted it.

At about that time, we were also getting really tight on space. Our complex had the sign man, John, next door on one side of me and a scale company on the other side, which had just gone out of business. Next door to the scale company was Mike, the welder, and next to him was Rob with Wheel Warehouse. We all got along really well and helped each other out whenever the occasion arose. I decided it was time to expand so I added the unit next door after the scale company moved out. As my buddy Jim likes to say, *"You busted through the wall."* We now had about 2,000 square feet.

I was out selling one day and somehow I landed The Broadway department stores as an account. Don't ask me how, but I did. We even made the cover of their monthly catalog several times. Things were really looking up so I started to look into trade shows and we did our very first one in Las Vegas - The Unfinished Furniture Show. From there, we started to land a few out-of-state accounts.

It took me a while but I finally figured out that the dealers would pay their own freight so my days of renting trailers and driving weekends were over. In came AB Transfer Company and my good friends, Mondo Sr. and Jr., the owners. Mom started working for me part-time doing invoicing and the books which was a relief and gave me more time to build and sell. It would take me hours to type up a few invoices. We had no computers back then and I don't type. Even worse, I can't spell.

By now, I was I looking into hiring some sales help. My first few reps were not too good and didn't last but something was better than nothing. I'll never forget my first show in San Francisco at the Concourse, a temporary exhibit building. I got a room at the Van Ness Motel, a flea bag with roaches the size of small mice. My two reps, George and Bob, shared a room there also. Between the three of us, we were pretty broke but we managed to get by. I had two pairs of slacks, tan and brown, and two sports jackets, again brown and tan. From that, I could make four outfits because the show was four days long. George and Bob shared ties for variety as well.

The show was a huge success for me. I landed several new customers and was writing about $3,000 to $4,000 a day in business; that's a lot of butcher blocks. I brought up my own temporary make-shift wall, sign, carpet and accessories so I didn't have to rent a thing other than space. I mean who could afford it? I rented a truck and loaded and unloaded everything by myself. I didn't care; work was no problem for me. I did what I had to do, whatever it takes.

As the year went on, we were doing pretty well but there was still never any real money left after the overhead. I ran a few bills through the company like our gas and car insurance but still, Chocolate was covering our butts. By now, the drive to work was killing us both. Most days she would get home around 7 and I would arrive between 8 and 9. We were tired, we were wearing out our cars and the worst thing of all, we were having less and less time together as a family. Chocolate decided it was time for us to move back to Orange County and it just made sense so I agreed.

Mikee hated the idea from the start. She had to give up her horse, pets, school and all of her friends. I understood, but what choice did we have? We figured we could sell the house for a large profit and buy something closer to our jobs and the private pre-school that Nicole attended. She was way too young to be in school, I must add. We reasoned that the gas and wear and tear was adding up and our time on the road could be better spent on the job, making money. We also didn't like being in Orange County and having Mikee alone in Pedley, over an hour away. More importantly, she was in junior high and heading into her teens. She had discovered boys and was now boy crazy so she would need to be monitored more closely. We made the tough decision and listed the house for $105,000.

Our Pedley home was a dollhouse. We spent four years in that home and we loved and cherished every minute of it. We became a family there, our baby was born there and we found ourselves in that house. We put every spare penny and a lot of blood, sweat and tears into it. This was no easy decision but somewhere I heard that you have to be willing to give up what you are today, to change in a moment's notice, if you're to be successful in life. We were ready, willing and able. Okay, except for Mikee. But she didn't have much choice because the house sold to the first people who looked at it.

We had 60 days to find a new home and move. We spent our Sundays with Dixie Cole, our real estate agent and friend. Everything we liked, we couldn't afford. Some things don't change; Orange County was still way more expensive than Pedley. We finally found a beautiful three-bedroom home in Anaheim Hills for $200,000. It had a pool and a nice view but we had to finance over $150,000 which made our payment about $2,000 a month. Two grand a month! That was almost six times our old payment. Chocolate had gotten a few raises and was making decent money but I still didn't know how we would be able to afford this payment. She thought she could make up the difference on some commission deals at work. As usual, she said we could do it so I went along with the program. I'd just have work harder and find a way to get more money out of our company.

It was very tough leaving our home. We had to board Mikee's horse, Tonopah, and get rid of her cats. I gave our goat, Peaches, and our chickens to my neighbor and good friend, Cap. The birds had died and so did one of my dogs, Sadie, but I had to part with Dallas. Bo and the fish tank were coming with us. There was no way we were parting with them.

As luck would have it, we signed all of the papers and bought the new house and 30 days later, the people who bought our house fell out of escrow. Oh noooo. We were moving into the new house and had to carry the old house until it sold again. So here we were with two house payments and both sets of utilities and insurance. We were beside ourselves but once again, we buckled down the chin straps and forged forward. The old house sold and was gone in about four months but, it was a struggle and a long, stressful four months. Poor Chocolate was going nuts trying to make money without putting too much pressure on me. She did a lot of praying and somehow *He* always answered.

As we settled into our new home, Mikee was having a tough go of it. She missed her friends and her old school, not to mention her horse. It was slow making new friends and she didn't care for her new school. I identified all too well. Then in late November, I got a call from the phone company; they wanted to know why we hadn't paid our phone bill for the past two months. I told them that they must be mistaken but they explained that we now owed them about $1,400 and had to pay it or they would disconnect our line.

I'll never forget that day. Chocolate and I were hanging wallpaper in our kitchen when we got the call. We knew right away who it must have been, Mikee. You see, Mikee would call her friends long distance every day after school. We had warned her several times about the bills that came in at over a hundred bucks. We tried to understand her loneliness and we cut her some slack but my God, $1,400 in two months? Yes, it can add up when you stay on the phone everyday for hours at a time. Mikee was sneaking bills out of the mail and hiding them so we wouldn't see them. I don't know what she was thinking. There was no way in the world we could afford this bill with Christmas right around the corner. Needless to say, it put a damper on our holiday season and long after. I made payments on that bill for six months before it was finally paid off.

I also made Mikee promise to pay me back someday and I'm still waiting…

Nicole's baptism with Godparents Sam and Dennis.

142

First Creative Ideas family photo - Chocolate, Me, Mikee and Nicole.

Chocolate, that's my girl - ain't she a beaut.

Me and the Brooklyn Bridge.

Grandpa Hoffmans bar and apartment on Furman Street.

The Cammarie Bakery on Henry Street.

CHAPTER 9
CREATIVE IDEAS

I guess I never mentioned the name of our company. It all started back when I worked at Overland Industries. I was working with this really nice, older guy named Larry. He had to be about 35, which is really old when you're 17. I remember thinking to myself; I wonder why this old guy is still working an entry-level job like me at his age. Well, Larry went through a nasty divorce and had a few other issues but that's not important here. I used to love to break his chops. I was always making things at work, like tool boxes, cabinets, junk like that. Every time I made something I would sign it like an artist would, *"Creations by Steve,"* and for some reason this would annoy him so I did it even more.

When it came time to name our company I had no clue what to call it so I told Chocolate about Creations by Steve. She said, *"That's nice honey, if you're opening a beauty parlor!"* She thought that title might not fit a furniture manufacturing company. She said, *"Let me think about it for a while."* I told her that I really liked the Creations part of the name and soon enough she had a few ideas. The first was Creative Designs, nah. The second was Creative Furniture; no, not at all. The third was *Creative Ideas* - now that just seemed right. I liked it the second she said it. ***"CREATIVE IDEAS"*** it was.

It's funny how after some time you can actually become your company and it takes on a piece of you. When I would write the name Creative Ideas it was like I was writing my own signature.

* * *

We were approaching the end of our third year in business and things were changing rapidly. By now, we had more than tripled our space and our sales from the first year to about $330,000 in business. Things were looking up. My buddy, Clint, gave me one of the wisest pieces of advice about owning and running a business when I first opened. He said, *"When you're busy you think it's never gonna stop but it always does."* This sage advice has served me well over the years because all businesses have their ups and downs; it's never a steady course. For me, it made me wise enough to ensure my bills were always paid and my expenses were always manageable. I also learned how to stash away a little for the slow seasons. Like summer, winter, spring and fall, there is *always* a slow season. You can count on it, but don't worry about it - just prepare for it.

* * *

This is as good a time as any for another *Stevism,* ***"There are three types of people in the world: those who make things happen, those who watch things happen and those who wonder what happened."***

To be successful at anything, especially in business, you better be in the first group and I was.

* * *

It was decision time; our leases were coming up soon and we needed to expand. The center we were in was being taken over by my buddy, Bob (Wheel Warehouse), and was much more conducive to retail sales anyhow. I felt we needed to be in an industrial area and started the search for a new shop. I found a new 6,500-square-foot building that I loved in Placentia, about five minutes from our house. I took Chocolate, Mikee and Nicole to see it and they all loved it.

The building was white with black doors and windows and a nine inch blue stripe all the way around it. The reason I mention this is because our daughter, Nicole, had seen another building in the complex that had a red stripe and she said, *"Daddy, I like the red one better."* I leased the building for three years and promised her we'd paint the stripe red and we did immediately. And that's how our new company colors, red and black, were born, thanks to our baby girl. We even came up with a new logo; a red brush-stroked Creative Ideas across a black-and-white graph with a red line heading up from left to right across the graph, kind of like watching stocks rise. So now we had a new building, company colors and a logo. All we needed was more business.

I was still battling sales with the butcher block carts. It seemed they were a seasonal product and would never get me where I wanted to go. I added some oak bars but that was just more of the same. I met a really nice man who was a buyer for a membership company that I was selling. One day, we were talking and he asked me, *"Have you ever thought of making a computer desk?" "What's that?"* I asked. He replied, *"I don't know but you should make one. I get requests for them often."* So I started to research the idea.

The only computers at that time, 1982, were IBM PCs and they were very expensive. Only professionals were able to afford them. But the more I thought about it, the more curious I became. I started to believe that someday very soon everyone would own a computer and, therefore, need a computer desk. I went to a store where they sold these computers and started asking questions. I came up with a few simple conclusions of my own.

First, I thought that since computers have a keyboard, maybe the desk should be the height of a typing table - not my best idea. Second, I learned that they have a brain and store their own information so there wasn't much need for a lot of file drawers, which was a relief because we weren't very good at making drawers. Third, I concluded that the monitor unit would be nice if it were higher than the keyboard so it was ergonomic. Tada! The hutch was born.

That was it! I made our first computer desk. I called it the *split level desk* and I made it available in two sizes, 36 inches and 48 inches. The front level was 27 inches high for the keyboard and the back 30 inches high for the monitor. But I didn't stop there; next I made the *computer desk*. It had a flat top and was 27 inches high, with two utility drawers and a shelf below for software. I offered this in two sizes also, 48 inches and 60 inches. Along with this desk I made two racks to support the monitor, a *low rack* and a *high rack*.

I'm sure you're quite impressed with these original names but, they worked so don't laugh. Then I added a tall *software hutch* in two sizes that could be used on the computer desks. Throw in a couple of *printer stands* and a few *bookcases* and what do you know, a computer furniture line was born. By the end of the month, we had created some of the first computer furniture to ever hit the market.

Jeff and I loaded up the rental truck and took this new line to the San Francisco Market and we were a smash. We sold the heck out of it in our first market debut. It was incredible! We were written up in the trade magazines and even won an award, *"The Schubie Award,"* for the best new design. And, go figure, it says right on the trophy, *"Third Annual Best Design Award."* Third, who would have guessed that?

A while back, I had fired all my reps and replaced them with a couple of young hot shot reps named Mark Archer and Gary Tripp. Mark had a partner named Cal Hardy who also was a part of my new California sales team. Gary had a good buddy named Roc Anderson, so I hired him for Washington and Oregon. These guys all worked for one of the hottest companies on the planet at the time so I thought they might be able to get me into places I'd never been.

Perception is everything.

I can't stress that enough. I'll never forget the first time Gary came to the old factory. He walked in and wanted to know where all the furniture was. I told him this was a small place and we shipped it as fast as we built it. He was not impressed. Shortly thereafter, the buyer for the Broadway Stores came out to the factory and he was in shock. He said he couldn't believe that he put his butt on the line for such a small company. He told me that had he known we were so small he never would have bought from us. Broadway had some 25 stores in California and about a dozen in Arizona; they were by far our largest account.

As luck would have it, I went up to Los Angeles to visit the buyer one day and to my surprise he had been replaced. I was able to get in to see the new furniture buyer and he informed me that he doesn't buy gourmet carts and that I'd have to deal with the kitchen buyer. I went in to see the kitchen buyer and she informed me that she doesn't buy furniture; I'd have to see the furniture buyer. I found myself back in the hall confused and befuddled and without a buyer for my product line. The new monthly catalog had just come out and we were on the front cover, go figure.

We were done. They sold off all of the carts and we lost our largest account. I was devastated. Now what? I had just signed a three-year lease on the new building and lost our biggest and best account. There was no time to ponder the past. I reminded myself of the saying, *"It's time to get busy living or get busy dying."* For me, it was time to get to work and get us moved. We moved the company over a weekend and were set up and ready to go by first thing Monday morning. We had about fifteen employees by then and mom was working five or six hours a day.

I never took a paycheck for most of the first five years in business but I always managed to make payroll, buy new equipment and grow the company. I actually started paying myself about $500 a week by the fifth year and moved it up to $1,000 by year seven. I would stay at that level for the next several years. So, if you average it out, I made about $500 a week for the first ten years I was in business. Now that's either dedication or just plain foolishness, I'll let you decide.

I always felt that if we did a good job, built quality product, took care of our customers and employees, paid our bills and ran a respectable company the money would follow. That is the foundation on which I built Creative Ideas. Back in the days when I worked for Overland, I would always say hello to the owners and I was lucky to get a nod out of them. I worked for these guys for some seven years and they hardly knew I existed. I told myself that if I ever had employees I would always treat them with respect and never get too full of myself. I only hope that I lived up to that but then that's for others to judge. I know I did my best.

* * *

My mom and dad were in their third apartment across from the Orange Mall and it was pretty nice. It was larger than the other apartments they had and was quite comfortable. My sister, Jackie, was still living at home, going to college and working part time. Dad was doing okay but his health was becoming an issue. I guess after so many years of drug abuse and chain-smoking it was to be expected. According to the doctors, he had a few small heart attacks, if you could call any heart attack *"small."*

My brother, Vito, was doing as well as can be expected. He didn't like all of the commotion and rules at CLIMB but he seemed to get along fine with the staff. He always had a favorite employee he talked about but forget it if someone touched or moved something of his. He threw a fit. You just can't believe how neat and organized this mentally handicapped, blind man was. I mean, if you opened his drawers he could tell you where everything was and what color they were by feel.

I didn't go visit him like I should. I used the excuse that I was too busy most days and I wanted Sundays to myself. That's a bunch of bullshit - I just hated going anywhere near those institutions and I didn't like seeing him all that much because it made me sad and I couldn't fix it. That's me, I'm a fixer. I fix things, I make things better, I build things. I just can't accept things the way they are; I always feel I can make them better. But, in Vito's case there wasn't much I could do and it frustrated and saddened me so I avoided him. Instead, I'd buy him a bed and a dresser, maybe a new TV or cassette player. Mom always brought him home for the holidays but that usually turned into a disaster. Vito can be a handful. He's difficult at best and needs constant attention. The bottom line is, we were all just too selfish, busy and set in our ways to deal with him.

When Vito did come home for a few days, mom had her hands full the whole time. Vito doesn't live by anyone's rules; he has a mind of his own. My dad was of no real help to her and he demanded time of his own. Jackie was either busy with school or work so it was all left up to mom. Vito needed someone to help him eat, dress, wash and go to the restroom. He could do most of this himself but not in unfamiliar territory and he was never home long enough to get properly acclimated.

Besides that, when he was home he wanted mom's attention all of the time. Who can blame him? He did without it for many years.

I remember one Christmas at my house when we all opening presents and throwing the wrapping paper away as we went. After Vito opened his presents he wanted the box that something came in. Now, mind you, he can't see and you wouldn't think he would remember the box in all the commotion but he did and he wanted it NOW. The whole family was there and we must have opened 50 presents. Chocolate and I started tearing the place apart looking for this box. Mom tried to calm him down but he became uncontrollable.

Dad threw a fit, which is what he did whenever things went poorly. Mom was crying and everyone was getting upset. I tore apart every bag of trash we had and we gave him a dozen different boxes but none of them would do. We never did find the correct box. I don't know where it could have gone or if he just imagined it. I can still hear him crying over and over, *"I want my box, I want my box."* Those words rip through my mind and heart and remind me just how helpless I felt whenever I was around him. The day was ruined for everyone. Vito carried on and on and made everyone feel terrible. That was the last Christmas Vito came home for more than just the day. From then on, I would pick him up in the morning and take him back that evening. It was just too much for my mother and better for everyone else this way, everyone except Vito.

* * *

Creative Ideas was growing and doing well in its third year; computer furniture was becoming quite a hit. When I say hit I mean it was more popular than butcher block carts. After all, this was 1983 and most people didn't even know who Bill Gates and Steve Jobs were yet. Still, there was a market for computer desks and seeing how we were the only ones making them we were getting most, if not all, of the business. It took some effort on my part to ensure we were getting noticed though. Most dealers would buy just one desk and maybe a printer stand and set up the display in the back of the store by the restroom, if we were lucky. I couldn't convince them to try more products and it frustrated me because we had lots of other sizes and styles.

"Necessity is the mother of invention."

I came up with a poster for dealers to use as a prop which showed all of the other items available. The posters I had hanging in our first shop gave me the idea. The problem was that most dealers, even though they really liked the posters, wouldn't bother to hang them or said they didn't have the wall space. Well, that would never do so I changed the poster to a desk blotter and wham, special orders started to pour in. With all of the special orders coming in, it became a little easier for us to get that second and third *SKU* (that's furniture talk for item) on the floor.

By that point, our company was really growing. I started buying machines, delivery trucks and forklifts. We were constantly adding more tools, lumber and supplies. It was so exciting to see my dream materializing before my eyes. To support the business we started doing the two San Francisco Markets (January and July) and the Computer Furniture Show in Monterey. I continued designing more and more items to add to our line which kept us valuable to our dealers. It's funny, we would be really busy from September until March and then all of a sudden, business would drop off. Every April, I'd freak out worrying about how we'd pay taxes and make it through the summer. I got to a point where I would bust my tail paying off everything I could while we were busy and then hunkering down for the summer. I could really manage and stretch a buck but that was no fun. In fact, it was really hard work and quite stressful.

* * *

One summer, we were doing the Unfinished Furniture Show at the Las Vegas Convention Center and unloading our rental truck when security told Chocolate and me that there were no children allowed in the building. In the early days, Chocolate and I that would drive to Vegas with our family and she and Mikee would help unload the truck and setup the display for the trade show. Back then, we couldn't afford any help.

Well, I went berserk; I said to the security men, *"What do you mean? Are you crazy? These are my kids. I have no place else for them to go."* They didn't seem to care and they made us put the kids in the hot cab of the truck while Choc and I finished unloading. Then, they made Chocolate and the kids leave the building while I set up the display alone. Now understand, this is hard work with help but alone, it's miserable. I worked the whole evening rolling out the carpet, setting up the furniture, building the display wall and hanging the signage. With Chocolate and Mikee to help this would have taken a few hours but alone, it took most of the night. Our furniture is big and heavy so by the time I was done I was exhausted and pissed off. I swore I'd never do another show by this company again and I never did.

The next morning, as I was heading in to my booth, I noticed that some of my furniture had been moved to another location. Now I was really seeing red! After closer examination, I noticed that what I was staring at wasn't my furniture at all. A man approached me and I said, *"What the hell are you doing with my furniture in your booth."* He told me to go to hell so I went after him - I wanted to knock him on his butt. Some sales reps intervened and I left but this was how I first learned of the term *"knockoffs."* It's a term used for copies made by those who can't or won't design their own product. Little did I know but this would happen to us over and over again throughout my career. Many have told me that's it's the *"greatest form of flattery"* but I've never believed that. I just think it's an easy form of thievery.

Now don't get me wrong, it's not that I'm a great designer or anything but I do have a knack for coming up with different, quality, marketable items. My tricks of the trade have always been that I listen to what people want or need. I have a good eye for design and I like balance. I can take many different elements from other things and put them together to create my own look or design.

Let's face it, there's nothing new under the sun. That being said, I didn't take myself too seriously as a designer but I did try to be unique and do my own thing. What separated me from the pack was my willingness to take risks. I dared to be different and eventually dominated the home office category. Heck, when I started building computer desks for the home, the term *"home office"* didn't even exist. Then, all of a sudden, it was the buzz of the industry. Home office eventually got its own tradeshow and a news magazine of its own. I took the bull by the horn and pushed this category down everyone's throat in the beginning when no one believed. I was willing to try many different sizes, shapes and finish colors when others didn't see the need. I built furniture with function and quality. I was always first to come out with the latest trends. Obviously, it pissed me off when others would just copy my work and call it their own. But again, that's life. Nobody gets the stage all to themselves, especially when there's a profit to be made.

Another time, we were at the Computer Furniture Show in Monterey when I introduced my very first executive desk, the 6030EX. I hosted our sales meeting the day before the show and my reps were very disappointed in the new desk, to say the least. That evening, I felt terrible. After months of designing and planning, this was not the reception I had expected. I was sure that this new desk and the price point were a good value but after their feedback, I began to doubt myself. The next morning, the criticism continued and the remarks were brutal. But I showed them. By the end of the show, we sold the heck out of that desk and it went on to be our best-selling executive desk ever.

The lesson I learned was twofold. First, never stop believing in yourself - push forward and keep pushing. And second, getting others' opinions is important and can be very useful, however you have to keep them in the proper perspective. Remember that opinions are like assholes, everybody has one.

As our business grew, so did the responsibilities of owning a manufacturing company in the state of California. California is one of the toughest states in the union to own and run a business, let alone a manufacturing business. All of a sudden we needed spray booth permits, propane tank permits, hazardous waste permits, A.Q.M.D. permits (Air Quality Management District), fire department permits and city permits. We needed permits for our air compressor tanks, dust collectors, sprinkler system, machines, air lines and electrical system in the factory. There was even a permit for the rain water that came off the roof, if you can believe that. There were forklift permits and resale permits. Business licenses for our factory and our showroom, special truck driver's licenses and upholstery licenses. We had Cal OSHA rules and regulations to learn and comply with and safety classes to attend.

And if that wasn't enough, there was insurance. I had to buy property insurance, fire and theft insurance, product liability insurance, truck and auto insurance, umbrella insurance and let's not forget the back breaker of all, workers' compensation insurance. Now, I'm not complaining but jeez, can't a guy get a break? Every time I'd get one thing squared away, they would think of another. I think someone just sits around making this stuff up; it's a real headache for any business, but especially a young company. I was learning a lot but I now needed the assistance of lawyers and consultants, which resulted in more expenses. I was young and full of piss and vinegar so I just kept on handling everything that came my way. I believed I could do it, and somehow I did.

I would like to add that we were *green* way before it became so popular. I was no saint but the state made sure we played by the rules when it came to the environment. And we took it to the next level. For example, we recycled everything. Sawdust became horse bedding or potting soil. Our lumber scraps went to Mexico and were made into moldings, while the wood chips were made into particle board. We rented our stain rags and they were cleaned and reused over and over again. We collected the pallets and metal drums and returned them to the suppliers. We purchased recycled cardboard and all of our scrap cardboard was stacked and recycled as well as glass and cans.

We did everything to play by the rules, avoid trouble and save or make a buck. Looking back, I'm glad we did with what we know now about our planet. I only hope we all wise up and make the necessary changes to save our planet. What we really lack in our country is good old **Common Sense**. Sometimes I think I should have been a politician but there's no room for honesty, integrity and sincerity in politics, is there? Grow up *Walter*.

* * *

Most of our reps were doing pretty well but a growing business always needs more sales. It's required to grow, become successful, make money and stay in business. I've always said, ***"The hardest thing about being in business is staying in business."*** If you can hang around long enough you stand a chance.

Also, ***"Life is like a ball, we spend very little time on top or on the bottom, we spend most of our time somewhere in between."*** My point is, don't get too high when you're on top or too low when you hit the bottom because things will change soon enough. Recessions come and go.

We needed more reps so we could acquire more sales, which allowed us to hire more people to do more work, so we could pay more bills, buy more materials and add more equipment. More, More, MORE!

At this point, I was having some problems with Gary Tripp, our Southern California rep. I felt that he really didn't regard the company or the product like he should. We got into it and I fired him or he quit; it depends on who's telling the story. We made up shortly thereafter and I told him that if he were ever to do well as a rep he needed to put his John Hancock on the bottom line of what he sold and who he represented. That's a lesson I feel all salespeople need to learn. If you don't believe in your company and product how in the world will you ever convince anyone else to?

Gary's a smart guy so he took the ball and ran with it. He went on to become my best salesman and one of the best sales reps in the furniture industry, in my opinion. My other reps were no slouches, either. Mark and Cal were great, and Don Ross replaced Roc Anderson up north. These four became the nucleus of my sales crew throughout the United States for many, many years. Let's face it, without good salespeople you can have the greatest product in the world and still go broke.

CHAPTER 10
THIRTY-SOMETHING

It's amazing how quickly time passes as you grow older. As kids, time goes by so slowly. Hmm, reminds me of lyrics of a song by the Righteous Brothers. But as responsible adults, that's another story. Days seems to blow by and we never have enough time for anything. I was 29 years old and Choc was in her 30s, we were both in our prime and we were making things happen. Chocolate was running the show at Precision Mortgage and she was growing and glowing, personally and professionally. She worked hard and smart, made good money, raised our family, took care of our home and has always been *"The wind beneath my wings."* (Thanks Bette Midler.)

Chocolate still paid the mortgage and a few of the bills but I started making a few bucks so the pressure eased up some. Without her, there was no way I could have accomplished what I had. I mean, let's get real: I was awfully young to begin with, uneducated, way undercapitalized and severely lacking in confidence. I had no sales training, little office experience and I knew nothing about manufacturing except how to work in a shop. Now that's the real makings of a successful businessman, wouldn't you say?

But Chocolate and I helped each other with everything. We discussed every move we made and she always knew the right things to say. Even if was just encouragement or a simple, *"You can do it."* We were always there for each other. *"We make one helluva team"* is written on a little statue of two mice that we have treasured for years. In fact, it was on the top of our wedding cake in place of the little bride and groom. Funny, but we often compare ourselves to the two mice Sniff and Scurry, in the book "Who Moved My Cheese?" by Dr. Spencer Johnson. It's a good read about change and how to cope and deal with it.

We bounce ideas and dreams off each other constantly. We would set goals and attack them like there was no tomorrow. I got to a point where I almost felt unstoppable, maybe even a little cocky. But then, life has a way of bringing you down a notch or two. It can be very humbling at times, if not downright cruel. I guess that's how Chocolate and I stayed humble and never forgot where we came from. A good lesson for all to learn, a little humility.

Creative Ideas continued to grow and we needed more space. What else is new? It wasn't too long before we *"busted through the wall,"* as Jim always says. I leased the 7,000-square-foot building next store to us and felt confident it would take us well into the future. We'd grown to more then 13,000 square feet and 40 people.

* * *

It was early December and I'd been saving for some time to buy myself a new car. I had never owned a new car in my life, and I'd always dreamed of owning a red Corvette. My auto shop teacher in high school had a Corvette and, for some reason, I'd always said that if I ever bought a new car it would be a Corvette. I had saved about $15,000 to put towards a large down payment. This was my 30th birthday present to myself and I deserved it. I reasoned that I owned a business and a home and we were doing pretty well. So, as long as I could keep the payments low and the insurance was affordable, why not? I worked hard and long and seldom thought of myself and Chocolate had a new company car, so we had no other payments.

It was just about two weeks before my birthday when I got the bad news. It seemed the insurance on a new Corvette would be about $1,500 a year. I knew that I had a few tickets but that was ridiculous. I couldn't do that to myself or my family and I wouldn't. We could use that extra money for so many more important things besides car insurance, so I decided to pass on the car.

That Friday night, I took Chocolate out on a shopping spree. I decided to blow some of my down payment on other things I'd always wanted. Chocolate tried her best to talk me out of it but I wouldn't listen. I bought a beautiful 14k gold Concord watch and a 72-inch projection color TV. From there, I wanted to share, so I bought her some boots and a coat. Chocolate was nagging me to stop buying things and asking to go home and I finally agreed. I was pretty excited and accepted that the old van would just have to do for a while longer.

When we got home, I opened the front door to *"Surprise!"* My house was full of family and friends, I was floored. Chocolate had planned a great surprise party for me - no wonder she wanted to go home. I was shocked to say the least.

Chocolate knew that I didn't like surprises or a big thing made about my birthday but she did it anyway. It was a really nice party. Everyone was dressed in black and there was a black coffin full of presents. There were black balloons and streamers everywhere. The cake was a tombstone and the party theme was *over the hill*. I got a real kick out of it and was pleasantly surprised.

After greeting everyone and visiting for a while, Chocolate asked me to go get a case of beer from the garage. As I opened the garage door, there sat a new red Corvette. I was overwhelmed. I couldn't control myself; all I could do was break down and cry. Believe it or not, as I write this I get misty-eyed even now. It seems, my girl thought I really deserved that car so she bought it, financed it and put the insurance in her name to get a much lower rate. I told you she was smart and re-lentless. I couldn't believe my eyes. My first new car was sitting in my garage and I just blew a bunch of money on other crap. That's where my mind went…that's how I think. I was starting to panic, wondering if I could return the other stuff, Chocolate just said; *"It's okay"* and so it was…

As the party continued, Chocolate had another surprise in store for me. She'd hired a palm reader as entertainment. I don't believe in or like this sort of thing so I said *"I'll pass."* However, after a little pressure, I went along with the program. I went into my daughter's dark bedroom and sat down. As soon as she picked up my hand, the palm reader said, *"I see blood, lots and lots of blood. Are you bleeding somewhere?"* I'll never forget those exact words. Now this was a little strange and scary. I had to stop and think about it for a second. I told her, *"I have hemorrhoids and they bleed from time to time but it's no big deal, they've bled for years."* Then she said, *"You need to see a doctor right away."* Well, needless to say, this was a little freaky and it unnerved me a bit but I didn't put too much stock in what this quack had to say. I mean, after all, this was a party palm reader. What does she really know?

As the weekend rolled by, I couldn't get her warning out of my head. I started thinking about everything. About how tired I'd been feeling and about how for-getful I was becoming. Some days I'd leave work and lock the front door, walk ten feet to my car and forget if I had locked the door. I'd go back and do it again, sometimes two and three times. When I'd get home I was so exhausted. I'd sit and watch TV but I couldn't hold my head up, I'd have to prop myself up with pillows. The really scary thing was that in the middle of the night I'd wake up and my arms, legs, hands and feet would be numb. I kept telling myself that I was just tired, stressed out from working so many long hours and having so much on my mind.

Chocolate was begging me to go see a doctor but I kept insisting that I was fine. After the palm reading, though, we were both starting to become concerned, so I decided to go to the doctor first thing that Monday morning. This time I wanted to see a proctologist, one who specializes in hemorrhoids. In the past, I'd seen doctors and they always said try this or that and recommended surgery (if it got worse). The very thought of surgery alone scared me so I tried all their remedies but they never seemed to work.

I went to see Dr. Aaron two weeks before my birthday. He ran a bunch of tests and told me that I might be a little anemic but he didn't think there was much to worry about. He said he'd know more about how to proceed in a few days when all the results came back. I felt better about things and went back to work.

That evening, I went home early to watch Monday Night Football with my buddy, Clint. It was about 7 o'clock when the phone rang - it was Dr. Aaron. He sounded a little excited and said that he wanted someone to drive me to Hoag Memorial Hospital and that he'd meet me there as soon as possible. I said, *"I can't. I have company and we're watching the game."* I told him, *"Besides, I need to open my factory in the morning. Can't it wait until after that?"* He replied, *"I'm at dinner with my family and I'm going to leave now. This is really serious. I need you to meet me there right now."* I still tried to argue and then he said, *"If you don't get to the hospital now, you may not make it through the night."* That was it; I think I went into a state of shock. I handed the phone to Chocolate and the rest gets a little blurry for me.

According to Chocolate, I fought her the whole way to the hospital. She said that all I would talk about was who was going to open the shop and what was going to happen if I had to be out for any length of time. She told me to shut up and stop worrying about work, that she would handle it. When we arrived, Dr Aaron was waiting for me and they rushed me into intensive care. They started giving me blood transfusions right away. I was in critical condition! Me! How could this happen? I was scared to death.

It seems I was bleeding so much and for so long that my blood count (hemoglobin) was down to 4.5. An average man is walking around at about 11 to 12 so to be at 4.5 is a really rare sight. They were amazed that I hadn't gone into shock or worse - had a heart attack, stroke or brain damage.

For the first five days, I went through a battery of tests and I was getting pints of blood daily. The doctors just could not and would not believe that I could lose so much blood from hemorrhoids. They thought I had cancer or bleeding ulcers. They put me through some of the most invasive and horrible tests a person can undergo. It was all so scary and embarrassing and I was so weak and tired. Getting sleep in the intensive care unit is virtually impossible. There's someone taking your vitals every 30 minutes and forget about the alarms and buzzers going off constantly.

I think three people died in that unit while I was there and I'll never forget watching all the commotion. Did I mention I was scared to death? I did a lot of praying and soul searching. I didn't want to die; I refused to die. When you're in that type of situation, you're so helpless, you have no idea what's going on and you lose all control. Everyone talks about you like you're not there and the nurses treat you like it's just a job to them, which it is. It's funny, but you take away a man's home and family, strip him of his car and clothes and what you have left is what I felt like, a slab of beef. The nurses would be talking about their boyfriends or what they did last night and here I was sick and possibly dying. But life goes on. The doctors would commiserate over me and talk about different tests and exams that they thought they should try next.

After five long days, they relented and finally came to the conclusion that I was losing the blood due to the hemorrhoids, *Duh!* That's what I'd been telling them all along. But in all honesty, I'm glad they took such precautions. Dr. Aaron saved my life. On the sixth day, they felt that I was stable enough to do the dreaded surgery. I'd feared this day for many years and by the time it came I was just happy that was all I needed. The surgery was a success and I found myself back in the intensive care unit. Chocolate was a mess on the inside but a trooper on the outside. Still, I could tell she was really scared.

Dr. Aaron met with us the next day but I was still pretty groggy from all the drugs and lack of rest. He told me I received nine-and-a-half pints of blood and that I was lucky to be alive. He also informed me that I could go home a few days later if I was stable and could pee on my own. I guess I was still too drugged to realize at that moment what he meant but I would figure it out soon enough.

Have you ever seen the clear air hose that they use on aquariums? I had one of those stuffed up my unit so I could pee. Every day they would pull it out (ouch!) and wait to see if I could pee that day. If I didn't, a cute, young nurse would come in and well, I think you get the picture. Let me tell you this is one painful, ugly, disgusting, embarrassing procedure and it went on and on for days. It got to the point where we were praying for me to pee. Seems that after this kind of surgery you swell up on the inside and it blocks off your stream. If you can't pee, infection can set in and you don't go home.

One morning, after they removed the hose, I went to take a shower, my first in quite a while. Chocolate was in the hall praying and low and behold, I began to pee. Yes, in the shower, disgusting I know but I didn't care. I was peeing and I was going home.

The next morning, Dr. Aaron came by to release me. What he had to say put a bit of a damper on the day. He told me that I needed bed rest for a month or more and I was to take it real slow and easy for the next year. He lectured me on how I had been neglecting my health and needed to take much better care of myself in the future. Yeah, I thought, can I go home now? And then he laid the big one on us. It seemed there was this new disease called AIDS, and after all the blood I had received I would need to be tested every year for the next five years. At that time, they weren't too hip on the disease and they hadn't started testing donated blood yet. I learned that I could have contracted this virus and it would take five years to ensure I was in the clear. Just what I needed, some uplifting news. But I was still thrilled to be going home. Happy birthday and you know what? It was like a new *birth-day* for me.

Thanks to the unknown Palm Reader and Dr. Aaron I was given a second chance. ***They saved my life.***

"Angels." I seem to get my share. ***Thank You, God.***

* * *

Some things don't change. The whole ride home I was quizzing Chocolate on what was happening at the shop, how the kids were doing, if she was okay and so on. By the time we got home, I was beat and it was back into bed, my bed, and it felt so good.

Now I'd like to kill a myth or two if I can. Hemorrhoid surgery is no picnic so don't get me wrong, but compared to some of my worst flare-ups, it's mild. I would suffer with some of the worst pain before the surgery, sometimes for days and weeks at a time. The surgery leaves you uncomfortable but at least everyday afterward you are improving and getting better and better. Yes, I'm a new asshole now, according to some.

I must apologize for ever doubting the Palm Reader and others like her. She saved my life and made a believer out of me. Obviously there are people out there with greater powers or senses than I understand but they exist. I still won't go to them; I still feel weird about it. I guess I don't want to know the future, but that's just me.

* * *

Chocolate had taken a leave of absence from her job to run our company and they were pleased to be getting her back soon. She was trying to care for me, cover Creative Ideas and still keep up with things at her own job. It was a very demanding schedule for her. She would get Mikee off to school in the morning, drop Nicole off at Montessori School and then go to our company. Once there, she had to figure out everything from scratch. All she knew at the time was what I told her over the years. From there, she'd run over to Precision Mortgage and spend an hour or so working. Then, back to Creative Ideas to close up, pick up Nicole and then home to fix dinner and tend to us all. Wow, I was married to Wonder Woman and didn't even know it.

Let's also give some credit where credit is due. Jeff, Pancho, Al, my mom and our crew really sucked it up and busted their butts to help Chocolate with everything while I was away. After about a month or so, I began to go into work late and leave early. It wasn't much, but it allowed Chocolate to go back to her job and took some of the pressure off her. I swore I would never work as hard with the kind of hours I had in the past. I learned my lesson (and if you believe that I have some beachfront property in Arizona I'd love to sell you).

You know that red Corvette I got for my birthday? Well, I had it for several months before I ever really got to drive it. It was too hard to get in and out of and too bumpy a ride for my butt. Then, the first time I took that baby out on the freeway a pallet fell off a truck in front of me at 70 mph. I jerked the steering wheel so hard that the car spun out of control several times down the freeway only to come to a halt about an inch from the center divider facing the wrong direction. Believe it or not, there wasn't a scratch on the car or me in spite of all the traffic and busted pieces of wood flying past. No harm, no foul. Amazingly enough, all I needed was a change of pants. *Angels!*

As time passed, I was getting stronger and feeling better but I did have some long-lasting damage. I would start to say something in conversation and forget what I was talking about (in mid-sentence). This really troubled me. What kind of a salesman and businessman could I be if I couldn't remember what I was talking about? Dr. Aaron warned me about this. He said that the memory loss might pass with time or it may never get better - it was all luck of the draw. I hated this but I was feeling better so I just hoped and prayed for the best.

Funny thing about turning 30, I somehow reasoned it would be lucky even after what had happened. I still felt that the 30s would be great years for me because they all started with the number three. Another factor was that my baby, Nicole, was three. I even named a new desk line the 300 series just because I loved the number. It turned out to be the best-selling group I ever designed. It's crazy what *positive thinking* can do.

After a few months, I was back to work full-time again; there was just too much to do. I did give up my workbench in the shop and moved up to the front office. I did that partly because I was too weak to stand all day and partly because as the company grew, there was just way too much office and phone work to be done. I was the plant manager, office manager, sales manager, designer, buyer and top salesman. I ran the collection department and the accounts payable department. I also handled all the plant engineering, sales and the marketing. I, too, was growing in many directions and I soaked it up like a sponge.

Mom started working full-time; she answered the phones, typed all of the orders and invoices, did the payroll, cut my checks and handled all of the filing and mail. Keep in mind, this was all before faxes and computers. We did it the old-fashioned way. We used adding machines and typewriters and between the two of us, we ran the whole front end of Creative Ideas for many years. It was very taxing but fun and exciting at the same time. I was finally living the life that *Walter Mitty* only dreamed about. Creative Ideas was my stage and I was the star in my show. I was really something and, if you don't believe me, just ask me.

As the company grew, the buildings were lacking in some important areas besides space. We had no truck docks or storage yard, parking was an issue and we were light on electrical power. We needed more restrooms, storage and office space. Our lease was coming up so it was time to think about moving again. We got lucky: the 18,000-square-foot building right across the street was coming up for lease right about the same time as ours. I couldn't pass this up. Besides, we could move over a weekend and didn't even need a truck. I also made sure we could have access to the other 15,000-square-foot building on the property when its lease expired in a few years. So we signed a five-year-lease with an option for the other building. Again, I thought this should take us well into the future.

Moving is always painful and very expensive even if it's right across the street. In an operation like ours, there is so much to do. Not only did we have to move everything but there was electrical, air lines and a dust collection system to set up. After we got in and were up and running, we all went brain dead for about two months. I don't know why but we couldn't get back to normal production no matter how hard we tried. We were getting behind and blowing lots of money on overtime. I just couldn't understand it; we had more space, more equipment and more manpower yet we couldn't produce. I was desperate and looking for some answers.

I know I'm not the brightest bulb in the box but I do have more common sense than most people and I never lacked for will power or desire. I have a theory, big surprise. Another *Stevism:* ***"Life is like a library, you don't have to read all of the books in the library to be smart, you just need to know where the library is so you can access them as needed."***

* * *

Well, I knew where the library was so I hired an old-timer who had a world of knowledge about building furniture as a consultant. He worked for me for about a month and I did get some good tips along the way but, for the most part, things just seemed to work themselves out. I learned that people work like they drive home in their car, on autopilot. When you move them, you disrupt the flow of things and you take away their routine. This disruption causes people to have to think about everything they do. The simplest tasks now become a chore - like where is the restroom, where are the supplies and so on. It just takes time for everyone to get used to their surroundings and get back to normal, back to autopilot. Believe me, this was an expensive lesson and I pass it along to everyone I know who is moving a company. Plan on the extra dollars for the learning curve; expect some downtime and most of all, be patient.

Another point about my library theory is that we spend way too much time trying to get better at things we don't do well or don't like to do at all. I read a book by Jim McIngvale, "Always Think Big!" Love that title. Jim was a good customer of ours and a friend; he's also one of the most successful furniture dealers in this country. Jim owns and runs Gallery Furniture in Houston. In his book, Jim talks about growing up and how we're always instructed to spend extra time on things we're not good at or don't have any interest in. He makes the point that if we spent more time on things we like and excel at, maybe we'd all be happier and more successful. A good quote from Jim and something we should all realize, *"If it is to be, it is up to me."*

After all, the library is always open; it's always there if you need to access it. I learned this valuable lesson and use it all of the time now: Do what you love to do and be the best at it. Don't spend too much time worrying about things you don't like, can't do or can't control.

* * *

Well, that's easier said than done. It took me a few more years to really learn that lesson and, at that time, I was just working my ass off. I was burning the candle at both ends again. I was still trying to spend time in the shop and run the sales and office in between and at night. I was doing all of the trade shows myself and, when I wasn't busy with that, I was designing new product and dealing with all of the government agencies. It seems I'd already forgotten and broken the one promise I'd made to myself in the hospital.

In the factory, things were growing and changing. We kept adding new machines and more dust collectors, forklifts and people. I would go to trade shows and on factory tours to learn more about modern machinery and new techniques. Our payroll was growing and, with it, the need for more management. Jeff, Al, Pancho and Abel were promoted to supervisors. Pancho ran the mill, Abel the pre-assembly, Al the assembly department and Jeff ran the finishing and shipping departments. Jeff was my contact to the shop and my right-hand man. Most of my employees were Hispanic and spoke little or no English. Meanwhile, my staff, Jeff and I were equally inept in Spanish. This made running a company of this magnitude a challenge. But that didn't slow me down. It was just another obstacle to overcome and we did. My supervisors learned some English and Jeff and I learned a few necessary words in Spanish. I just loved what we were building so nothing was going to discourage me. I really couldn't believe that this company was mine and that it was becoming such a force in the furniture industry.

I always felt that I was fooling everyone and that one day, they'd figure it out and I'd be done. That's the little fear that you live with when you own a company and it begins to do well. In your heart and head you can't believe what you have accomplished. As I mentioned earlier, for some people their company becomes them and they become the company. When you build something from scratch and put your heart and soul in it, when you love it and enjoy it, something happens. It's like you cross over and it becomes you and you become it. *"I was Creative Ideas; I will always be Creative Ideas."*

It gave me everything I needed in my younger years - success, money, pride, knowledge and the platform to strut my stuff. A place where I finally belonged. Most of all, it was helping me gain something I'd lacked most of life - confidence. I always dreamed of becoming a singer, drummer or baseball player. All that *Walter Mitty* lacked was talent, the kind of talent that you gained with years of practice, experience, love and support. I always wanted to be rich and famous, up on the big stage. Well, Creative Ideas was all that for me and more. I found my vehicle, my stage.

* * *

Tony Robbins always speaks about *"**Passion**"* and how you can't live without it and I'm a firm believer in passion. I believe that if you live a life without passion, you're not really living at all; you're just going through the motions. You have to have passion for everything - your marriage, your kids, your career, your home and so on. And you have to give them all quality time and attention. Try not caring about your car and see what it looks like and runs like in a few years. Now apply that to your spouse, family, business, etc.

The true key to my success is that I'm more passionate than most people. If I do anything, I want to do it to the best of my ability and then some. I demand the best of myself and the people around me. I strive for perfection but I think about others along the way also. Passion and compassion, in my mind, go hand in hand. They are not things you can acquire or buy - you either have them or you don't. We all have a passion for something. Some of us are lucky enough to find it and some never will. You just have to keep looking and trying.

"Never give up and never give in."

These are the words that I pass along to my daughters as often as possible; yes, another *Stevism*. Find something or someone you love and throw your complete being into it. Only then will your journey through this life seem complete. My wife completes me, my family and friends complete me, my career completes me. This book completes me, my life defines me. I am a lucky man because I have a passion and compassion for everything and everybody. I never give up and I never give in. True grit. That, if any one thing, was the key to my success.

* * *

By 32, I'd passed my first couple of HIV tests. I was clean. The couple of months leading up to each test were nerve-racking, to say the least. I would actually start feeling sick as the deadline approached and then, after the test came back negative, I'd miraculously be just fine. The mind can play such wicked games. I was feeling strong again, working out regularly and playing racquetball as often as I could, though I was still having trouble with short-term memory. It was better but I would still lose myself in mid-sentence all too often. I had to really think and concentrate hard during conversations, especially during business conversations.

Dad was in and out of the hospital with heart ailments. He kept having small heart attacks and the doctors said he couldn't have angioplasty because his heart was too weak and he might not make it through the procedure. That totally ruled out any open heart surgery, so all they could do was try to treat him with medicine, exercise and rest. They instructed him to quit smoking and lose a few pounds but it went in one ear and out the other. Dad always did as he pleased; he had a mind of his own.

Mom was still working for me and I think she liked it because it got her out of the house and away from my dad. Even when he was on his best behavior, dad was a real pain in the ass. He got bored easily and was always sick, so she had her hands full with him all of the time. He continued to control her and didn't want her to go anywhere alone so he either went with her or made my sister go. Dad came down to the shop almost daily to check on us and hang out. He'd visit with my mom for a while and then with me. When I told him I had work to do, he'd go out to the factory and watch the guys for a while. Dad spoke Italian fluently so he could communicate with the workers and he'd always tell them how lucky they were to work for me. That's my dad; what can I say?

Do you remember the song "Cat's in the Cradle" by Harry Chapin? That song explained my relationship with my dad perfectly. When I was young and I needed him he was never around. He was either too busy or too screwed up or in jail. Once he finally settled down, he saw all he'd missed and wanted to be a dad. By then, I'd grown up and didn't need him. I was bitter from the past and way too busy to make time for him. I had my own family, friends and my business and sadly, I only spared him a little time here and there.

Now, don't get me wrong, I loved my dad as much as I've ever loved anyone in my life. I always wanted to be like him - the good parts of him that is - but I also hated him more than anyone else. I was unable to really get over all that had happened; I could never learn to trust him. I guess I never really forgave him for all of the pain and suffering he caused us. I wish I could have done better and believe me, I tried. I just couldn't get all the way there. Still, my dad was relentless; he'd call me two or three times a day just to ask, *"What are you doing?"* *"I'm working, dad. I'm busy, dad."* I'd snap back.

My sister, Jackie, was out of college and working full-time at a law office. She still lived at home to help my parents out and save some money. They planned to buy a house together someday. Jackie also saw a lot with my dad (she too had it very tough) but he loved her to death and she somehow managed to love, honor and forgive him. Meanwhile, Vito was still at CLIMB and doing alright. We saw him mostly on big holidays and on his birthday. But that was about it. Some things just don't change; he was still asking to come home.

As for Chocolate and my girls, well, Chocolate's company moved to larger quarters, added a new partner and lots of new people. Chocolate was managing the whole company like it was her own; she took it all so seriously. I kept telling her that she needed to push for more money because, as a company owner, I knew the true value of an employee like her. I wished I had one. But all in all, she was doing pretty damn well; she had a company car (Mercedes), life and health insurance for our entire family and earned more than $100,000 a year. Not bad for a little, barefoot, uneducated girl from Fontana. They treated her really well and she deserved it.

The funny thing was that every building I moved into, I'd always set up an office for Chocolate in hopes that one day she would join me and we could work together. I missed those days in Pedley when I would work in the garage and she was in the kitchen with the door open so we could be together all of the time. I'm a rare and lucky breed; I love my wife and kids more than life itself. I love being with Chocolate; she is my best friend. I was lucky that despite all of my faults and flaws she somehow saw the best in me and loved me, too. We are truly life partners, soul mates. Chocolate always compared us to lobsters. Apparently, they mate for life. I've always jokingly said that she's like the big crab with the one big claw, always keeping me in line with it.

Mikee was now a beautiful teenager. She had her up and downs but overall she was a really good kid. She was doing okay in high school but somewhere between boys and fun she lost interest in school. Like her parents, she thought she knew it all and was very impatient with authority and direction. As with most teenagers, someone has to be the bad guy and, in our house, that be me. I was a real pain in her ass but I just wanted to teach her responsibility and self-discipline. I've always felt that kids need these things in order to become responsible adults and cope with the stresses of life, work and family.

Nicole was a bundle of joy; she was so cute and gullible and we teased her every chance we got. She made us happy and we laughed all of the time. But she too was a pain; she wanted to play games every night when we got home from work. Most nights we were just so tired but she nagged us to play anyway. And get this, she made us play and then she cheated. She couldn't stand losing; I wonder where she got that from? Whenever we played Monopoly, she came up with extra money out of nowhere.

Nicole had slept in our bed since she was born. I guess I never got over that bad experience in the hospital and I worried about crib death. That wasn't going to happen on my watch. As a kid, I could sleep through a hurricane but, as a dad, if you dropped a pin I was up checking the house and patrolling.

We were asleep one night when I heard a crash like someone had smashed through a window. I jumped out of bed and the only weapon Chocolate could find was an aluminum ski pole. So, here I was going room to room carrying a ski pole and wearing little more than my birthday suit. I couldn't find anything; everyone was safe and sound asleep. I even checked outside and all was calm. Finally, as we were about to go back to bed, Chocolate went into the guest bathroom only to find that the shelves in the medicine cabinet had collapsed onto the countertop. A short time later, the Night Stalker made the headlines and I bought my first gun, a 9mm Beretta. As I said, not on my watch!

* * *

We were going on four years in our Anaheim Hills house and the payments were now very affordable. We were living well, so Chocolate thought it was time for us to move up. That's my girl, always pushing us to new heights. We liked our Anaheim Hills home; it was a nice property on a hill, with a pool and a view of the city. It was very comfortable, in a great neighborhood and close to work. *"So, why do we have to move?"* I asked.

Chocolate mentioned to our friend, Dixie, that we were thinking about moving and that's all it took. Within a week, Dixie drove a couple by our house and they fell in love with it and made us an offer of $225,000. Hell, we hadn't even listed the house and I wasn't sure I even wanted to sell and it sold. Now, we were looking for a new place within 60 days, this was always fun. The new owners wanted to move in by December for the holidays, so we searched high and low. We wanted a bigger house, with more property and a pool. We wanted something newer so we wouldn't have much work to do. Let's face it, we were busy enough. We must have looked at 50 houses and, as usual, the only ones I liked were way out of our league.

Then, one afternoon, we went to Yorba Linda to see a house on Summerwood Lane. It was a nice, big house but it was selling for $575,000, way out of our budget. We needed to keep the price around $350,000 to qualify for a loan. As we were leaving, I noticed a *"For Sale"* sign through the overgrown shrubs and bushes at the corner house. Dixie looked it up in the listing book: five bedrooms, six baths, large bonus room, formal living and dining room, large family room and over a half acre of horse property. The house was just three years old, 5,000 square feet with a large master suite and a walk-in closet. It was priced at $415,000 after several reductions. I said, *"Let's look at it."*

As we walked through the house, I kept suggesting all the improvements we could make. I fell in love with the place. Chocolate, on the other hand, was not so sure. She said it was dark and dreary, needed lots of work, with an overgrown landscape and dirt for a backyard. Yes, but I pointed out the horse property, the 5,000 square feet, the upstairs bonus room and the large master bedroom and walk-in closet. We knew the houses on the same street were much higher in price and we would make money the second we closed the deal. I convinced her and Dixie to submit an offer of $350,000. *"What do we have to lose?"* I said. We were taking a shot in the dark. After several offers back and forth, we settled on a price of $385,000 as long as the owner would carry a second mortgage of $15,000.

The owner of the house was a very young man, maybe 19 at the time. He had come into a lot of money after losing his parents and grandparents at a very young age. The reason the house sold for so little was two-fold. One, his agents were a couple of crooks. They just wanted to make a quick buck and didn't care who got hurt along the way, so they kept convincing him to lower the price. Second, he was a bit of a head case; he played in a band and used way too many drugs. He kept telling potential buyers that the house was haunted and scaring them off. He even had Chocolate and my girls nervous but I reassured them that the only haunting in the house was between his ears, drugs...

We closed escrow in 30 days and moved in Dec. 1. We always seemed to be moving around the holidays. Isn't that the time of year for peace and quiet? Well, not in our house. After arriving in the new house we realized that all the furniture we bought for the old house didn't work so now we needed to buy everything all over again. Do you have any idea how much stuff you need in a 5,000-square-foot house? A lot! Little by little though, we started furnishing and remodeling the house. But we had some serious house payments to contend with at the same time - $3,500 a month plus we had to pay off the $15,000 second mortgage within the first year. We went from a very comfortable lifestyle to being strapped all over again.

I was making $1,000 a week so we split all of the bills down the middle. Choc would pay half the mortgage, buy the groceries and tend to the kids and I would pay the other half of the mortgage and the rest of the bills. Once again, we were broke all the time but that never slowed us down - it just made us more determined. We just worked harder, smarter and earned more; that was always our answer to everything.

After about a year, we were able to refinance the house and drop our payment to $2,800 a month. We paid off the second so things were getting much better. But up popped the devil! During the refinancing, the appraiser said the house was only 4,350 square feet. I argued with him, told him he was crazy. I demanded he redo his appraisal. I was positive it was 5,000 square feet. Well, remember the crooked agents. It seemed they embellished by about 650 square feet or so. I was so pissed off that I sued the real estate company.

I also learned a valuable lesson: *"Buyer Beware."*

Just because it says something on an ad sheet and in the listing book doesn't mean it's the real deal. You can't even trust the wording on most contracts. People are looking to get over on you everywhere you go in life. It's a shame but you have to be very careful and do your homework.

Chocolate and I decided that we were so used to paying the $3,500 a month payment that we might as well keep paying it and pay off our house more quickly. Once again, we were possessed, putting every extra penny we made into the mortgage. It was like a game to us. We paid that house off completely in less than nine years. All the while, we refurnished and remodeled along the way. I told you, I could really manage a buck.

A friend of ours, Mark Patton, thought we worked too hard and played too little. He gave me a tip that I still use to this day. Mark said, *"If you make three dollars, you should spend one on bills, save one and reward yourself with the last one. Have some fun, life is too short."* This was a very good piece of advice, one that all should heed. I never did get that crazy. I'd blow maybe a half a dollar on fun but we never lacked for anything. We even began to take a vacation from time to time. After the house payment was gone, I would save all I could and when we did splurge, it was for tangible items such as furniture, art or clothing. I even bought Chocolate some nice jewelry and we had new cars all of the time. That summer, I took us to Hawaii for our first real family vacation, the Hilton Hawaiian Village in Honolulu. We had a blast; it was just the five of us: Chocolate, the girls, me and Uncle Tris. Yes, Uncle Tris, my best friend, went everywhere with us for many years. He was then, and always will be, a major part of our family.

* * *

As I said earlier, life is funny. Every time things get going in one direction, up pops the devil. The good old Yin and Yang, you can't have one without the other. While in my 30s, a lot of family members started to expire. I guess, you can't have life without death.

My Uncle Philly had a massive heart attack and died without warning in his 50s. He left behind my Aunt Joan (mom's sister) and seven children. Shortly thereafter, my Uncle Dominick had a heart attack while on a hunting trip and passed away. He was just 59. This sent shock waves through the Balsamo family. My Uncle Dominick was the oldest and wisest of the Balsamos. He was the family patriarch and everyone looked up to him ever since their parents died. He left Aunt Francie and their seven children behind.

My dad was distraught over the loss of his older brother and wanted to go to New York for the funeral. He really wasn't up for the trip. Between his heart condition and financial status, he couldn't afford it so I volunteered to take him, after a little urging from Chocolate. We were just going for a few days; we'd attend the funeral, visit for a bit and then get out of there. I was sad for my father but I was also excited and nervous to go back home to Brooklyn for the first time since I was 14. I didn't know what to expect, I wondered how much had changed and how the family would react to me. After all, when I left, I was fairly close to all of them and, over the years, I had basically disowned them. I grew away and apart from them. Maybe it was what I needed to do, my way of breaking the mold and becoming my own man.

Once we arrived in Brooklyn, I wanted to get a hotel room near my Aunt Rosie's house, which was close to everything. But typical of an Italian family, my aunt insisted that we stay in her spare bedroom. Now, I had many problems with this. First, I didn't want to impose on anyone. Second, I wasn't comfortable in other people's homes. Third, I liked the space and freedom a hotel provides. Fourth, it was a tiny room, which meant I'd have to sleep with my father. Are you kidding me? I could go on and on but why bore you? My aunt insisted, my dad insisted, and we stayed there.

From the second we made contact with any of the family, my dad changed. All of a sudden, he was bossy, possessive and clung to me like nothing I'd ever seen before. I thought to myself, *"Back off"* but I went along with it because I wanted him to feel good and I wanted the family to see that I respected my father. Once we got to the funeral, it was surreal. Everyone was there only they were all so much older than I remembered. I was meeting the kids I grew up with for the first time as adults and meeting their children at the same time, very strange indeed.

My dad was constantly demanding that I stay by his side. I never did quite understand why but I did my best to appease him. It was great to see my Aunt Mary and my Cousin Vito. Boy, how I loved and missed them. But it felt weird to express that since I had deserted them so many years before. I could have called, written or came back for a visit but I didn't. I swore the day they dragged me away from Brooklyn that I'd be back as soon as I was 18 but here I was in my 30s and the only reason I was back was for my dad and a funeral. Shame on me. Guilty as charged.

I tried to catch up with everyone but there wasn't much time and my father wouldn't let me out of his sight but for a few minutes here and there. It was incredible to see so much of the family in one place and how much they had all changed. I'd forgotten just how big our family was. We left a few days later and we all planned to keep in touch. But you know how that goes; we're blood but we hardly know each other and there were 3,500 miles and many years between us.

Over the years my Cousin Baby Vito and I talked from time to time and even now, I visit him and his lovely wife, Joby, whenever I go to New York but that's not often enough. He has a great wealth of knowledge about our family since he lived in Brooklyn long after I left. Vito had it pretty rough as a kid also. My Uncle Sally was very tough on him but that's a whole other book and he'll need to write that one. He has been very helpful to me in filling in some of the blanks as I write this book. As for the rest of the family, sad to say things went back to normal, the promises to keep in touch never transpired.

Not long after we got back home, I heard that my Uncle Red had died. Not long after that, his son, Donny, died also. Donny died a slow and painful death from AIDS; he was, unfortunately, a drug user. This scared the hell out of me since I still had a few years of AIDS testing to go. Donny was just a young man in his 40s. His brother, Vito, cared for him daily until the day he died. Donnie left behind my cousin, Marylou, and their two young children, Vito and Christina. My Aunt Mary was distraught over this terrible turn of events and never did recover. Losing both her husband and eldest son really took its toll on her both mentally and physically.

Next was my godfather, Bennie Balsamo, another heart attack victim. He, too, was in his 50s and he left behind his wife Louise and their two boys, Vito and Vincent. It seemed like the men in our family all died way to young; they all had very bad hearts and drug abuse seemed to run in the family.

They say you can never go home again and I guess there's some truth to that statement. My home was in Southern California with my wife, kids and family and

I was glad. Brooklyn was once my home, my roots, but that was a long, long time ago. I didn't belong there anymore. I was different from the rest of the Balsamos. I earned my living the old-fashioned way. I worked my ass off and I held my head up high, I was legit. I loved my family and their history but I had to do things my way. Kind of like the song, "My Way," sung by old blue eyes, Frank Sinatra. I love Sinatra and his music and that song is truly how I live my life, my way. Of course, you know that I grew up listening to it as a kid so how else would you expect *Walter Mitty* to do it?

* * *

Things were starting to settle down again and summer was right around the corner when I got the worst call of my life. Dad had just returned from the doctor's office where he was diagnosed with cancer. Lung cancer! I was stunned, shocked and full of questions. How bad? Could it be treated? Mom, Jackie and I all went with him to see a cancer specialist the next day. He told my dad that they caught the condition fairly early and it could be cured with radiation treatments. Chemotherapy was out of the question because of his heart condition. The doctor thought his chances were very good. As we got back into the car, all my dad could say was, *"I guess I can't get out of this one."* Then he predicted, *"I won't make it to Christmas."*

My pop had gotten out of everything over the years - school, work, marriage, raising a family, the neighborhood and even prison. He survived drug addiction, drug overdoses, heart attacks, living on the streets and the mob almost killing him. It seems my dad was very close with the head guy in Brooklyn so, when he screwed up instead of killing him they just beat him severely. They knocked out all his teeth, flattened his nose and beat him so bad that he almost died. But he was like a cat with nine lives, and he bounced back. Unfortunately for him, this must have been life number nine.

It was a very long and somber ride home. Dad started going for the radiation treatments but hated them and complained that they were killing him faster. I tried to stop by his house daily and spend time with him but he was very depressed and in a great deal of pain. It was really difficult and depressing just being around him. And my dad, God bless him, was not about to go quietly into the abyss. No, he was going to make sure we all suffered alongside of him.

My sister, Jackie, was heartbroken. She'd been seeing a nice man named Mike Couden and they were planning to get married that year. She was praying my dad would hang on long enough to walk her down the aisle. Dad made the wedding and it was a glorious day. Mike and Jackie continued to live with mom and dad in the home that they purchased together. In the end, my dad finally got to own a home, see his daughter marry and spend time with his granddaughter, Nicole. But then just when we started losing hope, the cancer specialist told us that he thought he got the tumor and that it was gone. Great news!

* * *

It was Nov. 25, 1987; I was just 32 years old. Thanksgiving was tomorrow and we were all at the hospital visiting my dad. He was in terrible shape, drugged so much that he hardly noticed we were there anymore. He was in such pain and all he could say was, *"Drag, drag, drag."* He wanted a hit off a cigarette even in his dying hours. I would light one and hold it to his mouth. His dying request was a cigarette, the very thing that was killing him. Go figure.

We were all planning a big Thanksgiving dinner at the hospital so we could all be together. The hospital was nice enough to provide us a room to use and everything. But now that seemed like a moot point. One of my dad's last requests was to give Nicole her Christmas present early; he was so afraid he wouldn't make it to Christmas. He gave her this pillow person that had a face, legs and arms. He had bought it for her months earlier. She called that pillow her *"Grandpa doll"* and she still has it to this day. It has traveled the world with her; it's never too far from her reach.

That night, as we were all leaving the hospital, I asked the nurse to let the doctor know, *"It was time."* The doctor told me that he could give him something to help with the pain but it could cause him to drift off for good. He told me to just let him know when we were ready. I didn't tell the others, I just did what I had to do. It was time. The pain for him and our family was more than anyone could take. He'd reached a point where he really didn't know anyone or anything but pain anymore.

It was about 5 o'clock in the morning when my phone rang, it was my mom. I'd been lying there awake all night expecting that call at any moment. My dad had passed away. They said that he had a heart attack in his sleep but I knew the truth. So it was finally over - my daddy was gone for good. Dad always had a flare for the dramatic and even in death, he made it forever memorable. *Happy Thanksgiving!*

We will think of him on Thanksgiving for the rest of our lives. I like to think he somehow planned it that way and is very pleased with himself. In fact, I'm sure of it. In the end, my dad didn't last six months. He was right; he never did make it to Christmas. As for the doctor, I guess he didn't get the tumor after all.

There was a lot to do and I didn't want my mom and sister to have to worry about anything except dealing with their own grief. I made all of the arrangements. I went out and bought him a suit; he didn't even own one. I had to arrange the coffin, cemetery, plot, headstone and the funeral home and service. I had to be the strong one, and as usual, I was up for the challenge. I did it all and I tried to be there for everyone.

My dad was quite a guy. He was smart, cunning and extremely likeable and he had a lot of common sense. Dad was the one who set the tradition in our family, insisting that we always spend holidays together. No matter what he ever did, he always made sure the family stayed together and believe me, we had plenty of reasons to grow apart. Even among his brothers, sisters, nieces and nephews, Tony was always everyone's favorite. That's because he truly loved everyone and never meant to hurt anyone; it was just the drugs, *the devil.*

Before dad died, he sat with all of us and made us promise different things to him. My mom promised to always love and remember him. Jackie promised to take care of my mom and herself. Chocolate promised to be friends with my mom and take care of me. My brother-in-law, Mike, promised that he would always let mom live with them. Nicole promised to always remember and love her Grandpa. As for me, there was a list of things. I promised to take care of the family, keep us all together, watch out for my mom and sister and to take care of myself, Chocolate and his granddaughters. That was just the beginning.

He made me promise to be with him in the funeral home when they did their thing behind the curtains, because he didn't want to be alone. I did it in spite of the funeral director's advice but it was one of the toughest things I've ever had to do. He asked me to bury him in California where he could be close to us and to promise that my mom would be buried in the same plot as him. I've done my best to keep my word on all counts and so has everyone else. A promise is a promise.

Dad's funeral was pretty small. None of his family from New York came; they just sent some flowers. Mostly, it was just a few of his old local friends, our immediate family and my four buddies. That was the first time I can ever remember the five of us crying together. We were at the cemetery and Dennis, Tris, Jim, Clint and I huddled together and cried. Over the years, we would repeat this more often than I care to remember as our parents and loved ones passed and left us behind to pick up the pieces. I was glad they were there and I'll always be there for them… *Always.*

* * *

About six months later, I heard a song on the radio that just floored me. It was "The Living Years" by Mike and the Mechanics. In the song, Mike Rutherford talks about not being there the morning his dad passed away and I wasn't. He also expresses how he never really got to tell his dad all the things he had to say, and I didn't.

Those lyrics ripped through my heart and really touched home with me. I cried. I'd been feeling pretty low and was depressed all of the time. All I wanted to do was sleep. I couldn't wait until the day was over so I could go to bed and I didn't want to wake up in the morning. I was even losing interest in my business and food, which is how I knew that things were getting serious. I couldn't explain it. I had everything to live for - my family was great, my business was successful, I was healthy, I had money, a nice home and cars but nothing seemed to matter. I was losing it.

Chocolate convinced me to go see an old therapist friend of ours, Susan. As soon as I told her my symptoms, she told me that I was in mourning for my dad. That was crazy - it had been six months. She explained that some people try to be so strong during a tragedy that they just suck it up and bury their own feelings. We put our feelings on hold until everyone else is safe and sound and doing alright and then they come out to haunt us at a later date.

So, I was in mourning. I was really, really sad and I missed my dad. It was finally my turn to cry, have regrets and feel the pain of losing a -parent. I missed his pain-in-the-ass visits and constant annoying phone calls. I missed all of his dumb clichés, his silly sayings, his superstitions and his over-opinionated advice. I missed the way he always tried to hug me and tell me that he loved me. I missed his favorite subject, which was food. *"What's for dinner?"* He'd always ask. And Lord knows, I missed his cooking. The man could take anything throw it in a pot and make a fantastic meal appear. It would take me many years to realize just how much I loved him and how much of each other's lives we'd missed. Funny, but I was just like him. I was everything he wished he could be. I became the man he should have been. I took his best traits and exploited them. I took his worst traits and learned from them and avoided them.

As it turns out, my dad was my true mentor, the person I emulated most in life. Thanks to him, I'm the person I am today. Thanks to my childhood, I grew up to accomplish all I have. Lessons are funny, you just never know where, what and when you're going to learn some of the most important ones. I just wish I could have forgiven my dad while he was still here. I wish I would have loved him more and showed it better. I wish I could have been a bigger man. I wish. And wish.

* * *

I'm reading a book called "Outliers" by Malcolm Gladwell which has helped solidify something I believed all along. You just never know what will be the lucky break that will lead to success or happiness. Everything that happens to us, good or bad, greatly influences our future and leads to our success or failure. It all depends on how we handle the experiences. Looking back over my life, there's lot of pain and suffering and a list of things that went wrong. Still, many of those so-called bad breaks helped put me on the path toward success and happiness. *Lemons to Lemonade.*

If my dad had never gotten involved with drugs and gone to prison, my mom would have never moved us to California. I wouldn't have met my wife and had my girls. I may never have been encouraged to start my own business and so on and so forth. Every successful person has had a series of lucky and unlucky breaks that have helped lead them to success. Most of us just don't realize it or think much about it. Sometimes, the worst break can turn out to be the best.

I believe that one left turn instead of a right may change the whole course of life. You just never know what's around the next bend. That's why I always say, **"I have no regrets."** In his book, Gladwell gives us examples of some geniuses who go on to live below-average lives because of the path their lives take. He also shows bad breaks that happened to people like Bill Gates of Microsoft that turned into the luckiest of breaks because of timing, passion and determination. You just never know - that's life. What I do know is that I'm happy to be here.

All in all, my 30s were an absolutely wonderful set of years. Sure, there were too many deaths, some illnesses and sadness but someone once told me that *"Life is a journey"* and on this wonderful journey, we encounter many storms and rocky roads. In my 30s, I learned that I would never stop missing my dad and the others who passed away. I learned that I am eternally grateful that my wife made it through a very rough patch with a hysterectomy and then a tumor the size of a small chicken. I learned how to work to live but not live to work.

The 30s were very good to me and my family, all in all. We persevered, we survived and we lived on. When I look back, I realize that the good times make us smile and give us warm pleasant memories while the tough times make us wise. And it's important that we never, ever forget.

* * *

"Life is not a sprint, it's a marathon."

**Family vacation in Hawaii 1988,
and the Grandpa doll in Nicole's arms.**

Me and Chocolate on her birthday in the back of a limo.

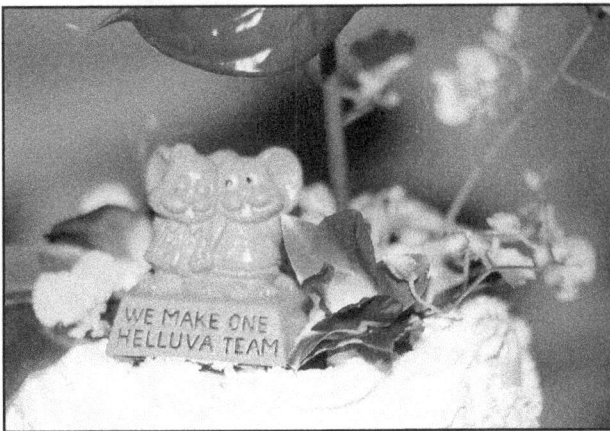

Our wedding cake topper and our saying.

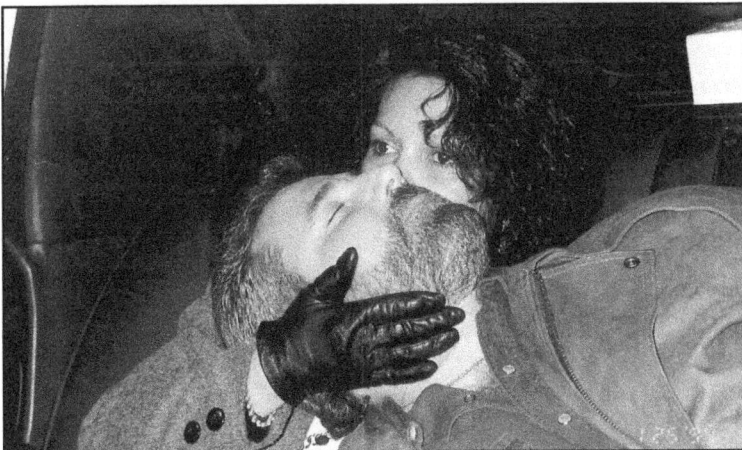

Me and Chocolate after a S.F. Market in the airport, beat as usual.

Mom and Dad at Jackies wedding…he made it.

Nicole vacationing in N.Y, visiting Cousin Vito.

CHAPTER 11
BACK TO BASICS

So let's take a second to review. My childhood was confusing and scary, a bit of a nightmare to say the least. Most of what I remember were the hard times but these experiences are where I picked up many of my family values and traditions as well as my passion and compassion. My teens were tough, lonely and sad, for the most part. One of the best things that ever happened to me back then was my relationship with Carrie, and she broke my heart. Still, I learned about love, met some life-long friends and fell in love with my wife. All in all, not so bad.

I started to find a direction for myself in my early 20s but that's still a very tough period for most of us. But after all, I did buy my first home and started building a future and a family by 22. In my mid-to-late 20s, I began to focus and started on the path that has led me here to you today. By 26, I'd opened Creative Ideas, had a child and found the road to success through the masters of positive thinking: Dr. Murphy, Tony Robbins, et al.

I knew that the 30s were going to be lucky for me. I finally got my first new car but I also nearly died. I bought a new house, and I lost my dad. My business was booming but we were killing ourselves running it. The Yin and Yang of life, I guess.

In my 30s, some of my wishes also came true. You see, when dad was diagnosed with lung cancer my mom started working less hours and taking more time off. I was trying to hold down the fort alone but it was way more than I could handle. Our company was quite large by this point and we were very busy. There was no way in the world two people could handle that office, let alone one. Chocolate and I discussed hiring someone but whom? After much discussion and soul-searching we decided the best and only person qualified for the job would be her. I was thrilled! Chocolate…not so much.

She traded in her business suits, the company car and her nice office with her educated peers and friends for a pair of jeans, a noisy factory, less pay and a shit-load of immigrant workers who didn't speak English. I'd become a very good salesman, I guess. I managed to convince her that this was the right thing to do. But really, she knew in her heart and head that this was the only thing to do if we were going to take the company to the next level. Chocolate, grudgingly, gave her 30-day notice and moved over to Creative Ideas. The folks at her old company were heart-broken and sad to see her leave. I think that was the beginning of the end for Precision Mortgage. They lost their spiritual leader and the soul of the company but hey, that's just my opinion.

Now understand that this was no picnic for either of us at first. In fact, the first year or so was quite challenging, to say the least. Here were two very strong-minded, young people who were used to running things and getting their own way. There was a tremendous adjustment and learning curve for both of us. Chocolate truly missed the professional side of her old job and all of her business and banking connections. She was stuck in a factory with no real contact with the public except over the phone. The two of us were spending 24 hours a day, seven days a week together. There were many clashes and many times when we butted heads but, as always, we sucked it up. We refused to quit and the more people told us, "*This will never work,*" the more determined we became.

Like water seeks its level, we learned how to work together and how to split the company into two parts - hers and mine. Chocolate took over the office, including collections, payroll and customer service. I, on the other hand, managed the factory, payables, sales and marketing and new product development. Before I knew it, Chocolate hired an assistant for me, Penny Griffin. Penny was my oldest daughter Mikee's best friend. She was a great kid, learned fast and was a dependable worker. Besides all that, she was like family to us so she fit right in. Penny relieved me of a lot of my tedious duties and with her on board, I learned how to delegate…okay, a little.

Shortly after Penny arrived, Chocolate hired Mikee as her assistant. Now we were cooking, we really had a staff. Between Chocolate and the girls we had everything covered and made a heck of a team. Mikee was a quick study and she took on a lot of Chocolate and mom's responsibilities right away. With the staff now in place, I was free to explore new ways to improve and grow our company.

I started to hire some new reps because it was about time to expand our company into more regions. This would help keep us recession proof, I thought. On came Mike McCartney for Arizona and New Mexico, Mike Clark for Colorado and Utah and big George Arbeiter for the Midwestern states. All three were very good men and real smart hires on my part.

George was the real break-through rep for our company. He helped us pioneer the whole Midwest and he did what the two reps before him had failed to do, sell and land great accounts. Through George and many others like him, we landed most of the Top 20 accounts in the country. After a while, we had quite a sales crew and an impressive account list. I would always say we had the best accounts and best sales reps in the business, because we did.

Creative Ideas was really becoming a leader in the furniture industry. I was designing new items, styles and finishes constantly. I loved being first to the market with everything, including new marketing and sales tools. Just being considered a *"designer"* made the *Walter Mitty* in me feel like a million bucks and pushed me to higher levels. Creative Ideas was the first company to offer truly functional computer furniture with keyboard pullouts, printer drawers, surge protectors, CPU cabinets and much more. Over the years, I designed some of the first partner's desks, the fan-angle desk, corner groups, accessory cabinets and a ton of software hutches and protocols. We created the hide-a-desk and hide-a-chair, the pop-top desk and our most popular item, the angle desk, not to mention numerous computer credenzas.

We were the first to do Mission and Shaker style lines and offered matching office chairs for everything we designed. We dared to try different species of wood like maple, alder and quarter-sawn oak, when everyone else had their heads in the sand with plain oak. We were first with two-tone finish colors, solid-wood desk tops and a large variety of sizes, shapes and finishes. Later on, I was even bold enough to name one of our finishes after my wife, Chocolate, and it went on to be our best-selling and most-copied finish.

Creative Ideas was the first company to combine home office with home entertainment. We gave our dealers and the consumer something they lacked before us - choices, options and customization. We offered more files, chairs, bookcases and accessory items than most of our competitors combined and we did all of this with quality, integrity and an excellent delivery schedule.

As far as marketing tools go, we made a great catalog, desk blotters, tear sheets and Made in America hangtags. And we offered the best warranty in the industry, a lifetime warranty. Why not? We built some of the highest quality furniture and our products were pretty indestructible. Believe it or not, some of these sales aids were actually considered ground-breaking at the time. Early in my career, I felt that the furniture industry was very immature in its packaging and presentation; it was as if you were buying used furniture. I purchased a microwave oven for the office and

I noticed its packaging and I thought how professional it all looked so I strived to bring that to our products. We started to add things like directions, warning stickers and labels, care cards, warranty cards and name-branding to all of our products and packaging materials.

I was giving the dealers "Creative Ideas - Home Office Gallery" neon signs for their stores, sales podiums to hold our catalogs and full-color brochures and tear sheets to hand out to their customers. As I said earlier, when my competition was resting, I was working. When they were sleeping, I was thinking, plotting and planning. I was unflappable and unstoppable. I think I was a thorn in their sides but I gave them plenty to copy; I made it easy on them.

It took me a while but I finally realized that we couldn't make everything and I couldn't sell to everybody so the knock-offs didn't bother me as much anymore. It was a big country and there were plenty of dealers to go around for all of us and we, at Creative Ideas, got more than our share. With that said, Creative Ideas single-handily led the way and created a whole new industry within the furniture industry, "home office." But I had some huge advantages over all of my competitors, I loved my job, I had a great partner by my side, a great home life and *Walter;* he never failed me. *His* vivid imagination, desire and dreams kept me hungry and anxious for more.

* * *

As always, with the good times come the bad. Jeff, my key supervisor for years, was having some personal problems. Needless to say, this was affecting his performance and, though I tried, I could not get him to straighten out. I had to make one of my first really tough personnel decisions; I had to let him go. I'd been told more than once that you have to *"separate the emotion from the decision making"* or as they say in the "Godfather" movies just before they shoot you, *"It's not personal, its business."* But for me, everything was personal. I didn't believe in the cold, corporate way of doing things.

My dad used to say, *"You catch more flies with honey"* so I believed in treating people the way I wanted to be treated. I can hear the cliché in my head as I'm writing, *"Be careful how you treat people on the way up because you never know who you will meet again on the way down."* I'd never planned on the going down phase but I do believe in treating people fairly.

* * *

They say, *"People will forget what you say, they'll forget what you do but they will never forget how you made them feel."*

Another *Stevism* and I truly believe that. I called Jeff into my office and we discussed the situation. I gave him a few weeks' severance pay and thanked him for his years of fine service to me and our company. We cried together that day but he knew that he left me no choice. I missed Jeff for the longest time and I still think of him fondly from time to time. Jeff was a great kid and he played a huge part in getting Creative Ideas off the ground. But in business as in life, sometimes you have to cut your losses and move on and so I did.

We really needed a replacement for Jeff and so I started asking around. Gary, our local rep, knew of a guy who applied for a production manager job at another company and came in second. His name was Jerry McFarland. Jerry, like a lot of my reps and crew, had kicked around from job to job just looking for a home, a place to make his own. Well, welcome home Jerry. I hired him to be our first and only production manager.

At Creative Ideas, I always said, *"We build more than furniture, we build people."* Everyone who ever worked for us found a home, even if it was temporary. We weren't the best-paying company and we didn't offer the most benefits but, for our industry, we did very well and we cared about our people. We always treated them with respect and dignity; we always looked out for them. I always promoted from within and gave opportunity and training to everyone who passed through our doors. We were color blind; we didn't care about your race, religion, gender or sexual preference. We accepted everyone for who they were and tried our best to make them a part of something larger, our company and our family.

Over the years, we helped our people in more ways than you can imagine. I gave them more than just a job, I always say *"I gave them a hand up, not a hand out."* We gave them a safe haven, security, a steady paycheck and a home base. I advanced them money on future earnings and I lent them tools, equipment and trucks to move. I gave away furniture, clothes and gifts for their kids on holidays and birthdays. We witnessed many weddings, funerals and births. We got to know their families and friends intimately. I helped employees buy cars, rent apartments and buy their first homes. Besides helping with the paperwork and credit, I even lent money for a few down payments. I gave time off to move, for family illness and bereavement long before it was popular. I bailed a few of our employees out of some really bad jams. I bought cars for more than a few and helped fix more than I care to remember. I never asked anyone to do anything that I wouldn't do myself. We hired inexperienced, down-on-their-luck people at times because they really needed a job and we carried some for much longer than most would. More than anything, we gave freely of our love and friendship.

Now don't get me wrong, I'm not claiming to be a saint. I'm not - I'm a businessman. But I'm also a pretty good guy and I truly cared about our people. The last thing in the world I ever wanted to do was hurt any of them. I knew that I was a bit of a fool as a youngster and I hurt a few folks along the way but we all grow up sooner or later. Because of my life and my wife, I saw the light sooner than most. I knew you couldn't expect employees of a large company to be a family. I'm a realist but what the heck, why not try?

* * *

Another *Stevism*: **"Shoot for the moon. If you land on a star, look at how far you've come."**

* * *

I expected everyone in our company to do their best and be their best. I tried to get them to understand that you have to show up to work for eight hours anyway so why not try your hardest while you're there? Work toward improving yourself and your company while you're at it. If you have to be there anyway, why not make the best of it and the best of yourself. As a boss, we always notice the extra effort, the guy who stays a little late or the girl who works through lunch to finish a task. Those with the good attitude, company sprit, the team players, sometimes they get the promotion even when they are not the most experienced or the best person for the job. As a boss, we see the effort, the desire and the fact that they will go the extra mile; that's who we want on our team.

I also demanded that everyone show respect to one another and that had to start at the very top, with me leading by example. One time, I got wind that our janitor, who was an older man, was being harassed by the younger workers whenever he cleaned the restrooms. I was furious and in our very next managers' meeting I told all of our supervisors to correct this immediately. I told them that if I heard of it again, each of them would take a turn cleaning the restrooms to see how he feels. I preached to them how good they had it and how hard it must be for this man to come to work every day and clean our toilets. He did it to feed his family and the very least we could do was respect him for doing something none of us would do. I told them I had more respect for him than I had for any of them right now.

Within days, they installed signs and barriers to lock the employees out of the restrooms while this man did his job. I never heard of another issue like that again in all my years of running Creative Ideas. We all learned a great lesson that day, myself included. We're all created equal and we all deserve respect, even if we do have different posts in life. Sometimes I, too, stumble over things on my way to learning but I eventually learn from them.

I felt like I was really armed and dangerous. I had Chocolate as my right hand and Jerry as my left, there was no stopping us now. Me and my big mouth. It was somewhere around mid-1989 when sales began to slow. We were heading into another recession. Great, I thought, it seems like we'd just gotten over the last one and here we go again. Little did I know that a war was just around the corner. Sometimes ignorance is bliss.

Our sales started to fall off and our dealers and competitors began to drop like flies. Things got pretty rough for a while. But when we lost a competitor I figured we'd pick up some of their business. We did, but our sales continued to drop for two years in a row - 1989 and 1990. But compared to most, our drop-off wasn't that bad. It was just 2% in 1989 and about 13% in 1990 compared to our best year ever.

Believe me, I was still scared to death. So, as the old saying goes, *"When the going gets rough, the tough get going."* I just switched to another gear. I didn't know I had another gear but *"Necessity is the mother of invention."*

* * *

It's really amazing what you can accomplish when you set your mind to it. Far too many people throw in the towel at the first sign of trouble. You can't quit, no matter what the circumstances. I have another *Stevism:* **"Get mad, get sad and then get going."**

* * *

This is a really good one and it's how I live my life and how I've learned to overcome the pitfalls and disappointments along the way. Trust me, if you're alive you will have many. It's all in how you deal with them. Let's face it, no matter what the problem, whether you just got fired, lost money in the market, got dumped by your boyfriend, got in a wreck or even (God forbid) lost a loved one, the immediate reaction is always the same, at least for me.

First, we **get mad.** You're pissed at the boss, your broker, the ex, the idiot who cut you off, maybe even God. Well, this is natural. Our first reaction is always anger because we can't believe what happened to us. We're shocked and we don't want to accept it. Anger allows us to deal with the situation without getting too close. There's also the blame game. It's always someone else's fault when things go wrong, so we're pissed at whomever. That's much easier than taking responsibility or accepting the fact that shit happens or maybe we just screwed up.

Next, we *get sad*. This is the reaction that comes after we've had some time to calm down and stop blaming the world. It's the normal reaction we have when we start to face the facts about what happened and we have to accept it. The sad part usually comes within the first 24 to 48 hours, maybe after a sleepless night or a few too many drinks. It's when we begin to contemplate the future and realize that things have changed and that this is reality. Let's face it: Who isn't sad after losing a job, money or a loved one? It's also the time when we begin to feel sorry for ourselves, maybe a little guilty and maybe we even take a little responsibility for our actions or lack of them.

Last, but not least, and the toughest of the three, is to *get going*. Anyone can get mad and anyone can get sad - these emotions are easy and they come to us naturally. Heck, we don't even have to do much at all to stay angry or brood. Sadness and anger are okay if we learn to how funnel them and how to put them in their proper perspective. They can actually help you through the toughest of times, so they are a necessary evil.

But you have to move on; you can't allow yourself to get stuck. You have to push yourself past a bad situation or you're destined for failure. You have to get out and look for a new job or meet someone new. You have to accept that a car or girlfriend or parent is gone and they aren't coming back. You and only you have to help yourself. Now don't misunderstand me. I firmly believe its good to get mad and then sad. Heck, I preach it, but you have to pick yourself up and get going and the sooner the better. For me, a recession was just another period to push through.

At some point, we have to let it go and move on with our lives. To succeed in life, you must learn how to deal with pain and failure and when you fail you must learn from your mistakes and keep going, keep trying. This is how I built my family, my business, my wealth and my life. Every time I fell, I got up and pushed forward. I always believed, *"If you can do it, I can do it."* I've fallen more than most but that's because I've dared to try more than most. That's living! Heck, this is how I'm writing this book. Tripping and falling along the way but determined to learn, make it and refusing to quit.

* * *

I learned from Tony Robbins that people will do more to avoid pain than they will ever do to gain pleasure. It's funny but true. Fear is a great motivator. We will do almost anything to avoid pain or failure but little or nothing to succeed or gain happiness. For me, failure was never an option. I just believed that we could overcome any obstacles and so we did. I say, **"You can't lose unless you give up; as long as you keep trying you're still in the game."**

* * *

I have a plaque in my home office that reads, *"Success seems largely a matter of holding on long after others have let go."* It's very true. Recessions come and go. We all fall and make mistakes along the way. However, the folks who succeed are the ones that keep trying and learn from their mistakes. You have to pick yourself up, dust yourself off and *"Keep moving, it's hard to hit a moving target."*

* * *

By 1991, we were on the move again. The other building was available, so we took it. We now had *33,000* square feet. Again with the threes, I'm not making this up, I just notice. It's like when you buy a new car and all of a sudden you see them everywhere when before you hardly noticed. We signed a new five-year lease for both buildings with a five-year option and we were set. Over the next few years, we kept growing - more employees, more product, more customers and more equipment.

With more growth came more government agencies and more headaches. The larger you get, the more our government wants to get into your pocket and control you. It's not bad enough that the government is a silent partner that takes half of our profits in taxes. No, they have to cause us grief and take even more through permits, fees, licenses and crazy rules and regulations. But I did what they said and played by the rules but I always had one foot on the line, so to speak.

It didn't take long before we were beginning to outgrow both buildings again. Crazy, I know. I didn't ever want to move again; it was way too painful and costly. To put it off as long as possible, Jerry and I decided to start a night shift, a small group to do the things we couldn't get done during the day. For years, we worked from 9 a.m.to 5:30 p.m. so I could be there at all times. Then, Jerry came on board and convinced me that a 7 to 3:30 shift would make for happier employees, so we switched. I didn't care, we still ran the office 9 to 5 and I worked from about 8 to

8 most days anyway. But little did I know how fast we'd grow the night shift and how many more hours I'd have to work to keep up.

I also never imagined the additional aggravation and trouble this would cause. With a second shift, we needed more management and additional employees. I promoted a sharp kid named Octavio Aguilar to supervisor and he and Abel became our night managers. Still, we couldn't get any of our employees to switch to the second shift so I came up with a 50 cent per hour night shift premium. Amazing how that worked - suddenly we had volunteers. But the two shifts started blaming each other for quality issues or things going wrong. The nightshift employees never stayed long, so turnover was high and good people became harder and harder to find.

Our biggest problem was that our buildings were adjacent to an older, small neighborhood in Placentia called Atwood. Atwood was well known for a Hispanic gang that caused lots of trouble and violence. Why in the world would cities allow factories to be build so close to neighborhoods? Over the years, I've asked this question many times and I still don't have a clue to the answer. With all of the available land, you would think our local governments would plan better. Why not make a certain amount of space mandatory between residential and industrial parks? All that separated our factory from the neighbors' homes was a 12-foot concrete wall and a patch of grass. The neighborhood already resented the fact that industrial buildings were built so close to their homes and here we were running a night shift.

Throughout the years, we had some problems with the Atwood neighborhood but we always tried to keep the peace and mind our own business. For years, we tolerated broken bottles and rocks pitched over the wall into our parking lot or on to our roof. It got so bad that the north side of our parking lot was actually unusable. Abandoned cars, trash and furniture on our property became the norm.

I even had more than few run-ins with the neighbors. They seemed to think it was okay to turn on our sprinklers and allow their kids to play in them. I really didn't mind all that much; I was all for the kids playing and having a good time (remembering my Johnny Pump days). I just wished they would remember to shut them off once in a while. They didn't and I would get water bills in the thousands of dollars for sprinklers that would run all weekend long.

We also repainted the graffiti on our walls often and security was always an added expense. I tried to remember that this was their neighborhood and we were the intruders so we did our best to be good neighbors. It was only a matter of time before this became unbearable and even dangerous.

* * *

With dad gone, mom's life seemed to even out some. Don't get me wrong, she still missed him from time to time but, all in all, her life was finally peaceful and she had the freedom to do as she pleased. She was working for Creative Ideas full-time and happily contributed to our success. Meanwhile, we loved having her around and the additional help. She liked having her own money, office, a new car and the free time to spend with Jackie without dad's interference.

Jackie and Mike had a beautiful wedding and she was pleased that dad was alive on the most important day of her life. A few years after dad died, Jackie had a son, Anthony Michael Couden (Tony). My dad would have been so proud, his first grandson and named after him, no less. There is no greater honor in this world than to have your children name their first child after you. For us Italians, this is an old family tradition. Dad was somewhere looking down with a great big smile on his face the day my godson was born. Jackie had another son, Nicholas Stephen Couden a few years later. He was named partially after my daughter, his godmother, Nicole, and because they just liked the name Nicholas. Very nice, we were keeping it all in the family. My dad would have liked that also.

* * *

I have been blessed to be a godfather three times so far in my life (three again, hmmm). My first, Dennis and Nancy's son, Devin Cranford, was born three years after Nicole. Three years later, came our girlfriend Sam's son, Chayson Descisciolo, and several years after Chayson, my nephew, Tony. As I said, I'm truly blessed and honored to have these three young men call me godfather.

It wasn't too long after that I became a grandpa for the first time. Mikee had a son, Steven Michael Stacy - Steven after me and Michael after her dad. Steven was born Feb. 24, 1994. It was truly a proud moment for me and my daughter didn't forget either of her dads. She honored both of us which I thought was very special. Later on, Mikee blessed us all with another little angel, Mikela Marie, named after Mikee and Kelly (her ex) and Marie after my wife, Chocolate.

Our family was growing and growing and the holidays were great with every-one coming and going all the time. Chocolate and I took over the family traditions long ago of having everyone to our home for holidays. Everyone was welcome. If we ever ran into someone who we thought had nowhere to go well, they ended up at our table. On Christmas Eve, for more years than I care to remember, we've had an open house. The rules were to come and join us for some food, drinks and Christmas cheer. Everyone was encouraged to bring their families, children and friends - the more the merrier. We would say, *"Feel free to come for five minutes or five hours."* And we always made sure we had Santa show up for the kids. To this day, Chocolate has extra Christmas presents in our attic just in case someone shows up that we weren't expecting.

Nicole was happy and doing well in high school, finally. It took three schools to find one that she liked where she could be herself. Nicole always went to private school so she had a tough time adjusting to a public high school and all of the new kids. It seemed that it was a challenge to be a really good student and cool at the same time. At *Colie's* (our nickname for Nicole - her friends call her *"Balls,"* sound familiar?) old school she was an A student and one of the coolest kids in the school. All of a sudden, she was thrust into a high school where if you're smart you get harassed and picked on. And drugs were everywhere.

As soon as we noticed, we got her out of there and into a school she liked and could excel at both academically and socially. Poor Chocolate, though. She had to drive her to and from school everyday for three years but she felt it was worth the time and effort. Lucky for us, we owned our own business and she could adjust her schedule accordingly. Nicole ended up getting great grades and was involved in student government, theater arts and everything else you can imagine. We lived vicariously through her; she made us realize all that we missed out on in our high school years. She was already picking out colleges; she started that at eight years old and that's about the time I started saving for just that occasion. We always knew Nicole would go on to college so I wanted to be prepared. She just couldn't wait, she was so impatient. I wonder where she got that from?

As for the rest of our gang, Clint got divorced, married and divorced again. Cathy, his second, didn't last long. They were way too different and argued all of the time. On his wedding night, they drove to San Diego for their honeymoon and he was banging on the steering wheel yelling, *"What the hell did I just do?"* Not the best way to start a future together. I did give a nice toast at the wedding, though who knows? Maybe I jinxed them. Clint met a great new gal named Jana and they eloped. For Clinty-boy, the third time was a charm; this one stuck. He finally found a woman who could love him for him and keep him in line at the same time. They would go on to have three girls - Carly, Stevie (named after yours truly) and Christa. Unfortunately, little Stevie never had a chance. The good Lord had better plans for her and she died at birth. She will live on in our hearts and minds.

194

Dennis was on his third marriage to our friend, Nancy, and they had my god-son, Devin. Dennis was in the tux business after a failed venture in Palm Springs, a cowboy night club called Bronco Billy's, with a bull ride and all. A few years earlier, Dennis asked Choc and me to invest in this nightclub but when I heard it was in Palm Springs I declined. I tried to reason with Dennis and tell him that Palm Springs was a retirement community. Who the hell was going to ride a bull? Dennis, stubborn as usual, invested a bunch of money into the place and it was fabulous but it lasted just eight months.

Jim was on round three also and sorry to say but Carol was just another failed marriage. I love Jimmy but he drank and partied too much for his own good. There's one in every group and Jimmy was ours. Jim owned a tux shop in Santa Ana called Steppin' Out Formal Wear (what's with all the tux shops? Monkey see, monkey do). Great name, nice shop but Jim spent far too much time at the pizza joint next door drinking to really attend to business or his marriage.

My good buddy, Tris, was still kicking around the clubs and looking for Mrs. Right. He got pretty hot and heavy with a girl named Josta for a while but, unfortunately, that ended. But, he always had us and my girls adored their Uncle Tris. We couldn't go anywhere without them asking, *"Where's Uncle Tris?"* He and his roommate started a door and frame business together. I continued to hope that he and the rest of my friends would find happiness with the right woman. Fingers crossed.

Chet and Nancy and their three kids, Steven, Daniela and Meredith moved to Yorba Linda and they were doing fine. Chet was finally a lot closer to his job but then he got a new job and had to commute to San Diego. He was putting in well over an hour and a half each way something's don't change. We didn't see them as much as I would've liked. Our lives took different paths but we talk from time to time and he'll always be one of my oldest and dearest friends.

Sam and Chuck Cliff were married, living in Anaheim Hills and raising my other godson, Chayson. They seemed quite happy and that's all that matters. They were always close by as Sam is Chocolate's best friend and Nicole's godmother.

We have many other good friends also - too many to mention. This group, however, was our family, a family of choice. A family that has stayed together through the best and worst of times when we had no real ties except love and re-spect for one another. Now that's the *yin* but here comes the *yang*. As new lives enter this world, we must also say farewell to some of our family and friends. I always said that God has a master plan. I don't always understand the plan or agree with it (see Vito or Stevie) but there is a plan for all of us.

* * *

I believe that when we are born, our parents love us and get so close to us that the bond seems unbreakable. Then we become teenagers, which seems to be God's natural way of breaking the bond so that we can move on in life without too much heartbreak. As we become adults, we seem to reconnect with our folks and become much closer again. Once again, God steps in years later with His master plan. As our parents age, they become frail, forgetful and somewhat difficult for us to be around. This is how the bond is broken once more, allowing us to accept their passing. This is just my theory and what do I know? But it sure seems like the way things work out most of the time.

* * *

After my dad passed, many of my relatives closely followed. First, there were my mom's parents, Grandpa and Grandma Hoffman. Grandpa never did buy the liquor store but he managed to live out his retirement years without ever asking for a nickel from anyone. Mom tended to both of them by herself up to the bitter end and they didn't leave much but memories when they expired. Grandpa just wore out, and grandma suffered from dementia. They both lived long lives and died in their 80s. Grandpa died with his home fully paid for and a few bucks in the bank. Grandma died five years later and he paid their way until their final days.

My Uncle Sally was not so lucky. Like my dad, he also died of lung cancer at just 56. Uncle Sally was a brut of a man in life. He was tough and sometimes mean but he loved and took care of his family. He was another uneducated and illiterate Balsamo, but he also was a hard-working, street-smart, common-sense type of guy. Somehow, he managed to leave his family a home, a car service, money and some real estate all bought and paid for in full.

Next was my Uncle Joey, the youngest of the Balsamo boys; he also died of lung cancer. Like my dad he was just 55. Uncle Joey was also a really tough man but deep down inside, he was a pretty good guy. Now don't get me wrong, Uncle Joey would just as soon shoot you as look at you if you did him or anyone in our family wrong. I often felt sorry for my uncle because he made some terrible mistakes in his youth (many didn't live to tell about them) and he lived with the tormenting memories and regret until the end of his life. I know he asked the good Lord for forgiveness many times over the years but I just don't know if the Lord is that forgiving. I hope so. Like my other uncles, he also died owning two homes, a condo and a small business all paid for in full.

I got a call late one evening, from Aunt Debbie. She said, *"Uncle Joey is in really bad shape and they don't think he will make it through the weekend."* She told me, *"He really wants to see you."* I replied, *"Tell him to hang on, I'm on my way."* The second we hung up the phone we were making arrangements to fly out first thing in the morning. I went straight from JFK airport to the hospital and sat with my uncle. We visited for a long while talking about our family. I stayed by his side until he went to sleep for the night.

Shortly after we got back to the hotel the phone rang. It was Aunt Debbie. She just said, *"He's gone Steven, he's gone."* I was glad I made it in time; it seemed like I granted his last wish and allowed him to go peacefully into the night. From the time the doctors diagnosed his lung cancer, he lasted just three months.

Chocolate and I stayed for the funeral and attended the wake at an old funeral home in Brooklyn, on Court Street. I can't tell you how many wise guys passed through those doors over the years (both alive and dead) but that day there were many. I was actually scared to death being there, you just never know with these people…

* * *

Thinking about Uncle Joey takes me back to a time when he came to California to visit my dad. He was getting away from Brooklyn to hide out somewhere safe for awhile. And to recover from losing his eye, were not sure how, as he never wanted to talk about it but I think it had to do with the mob. Seems like Uncle Joey was always looking over his shoulder, never knowing when the next shoe would drop. As I mentioned earlier, he belonged to a gang that was being eliminated so being careless could've been very dangerous for him. He either traveled with a buddy (bodyguard) or when he was with my aunt, and he always carried a gun, usually in her purse.

Uncle Joey stayed with my parents for a week or so and when that got to be too much for my mom, I made the critical error of offering my home for a day or two. Being the ever respectful nephew, I offered them our bedroom while Chocolate and I camped out on the floor in the living room. My uncle and aunt made themselves at home while Chocolate and I got up each day and went to work. When we returned each night, my uncle (another great cook) had a feast prepared; he'd have the music blaring, the place a mess and think we were there to entertain him well into the wee hours of the morning.

At first, this was fun, and the food, stories and company were great. But after a few days, we were tired all of the time and sleeping on the floor with no access to our closet and bathroom was getting really old. And it didn't look like they were leaving anytime soon. I can't remember how long they stayed but it seemed like weeks (it wasn't). Finally, one day, they got into a big fight and decided to go home in the morning. Chocolate and I were thrilled; we were getting our home and privacy back.

On the way to the airport the next day, my uncle and aunt made up and talked about staying. We were in the front seat praying they'd start fighting again. They went home, thankfully, and from then on, any relatives who came to town went straight to a motel.

* * *

The Balsamo boys all figured out how to succeed without much schooling or assistance. Obviously, education isn't everything but it certainly doesn't hurt. Everyone in my dad's family was overweight and smoked like a chimney with no rhyme or reason for their eating, drinking or sleeping habits. All of the men developed heart conditions in their 40s and three of four had cancer by their mid-50s. For the men, this would prove to be fatal and, for the women, that was another story.

My Aunt Mary lived to be 79 before she finally ran out of life and the will to carry on. Losing her husband and oldest son was more then she could cope with and, in the end, she was bitter and frail. Aunt Mary came to California to visit my dad when he was ill. I was so excited to see her and show her all that I had become. I just knew that she'd be so proud of me. Oddly enough, she didn't want to spend any real time with me or my family and she refused to come to my home or business. I was crushed and angry at first but, somehow, I understood. I don't think she could be happy for me and my success when she had suffered so many losses and gone through so much pain with her family. I found that very sad for both of us. I so wanted her to be proud. I guess I was still looking for someone to recognize my achievements even after all I'd accomplished.

My Aunt Rosie made it into her 80s before her heart gave out but she lived a good long life. Her husband, Uncle Sammy, died years earlier in his late 70s. When he passed, it caused quite a stir in the Balsamo family. Years before, grandma purchased family plots (and a giant tombstone) for grandpa, all her children and their spouses. The boys and their wives were to go on one side with my grandparents and the daughters and their spouses were to go on the other.

Well, the Balsamos weren't too happy about a Russo going into the family burial site and they were enraged when Aunt Rosie tried to get Uncle Sammy on the side with their parents. She wanted to be on that side eventually and she insisted he go there with her. My Grandma's wishes eventually won out and he was placed to rest on the other side, but it got ugly for a while. Years later, my cousin, Butchie, her eldest son and the lawyer in the family, passed away; he was just 59.

Closer to home, Chocolate's mom had a massive stroke and passed about five years later. Ruth was 78 and her final years were painful for her and those of us who loved her. She was bedridden and paralyzed on one side of her body. She could barely whisper but you could still feel her love. In fact, some of her final words to me were, *"Take care of my baby."*

Chocolate's dad lived on until he had a heart attack in the middle of the night nearly nine years later. He was 87. Ray was another one of those men who never borrowed a nickel from anyone. Here was a man who lived on the street as a kid, survived the Great Depression as a young man and had no formal education. Self-taught, he build his first home with his own two hands and worked hard his entire life. Ray, always patriotic, attempted to serve in our military but was turned down for medical reasons. Against all odds, Ray somehow still managed to die a home-owner with cars, a motor home and some cash in the bank. They don't make 'em like that anymore.

After Ray passed, he left his home and their belongings to his two daughters, Chocolate and Esther. Ray had written Ray Jr. out of his will long before over one spat or another. Not needing her share, Chocolate passed hers on to her older broth-er and we bought out Esther's share of the home so Ray Jr. could live there in peace without worrying about payments. Chocolate covered the bills and looked out for her brother until he passed away several years later. Ray Jr. made it to 68 but he should have lived much longer. The problem was that Ray was always forgetful and he just could never remember to take care of himself or take his medicine, so his diabetes finally got the best of him. Ray basically just gave up on life; he grew tired and old and I think he just quit trying.

Chocolate's favorite brother, Johnny, passed many years earlier. Again, way too young. After Johnny got out of the military he never could find his way. He abused himself and alcohol for too many years and it finally caught up with him. Johnny died of liver disease in a hospital in Los Angeles; he was just 40 years old. He left behind two daughters, Tina and Kathy.

As for Chocolate's older sister, Esther, she's still kicking somewhere up north; Redding I think. We don't see or hear from her much anymore. I suppose families just grow apart sometimes. For Esther, this was best; I think she just needed to be alone, for whatever reason.

As for our buddies, they had a parade of family members passing. Denny's dad, Jim's parents and brother, Clint's mom, Sam's parents, Tris' dad, and Nancy's dad.

"And that's life, what can I tell you."

The longer we're lucky to live, the more loved ones we'll lose. My father-in-law used to say, *"I outlived everyone I knew."* In the end, he was just sad and lonely and waiting for the day he could reunite with his girl, Ruth. We come into this world alone and we leave the same way. All that's left behind are our family and friends and their memories of us. I remember those I've lost and their spirits live on through me and their loved ones.

* * *

By 1993, Creative Ideas had grown into a real respectable company. We were shipping furniture nationwide, our name and products were recognizable and we were really starting to make some money. Finally!

Gary Tripp, our top salesman, called us the ***"Ten-year - overnight sensation."*** It's funny but so true. When I first started designing and building computer furniture in 1982 I thought we would soar to the moon in no time. I was a little ahead of my time and it took a lot longer for technology to catch on. For the first ten years, we always seemed to be just plugging along. Don't get me wrong, we always made money, grew and kept the bills paid but we never could make very much or really get ahead of the game.

By 1994, we were doing over $6 million and growing at a rate of about 25% a year. That may not sound like much but, trust me, it's an awesome amount of growth in manufacturing. Each year, you need more equipment, employees, management staff, reps and space. In 1995, our sales grew to over $9 million and we added another small building for some finishing and packaging but that still wasn't enough.

Over the years, Creative Ideas grew so much that we required our own full-time showroom in San Francisco (on the sixth floor of the Furniture Mart). Like everything else, the showroom more than tripled in size. The years of the temporary shows were over for us and thank goodness, because they were a lot of work.

The crazy thing about the permanent showroom was that you'd use it just ten days a year and the rest of the time it would just sit idle. Still, the monthly rent was always due and it was quite expensive. For us, it was about $6,500 a month, not counting utilities, taxes and insurance.

The shows were a five-day extravaganza with dealers, sales reps and factory people coming from all over the United States and even the world. That short week would either make or break the next six months of your life. Because of the massive amount of preparation involved, these shows seemed to come every three months instead of six.

By the time market would start I was filled with nerves and anticipation. I was always the first in the building and the last to leave. And let me tell you there were times when I thought we were doomed. In the early years, before computers became such a hit, we had many long days. You just can't imagine what it's like to have everyone critique your every move. Dealers would file in and out all day long and I would just hang on their every word. Everyone thinks they're a designer and they're not shy about sharing.

By evening, I'd be exhausted; 12-hour days on hard floors in leather shoes, ouch. I refused to leave the showroom, even for a restroom break. It was rare that I'd sit or eat. I was so afraid I'd miss someone or something. By day's end, when all the other factory owners filed out to dinner with clients, we'd stay behind cleaning and vacuuming. And then, if I was lucky I'd spend the evening adding up the orders for the day and talking Chocolate's ear off.

For Creative Ideas, our shows were always a success because we always had a lot of new product and specials. I never took a chance, I always overdid it. I'd bring 20 to 30 new items to market while most would bring three or four. My reasoning, *"The more shit you throw at the wall the more likely something has to stick."* Often times, they all stuck.

Don't get me wrong, having a great show was very exciting and we certainly had more than our share. To do a million dollars in sales from a five-day show was incredible and rare. Creative Ideas did that three times: once for our 300 Series, a classic maple group; again for our 900 Series, an oak Arts-&-Crafts group; and then again, when I introduced our first *Signature Series* group. The S100 Series was a beautiful, expensive, traditional-style maple group with a chocolate finish. Those were the days; we were hotter than hell and they made up for all the years of waiting.

* * *

I always believed that what people see is what they perceive as the truth. The eyes don't lie. Even in the early dog days when we did our first shows, I tried to make us look as successful as possible. From that first show in San Francisco when I had two pairs of slacks and two sports jackets, I managed to change them up each day so I looked different and successful. No one knew that I stayed at the $29 flea bag motel or unloaded the truck and set up the display by myself. Each time we took our space at the Concourse, a temporary hall set up for the new comers (and the failing companies on the way out), I made sure we had a more prominent location and a larger space. I would bring more product, more props and more signage each and every time.

I just knew that if people believed we were growing each time they saw us, then we were doing something right and they would want to capitalize on our success. I was 100% correct. It worked as planned and we grew and prospered each and every year thereafter. ***Perception is reality.***

* * *

As for the *"Signature Series" by Steve Balsamo*, this was a concept that I stole from the art world. Being an art lover but unable to afford the real thing, I needed to buy serigraphs - signed copies of the original art made more affordable. Since there aren't enough of the originals to go around, serigraphs are a wonderful way for everyone to own art without the heavy price tag. My theory was that if people were willing to pay a premium for a reprint that's signed and numbered then, just maybe, those same people would want a *special edition* signed desk as well.

Once again, I was correct and our original Signature Series group was a big hit. After that, I designed three more Signature Ser*ies* lines over the years. None was as successful as the first but they all did quite well. I even went as far as to name them using my *Italian heritage* to add a little spice. Let's face it, everything Italian is great: food, shoes, suits, art, cars, music, women…so why not furniture?

I was also a little clever and creative in naming these groups after *"how I felt"* about my company. The first group was called *Mi Amore* – My Love, the second *Mia Passione* – My Passion and the third was *Mio Sogno* – My Dream (or for those who were in the know, My Nightmare). I always said that Creative Ideas was a mixed bag for me. It was my love, passion and my worst nightmare at times but customers may not have appreciated that so we went with My Dream instead. The final Signature Series group was called *Mio Retaggio* which has a few meanings, the first being My Heritage and second, My Legacy. Both were very fitting and poignant at the time that I designed it.

* * *

In 1996, we broke the $11 million mark and I had another real scare as a company and as a person. The Atwood neighborhood, where the company was located, had gotten worse over the years. Some of the kids who used to run and play in my sprinklers were growing up to be gang members. The rocks and beer bottles quadrupled with time. Just walking across our parking lot became a real adventure. The night shift was scared to come to work for fear of reprisals from the neighbors, and the complaints from the elders in the neighborhood reached new heights. It seemed like every government agency from the fire department to air quality control was called weekly with complaints about our factory's noise and the smell of chemicals.

Most of these complaints were unwarranted. I mean the building was already there and that was the real bone of contention. I just happened to lease a building in the wrong neighborhood at the wrong time. I didn't build it and, in my opinion, their real bitch should have been with the City of Placentia. As for noise, we were separated by 12-foot concrete walls and our night shift did its best to keep the noise to a minimum. It's a difficult task to run a large company and, under these circumstances, it was becoming impossible.

It was about 4:30 one afternoon when a low rider car pulled into the parking lot and three gang members piled out looking for trouble. Abel, my night manager, was scared to death and called over the radio to warn me. Fortunately, I met up with them before they could enter the factory. They immediately explained that we were making too much noise and keeping their grandparents awake at night. I assured them that we were doing our best to keep it quiet by turning off all noisy equipment and closing the doors by 8 p.m. I reminded them that I was a friend to the neighborhood, letting the kids use the sprinklers and buying them paint to cover the rival gang's graffiti. I also reminded them that I knew some of their elders and got along well with everyone. They accused me of having trucks honk their horns at all hours of the night. I tried desperately to explain that we had no trucking or deliveries after five but to no avail.

At one point a kid, maybe 15 and stoned out of his mind with his eyes rolling around in his head, pulled up his shirt to reveal a handgun in his waistband. I don't remember the exact words I used to calm him down but whatever I said, it worked because I'm still here today. I will tell you that from that moment on we all treaded very softly around there and I made it my goal to move us out of that neighborhood as soon as possible.

The very next day I pulled out our lease and noticed that we still had about a year-and-a-half remaining. I immediately called Pete, our landlord, and explained the incident and requested to terminate our agreement early. He wasn't overly sympathetic. Frustrated as hell, I called a real estate agent and started to search for a new property. I just figured I would deal with Pete and the lease when the time came.

Moving a large operation like ours was no easy task. Just finding the right building that met all of our electrical and trucking requirements was daunting and then I had to think about the 200 employees and their transportation needs. Most of our people came to work on foot or by carpool, bicycle or bus, so if we wandered too far, we'd lose a lot of good and experienced people. So I had my work cut out for me.

* * *

While making my rounds through the shop one day, a young assembler named Abel hit himself in the thumb with a hammer and passed out. When he hit the concrete floor he cracked his head open and lost consciousness. As I noticed the crowd beginning to gather, I pushed my way to the front only to find that he was bleeding and not breathing. I panicked! I screamed for Jerry to call 911 and then I started to do mouth-to-mouth resuscitation on him. The problem was that I could not get his mouth open; he had locked up like rigor mortis had set in. I started screaming for someone to help but they were all in a state of shock. No one moved a muscle, they just stood and stared. I guess the class we were required to take some years back paid off because I suddenly remembered how to revive someone by pumping their chest.

I started pumping away, the sweat pouring off me as I kept repeating, *"You're not gonna die on me. Not here, not now. You're not gonna die."* Finally, his heart started to beat but the second I'd stop so would his heart. I was exhausted; I continued for what seemed like an eternity but there was no one to take over so I pushed on. *"You're not gonna die"* I kept repeating as I pumped his chest for maybe 20 minutes until the paramedics arrived.

Once they did, I was relived and drained. I just sat back on the floor and I watched in horror as the firemen took turns working on this kid. The whole time

I was praying he'd be alright. Shortly after that, they hooked him up to a machine and wheeled him off to waiting ambulance. It was some months later that Abel returned to work; he recovered and was fine, thank God. Abel continued to work for me for years, growing into the assembly department supervisor. Often times, I wondered what would have happened if I weren't in the shop that day? What if I was out of town or just out to lunch? But I wasn't. *Angels.* I guess Abel had one that day.

* * *

It was mid-1996 when I inked a deal to build an 80,000-square-foot building on five acres in Corona; an up-and-coming city just 15 minutes up the 91 freeway. I had looked high and low and the only way I could get everything we required was to build my own building. I found a developer who would build it to my specs and lease me the building with an option to buy it after the first year if I could raise the money. This would prove to be quite the challenge, but we had two years. I gave this task to Chocolate telling her that I wanted to buy the building and wanted 100% financing - I didn't want to put anything down. Impossible? Yes. Do-able? You betcha!

Speaking of Corona, like I said, it was an up-and-coming city with tremendous growth potential and investment possibilities. Two of Orange County's finer cities, Yorba Linda and Anaheim Hills, bordered Corona making it even more attractive. It was also one of the closest points for the old companies in Los Angeles to relocate to a safer, cleaner and more affordable place with great freeway access. Corona was becoming the next best bedroom community for those who could not afford Orange County and now it had the one thing it lacked for many years - jobs.

Mom and my sister and brother-in-law were looking to move to a larger house in a newer neighborhood when we decided to move the company to Corona. I suggested that they look out there for two reasons. One, it would be much closer to work for mom and Mike, who was now my shipping manager. And two, they would get much more cluck for their buck. Sure enough, they found a new home in a great new neighborhood just ten minutes south of the new factory. They sold the old house in Anaheim and moved just around the time we moved the factory. Timing is everything. So Corona, here we come.

The final year-and-a-half in the old building was really painful but we endured. Between the neighbors and all of their complaints and the agencies popping in constantly, we were under a tremendous amount of stress. Add to that the fact that we were exploding at the seams; we were so busy that were turning down new dealers. Turning away business? I never thought I'd see the day.

I was out of the office a lot in meetings with the developer, the engineers, the city, the utility companies, etc. This was all so new to me but I was learning things at a brisk pace and loving it. My timing couldn't have been better. The new building was scheduled to be done at the beginning of November 1997 and my leases on all of the other buildings expired on Nov. 30. How's that for planning?

We started setting up the new facility in late October even though the building wasn't complete. I wanted to get a head start on the move, so I purchased a lot of new equipment, spray booths, air compressors and a dust collection system. I wanted to have as much in place and ready to roll by our move-in date as humanly possible. For the final months leading up to and including the move, I was working 14 hours a day, six and seven days a week; we were all putting in a lot of hours. When I wasn't at the old factory working on day-to-day business I was out at the new facility installing air and fluid lines with Mac, my maintenance manager, and his crew. Chocolate and Jerry were doing their best to hold down the fort and keep production flowing at a steady pace. I could never have pulled off a move of this magnitude without their help every step of the way.

On Nov. 30, 1997, I closed the doors of the old building for the last time and a new chapter in my life and career began. I was thrilled and relieved to be getting away from the neighborhood and all the friction that went with it. We were lucky no one ever got hurt. The new building was everything I dreamed of - it was absolutely beautiful and full of promise for a bright future. I had drawn that building on a napkin in a restaurant and handed it to an engineer a year-and-a-half earlier and now here it was - wow. *Walter* really outdid himself this time.

Did I mention that the closest residence was over a mile away? I guess I learned that lesson!

We had tons of new equipment and the set-up was designed perfectly for our production. I managed to lose very few of our 200 employees by offering a raise to cover their added transportation expenses. We got off to a great start. I was so proud and pleased with myself that we had a wonderful grand opening party for all of the management, customers, suppliers, reps and friends who could attend. Unfortunately, this euphoria didn't last long. It's funny how quickly I forgot the lesson I had learned years before. The moving lesson that I preached to anyone who would listen.

* * *

By the time Christmas rolled around, we were so far behind that it made our last move seem like a walk in the park. I know I preached patience but trust me, when you're in the eye of the storm the last thing you're thinking about is patience. At the time of the move I was just 43 years old. By that Christmas just 60 days later, I was forty-four going on sixty. Of the 200 original employees who came over with us, we lost about a 25% in the first month or so; the commute turned out to be too much. Later, I found out that the carpoolers were taking advantage of their riders and over-charging them. Not to mention, a large competitor located just blocks from our old factory had started hiring our people away from us with the lure of staying close to home.

My beautiful, supportive wife had just reached the magical age of 50 and she too was getting a little weary, to say the least. As usual, we survived the move and all of the obstacles that followed together, as a team. But I can assure you, it wasn't easy and each time, these things take a little more out of you. 1997 was a whirlwind year and one to remember. We built our new factory, moved in November, had our grand-opening party weeks later, celebrated both our birthdays and held our normal holiday celebrations with employees at the factory and friends and family at home. And if that weren't enough, we had to prepare for a major trade show in January. Talk about hectic, but that was our life.

Over the next few years, life changed tremendously. As a company, we were reaching new goals each and every year. In April 1996, we hit our first *Million Dollar Month* in the old factory, a true milestone. Just two years later on May 28, 1998, we had our first *Hundred Thousand Dollar* Day and then, just a year later in 1999, we hit an incredible *Two Million Dollar Month*. Wow.

Exciting to say the least, but let me tell you this was no easy task. It took lots of new equipment and manpower. Growing pains are just that, pains; you never seem to catch your breath. As soon as you get some new equipment, you need more people to run them. Then you need more income to make the payments and payroll. And then you need more customers and sales to cover the expenses. This means more salesmen, trade shows and product and so on and so forth. It's a neverending cycle. Seeing how I was still a young man and still full of passion for the industry (and the dough that came with it), I was moving at full speed ahead.

I was determined to reach that millionaire status even if it killed me. Not just on paper or through assets, I'd already done that. To feel really accomplished, I had to have a million dollars in cash in the bank at all times, which is much more of a challenge. Not too many people are sitting on a million bucks cash, trust me. There is always something to purchase or an investment that will keep you from reaching that status. But I was determined.

For a good portion of my business career, Ronald Reagan was our president and I loved him as much as I did JFK, no more. The big difference was that Reagan was really instrumental in my adult and business life. For the first time in my life, I campaigned for a candidate and I did it twice. Both times, as you know, President Reagan won. I always said that if Reagan could have gotten four more years I would have become a real multi-millionaire. Reagan was not only good for business, he was great for business. And he was great for our country he brought all of the old hippy, peace, love and dope types back into the fold. Okay, most of us - some are still way out there.

I, personally, felt that before President Reagan took office our country was slipping away. We were losing face with the world and *"We the people"* had lost the patriotic love for our country that made us a superpower. President Reagan brought not only a booming economy back to our nation but also the respect from the world and from our own people. President Reagan made me the patriot I am today. He taught us how to love and honor this great country we are so blessed to call home.

Go figure, my two favorite presidents were Kennedy, a Democrat, and Reagan, a Republican. I guess that leaves me somewhere in the middle and I'm fine with that. I'm for whoever will lead our nation with dignity, strength and a willingness to do whatever it takes to keep us safe and prosperous.

* * *

Meanwhile, our family was growing and prospering and the new house was working out great for mom and Jackie. Mike, Jackie's husband, was running our shipping department and doing a fine job. Mom was happy, maybe for the first time in her adult life. She had a new car, new home and life was finally peaceful and good to her; she deserved it. I can't thank my sister and brother-in-law enough for always being there and watching out for mom. It's funny, she was with Choc and me all day at work and then with Jackie and her family all night and on weekends. We were blessed.

My kids were doing well also. Mikee and my grandson were doing well and she still worked with us so we could keep an eye on her. Nicole graduated from high school and was on her way to the University of California at Berkeley, which brings up another reason why it's hard to save money and become rich. Kids. Between cars, clothes, insurance, college, books and dorms it all adds up. In the four years that Nicole attended Berkeley, she was a good student. However she added as many extra-curricular activities to her plate as possible, including a sorority and a six-month stint in Italy, so it was quite costly.

* * *

But paid for in full, thanks to Creative Ideas.

Uncle Sally (left) and Uncle Joey look like a couple of mobsters and you wonder why I was scared.

That's Chocolate, Uncle Joey, Me and Baby Vito visiting Uncle Joey in his New Jersey home.

Creative Ideas new factory construction 1997.

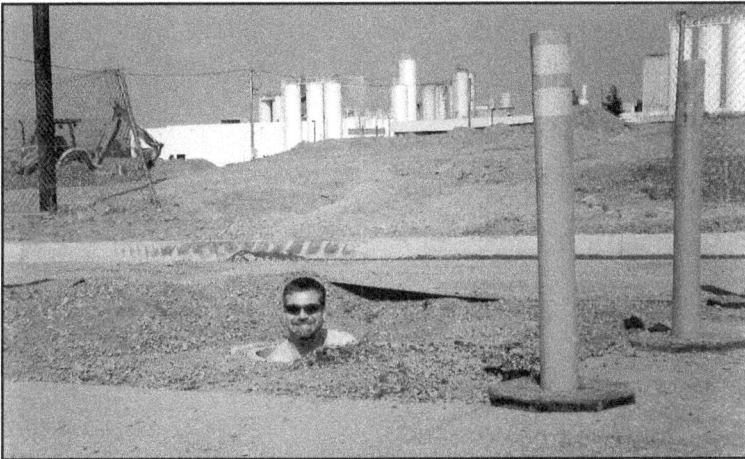

I told you I'm into everything, that's me checking out a manhole during construction.

Creative Ideas Corona facility, 130,000 sq. feet on 7 acres. Awesome!

CHAPTER 12
THE RISE AND FALL

PART 1 – THE RISE...

Ialways say, *"Into each life a little rain must fall, so pack an umbrella."* Throughout my professional career, I have had many ups and downs. It's inevitable, if you stick around long enough. By 1991, I'd owned and ran Creative Ideas for more than 20 years and it was the vehicle to my success. I owned a lovely home and my factory. I had a couple of great cars, money in the bank and best of all, a great home and family life. *Now that's success.*

Many years earlier, when Chocolate and I were just making our way back in Pedley, we didn't have much but we had each other and that was always more than enough. The rest, it's just the icing on the cake. However, I do like the icing; let's face it, I grew up without it. As a kid, we wondered what was for dinner on many a night and if the bills were going to be paid that month. Mom did her best to provide for us and, believe me, we never went without. Somehow, she always stretched a buck into enough food, clothes and the necessities and even a few goodies along the way. I don't know how she did it or where she got the strength from but I think I developed the same determination and endurance that she showed during the worst of times.

Because of my childhood, I grew up with a massive hunger for success and the more I got, the more I wanted. Not that this is a bad thing. After all, *"success breeds success."* When you have some success in your life you gain confidence and strive for more - it's only natural. There is no greater pleasure or reward than to set a goal and achieve it on your own. Every little victory builds upon itself and that foundation becomes who and what you are. I always said Creative Ideas was built on a foundation like a pyramid, making it very hard to bring down. For me personally, the more I achieved the more *Walter* imagined possible - *he* had no boundaries. I, too, was becoming a pyramid of sorts.

More allowed me to help not only myself but my family and others. It enabled me to build a home for my eldest daughter and my two grandkids just five doors down from ours in Yorba Linda. *More* enabled us to send my youngest daughter to the finest college and lend her a hand in buying her first home. *More* helped buy cars, furniture and necessities for my whole family over the years, and hopefully, made life a little easier for them along the way. *More* paid for my girls' weddings, some family vacations and several funerals. *More* allowed me to employ family members and pay them well. It's allowed me to save money for both of my nephews and my two grandkids so they will have an opportunity to go to college, something Chocolate and I never had.

Now understand, I don't believe in showering your children with everything just because you can. I'm an old-fashioned, conservative guy. I think they need to work and provide for themselves, how else would they gain any of life's experiences? I just wanted to lend a helping hand where and when I could.

However, I will say it's a tear! On one hand, you can afford to give them most anything and you want to but on the other, you know in your heart that if you do, you are stunting their personal growth. You are raising spoiled, undisciplined and, most times, unappreciative young adults who enter the world without a clue about how to fend for themselves. We've seen it all too often, just check out our young athletic superstars and how poorly most have handled their lives; too much, too quick.

I think it's extremely important that we teach our children how to become responsible adults and that starts when they are very young. I believe we need to discipline our children and give them some responsibilities, no matter how minor. We have to teach them the basics that we were taught as kids - love, respect, faith, honor, tradition and even desire (potty training is cool also). I truly believe it's important to know how and when to say *no* to our kids and not to give into their every whim. *"No"* has to mean no!" It's good to say, *"No, we can't afford that"* sometimes so they can learn to deal with disappointment once in a while. How else will they ever grow up to desire things enough to want to attend school and, later on, work for them?

I thank Chocolate for always doing a great job of practicing balance with our girls since I may have been an easy mark for them. That old, *"Do as I say, not as I do"* theory applied with me. My girls could melt my heart with a glance and I would just roll over and give into them. Not Chocolate - she kept us all in line with *The Look*. One raised eyebrow and we knew she meant business. Chocolate and I have been very careful to monitor and check ourselves with our two girls even 'til today and I can honestly say, both my girls honor us by being intelligent, self-sufficient and self-reliant. Neither of our girls ever asks nor expects anything from us or anyone else for that matter. Their only wish when you ask is for Chocolate and me to be healthy and happy, to relax, travel and enjoy the rest of our lives without stress. *Now thatsa nice...*

* * *

My 40s were by far the most successful and pleasurable years of my life to date. Creative Ideas grew into a formidable and profitable company and I was proud to be at its helm. It amazed me to see what we accomplished with this company that started in my garage years earlier. From a small business barely staying afloat, we grew to an enterprise that spent a couple of hundred thousand dollars a year on improvements and new machinery. Our sales and customer base grew each and every year as did our employee base.

In 1998, we did $17 million. In 1999, we soared to $21 million and, in 2000, we topped $26 million. Over the first three-year period in our new building, we were growing at an average of almost 31%. Incredible. Some of this was pent-up growth as we could only produce so much in the old building. And the rest? Well, I was finally in the right place at the right time. As the Internet exploded on to the scene.

Creative Ideas was now becoming a real furniture manufacturing company with all of the bells and whistles. I wish you could have seen this place, it was really something. We had this giant gray monstrosity of a dust collection system out back that I had purchased second-hand piece by piece at auctions over the years. To buy and build something like that new would have cost about $350,000. My team put it together, for less than $150,000 and it looked and worked like new. And the best part was it was paid for. Thanks to some wise shopping and the fact that our maintenance department had gotten so good we could do almost anything ourselves.

Between Jerry, Mac (Jerry's brother) and I there wasn't much we wouldn't tackle. And what we didn't know how to do, we learned. By the way, that dust collection system I was so proud of burnt to the ground twice in back-to-back weeks. Fortunately, it was mostly steel and we knew how to rebuild it but the first time I watched it burn, I cried. We had spent so much time and effort getting it just right that it broke my heart to helplessly watch it burn. All the fire department could do was to control the fire so it wouldn't spread to our factory. Then we spent the whole weekend working around the clock - rebuilding, painting and repairing it only for it to catch fire and burn again less than a week later.

That's my luck. I always say, *"If there are five doors but only one correct door I have to go through nine doors to find the correct one but I always find it."*

I always seemed to do things the hard way but I refused to give in. I knew I would always find that door. I've had friends who looked as though they stepped in shit, lifted their foot and a $100 bill was stuck to it. But then, I haven't walked a mile in their shoes so how would I know? I'm sure that many people believed the same thing about me but *"the harder you work, the luckier you get,"* and that's a fact.

* * *

We had two delivery trucks for local deliveries and three new forklifts to move around raw materials and it still wasn't enough. Inside the factory, we purchased and learned how to use the latest woodworking equipment available. Every year, we added computerized panel and chop saws, CNC routers, giant sanders, planers, edge-banders and more. I was amazed that our employees could learn to operate such sophisticated machinery. I can honestly say that even after all of my years of experience in the factory, I couldn't run half of them.

You know what's funny? I had a Corvette at the time that cost maybe $35,000 new and there was no way in the world I would allow one of my employees to drive it. However, I thought nothing of spending $150,000 on a new machine and turning it over to $12-an-hour kid who I barely knew. Go figure! That's manufacturing…

When we first moved into the new building, I installed a push conveyor system throughout our assembly and finish departments. That's where you push the product along on roller conveyors by hand from one station to another with no set timing or motors. With the advice of our new finishing supplier, I made sure we used everything that would be in compliance and work well with our new water-borne finishes. Then, after only two years they recommended that we switch to an automatic conveyor system.

Wanting to be proactive, I agreed. I desperately wanted to be up to speed by the time the new air-quality rule changes went into effect a few years later. Also, water-based finishes were better and safer for our people and our factory. Water doesn't burn, yet it was way more expensive - why is that?

Remember my library theory? Well, I didn't know too much about conveyor systems or water-based finishes and I was pretty much buried in the day-to-day business, so I turned to an old friend and industry leader, Tony Spriggs, to head up this project. What made this equipment sophisticated was the critical timing between each spray booth; it had to be accurate or your finishes could fail. So, we turned to the experts - our finishing supplier and the company that sold the conveyor equipment. Based on their recommendations, we purchased and installed about $400,000 worth of state-of-the-art equipment and revamped the whole finish department.

We added new spray booths, pumps and guns, a heat tunnel and swamp coolers for make-up air. It felt like we had just done this two years ago and that's because we had. But that's manufacturing, constantly changing and evolving. You change and grow or die.

Believe it or not, we had just turned the corner on 2000 when I realized that along with the new finishing line, which needed more space, we were starting to outgrow our building. I mean come on! I'd just spent $3.5 million and a year of my life on the building and another three-quarters of a million on moving, equipment and setup and we were already outgrowing it? Yep! So now what?

Never one to sit and ponder too long (you can't), I decided to purchase the land next door and add on because I never (did I say never?) wanted to move again and that was the promise I made to myself, never again. I decided (after a little begging and pleading with the little woman) to buy another two acres of land next door and add on another 50,000 square feet of factory space. In the end, we had 130,000 square feet under one roof, on seven acres.

After that, I made another promise to myself and my wife; I promised that *"This was it!"*

If we outgrew this factory then we'd have to just adjust the company's volume to fit. I reasoned that we could raise prices and eliminate and slow-paying customers when the time came but no more additions and no more moving. I had to promise Chocolate that for two reasons. First, to get her blessing on the new land and addition. And second, so she wouldn't kill me.

For years, it was Chocolate who was always on the move. She planted the seed that *we* wanted to buy a home and along came Pedley. Then she convinced me that, *"You can do it"* and wham, Creative Ideas. She was the one who reminded me that it was too far a drive from our home in Pedley to work each day so we sold that house and moved to Anaheim Hills. From there, it was her idea that we reinvest and move to a larger home so here we were in Yorba Linda. Every great idea I had seemed to come to me in my sleep. I always accused her of chanting her thoughts to me while I slept. Who knows? But things were changing and with the business it was me who was constantly on the move. Bigger showrooms, bigger factories, more people, more products, more equipment, customers, reps, etc.

* * *

For Chocolate, enough was becoming enough but not for me. I had grand business goals and I wanted to take Creative Ideas as far as I could, within reason. *Walter* believed we had enough space and equipment to take the company to $50 million in the coming years. Believe it or not, even with all the growth we were experiencing I was controlling it and holding us back. Any other businessman who was more aggressive and a bigger risk taker would have had us doing $50 million by then but not me. I liked slow, controlled growth and I believed in *pay as you go; pay as you grow.*

I refused to go into debt. My bills were always paid in a timely fashion and I took advantage of every early pay discount. I never used our credit lines or borrowed much at all. I got to the point where I wanted $300,000 cash in our company account at all times (cash flow) and then $400,000 and then $500,000, and I'd pretend we were broke if I had to spend a penny of that $500,000.

I liked being in control. No, I needed to be in control - there's a big difference. I had to control the growth so I could keep up with it financially and mentally. We had 300 factory workers, 25 managers and supervisors, nine office staff and about 25 salespeople throughout the United States. We were running two shifts and we had people in the plant from four in the morning until midnight daily and most Saturdays. It was getting hard to keep up.

* * *

Over the years, Chocolate and I discussed selling the company (another one of her ideas) and stopping to finally smell the roses and enjoy the fruits of our labor before it was too late. Like many times before, *"I was listening but not paying attention."* I never believed it would really happen so I agreed to do it if we could get the right price. Blah, blah, blah.

After getting the company just the way I wanted it (and peaking in all phases) *we* decided it was time to put it on the market. After an extensive search (by Chocolate), along came Tim McDonald, our broker and new friend. After all, I certainly was in no great hurry. Once again, I was listening but not paying attention. The company was listed and offers started to roll in immediately. Needless to say, I was both alarmed and excited at the same time.

Alarmed because this company was my baby, my life, my identity, my brainchild, *Walter's* stage. What in the world was I going to do if I weren't running Creative Ideas? Who would I be? How would I stay occupied? Those very thoughts scared the hell out of me.

Meanwhile, I was *excited* at the thought of settling down some without having the daily pressures of running a company of such a magnitude. The next show, the next design, bills, employees and so on. Security, that's a big one. And the thought of enjoying all of the great toys I owned but never had the time to use was alluring.

I was also excited because our very first offer was from another company in the furniture business and it was for $14 million. *Walter* started to envision a beach house for Chocolate and not some little place but a mansion on the water. *Walter* always thinks big! Next it was a Rolls Royce, then a boat, travel, the list was endless but I think you get the picture. It's that *more* thing…

* * *

The year 2000 was a very good year indeed, what I remember of it anyway. We had record months and days and the year was the biggest, best and most profitable to date. My daughter, Mikee, was working hard for us and had her second child, Mikela, that March. She was still living in an apartment and I hated the fact that my grandkids would have to grow up in an apartment atmosphere. Not that there's anything wrong with that. But I just wished they could be raised in a home like my kids were. I realized that Mikee and her husband would have a really tough time saving enough money to ever buy a house so Chocolate and I decided to help. I purchased a quarter acre of land just down the street from us and I decided to build her a home.

"Here's another fine mess you've gotten me into, Walter." Who didn't love Laurel and Hardy? Okay, I guess anyone under 40. That would go likewise for Abbott and Costello and The Three Stooges, all personal favorites of mine. But my all time favorite is Jerry Seinfeld. I love comedians and even you youngsters know who he is. Sorry, I'm drifting.

In 15 months time, I built an addition to our factory, started building my daughter, Mikee, a house, designed the first Signature Series line, remodeled the finishing department and put my company up for sale all while trying to keep up with the runaway train of a business. Yikes!!! I was busy to say the least and totally stressed but you never know just how hard it is when you're in the middle of it. It takes stopping and looking back to realize just how stressful life and work can become. For me, I was used to it. Like a weightlifter, I just learned how to handle more and more weight over the years. I would tell Chocolate, *"I can do this, I can stand on my head if I have to,"* and so I did.

* * *

At my 20-year high school reunion, an old chum of mine explained, *"I knew you in high school and you weren't that smart. How in the hell did you get to run a big company like this?"* I thought about his question for a second and then I heard myself flippantly answer, *"It's like eating an elephant, one bite at a time."* The funny thing is, as I look back now I honestly can say that I don't know how I did it either. I guess you just learn to adapt as you go. The bigger we got, the more of my small pea brain I managed to use. I even surprised myself but not Chocolate (or *Walter*).

I finished *Mikee's house* in December of 2000 and saw her moved in before Christmas, which was my goal. Start to finish, I built that house in six months after I got the plans approved. Fast, yes! Uneventful, no way! There were plenty of glitches since that was the first home I'd ever built myself. Let me clarify, unlike my father-in-law, Ray, who built his house with his bare hands, when I say I built this house I mean that I was the contractor. Big difference! I hired all of the sub-contractors, handled all the inspections and engineers and paid all of the bills. I was there on the job every morning, giving directions before I went to work, and then back every night to check on the day's progress and plan out my next move. On weekends, I shopped for toilets, hardware, doors, etc. I always loved building things and this was a real challenge for me since all I'd ever done before were room additions and remodeling.

As for the *factory addition,* that was nearly done as well. Two million dollars later and a year-and-a-half of planning, meetings, construction and lots of mistakes and dust and we had the addition finally complete. Now all we had to do was rearrange the whole factory which was like moving all over again. Honestly, we moved almost every machine, reran all the dust collection and air lines and rewired all of the electric. What a job and all while trying to keep up with record production.

This accomplishment warrants a shout-out to Jerry and all of my management crew; they really worked their asses off and did a great job! Poncho, my mill manager, used to say, *"You're always pushing us."* I pushed those ten guys - most of whom started as inexperienced workers barely speaking English and earning minimum wage - into managers of a large plant making more than $60,000 a year and owning their own cars and homes, amongst other things.

I would always tell them to work hard and learn English and they'd be able to do almost anything. After all, this is America and anything is possible if you can dream it and are willing to work for it. Look at me, I'm living proof. I got to see that day for all of them and many, many others who came through my doors, which was very gratifying indeed. I always reminded them that *"Once you're a manager, you're a manager for life. You take that with you wherever you go. You should never have to go backward."*

The *sale of the company* was moving right along also, if you call a half-dead snail's pace moving along. You just can't imagine all of the bullshit they put you through and the time that melts away as they do. The letters, memos, files and ten years worth of records that they needed to review. The lawyers, insurance agents, bankers, CPAs, partners and their staff that you have to entertain. The documents you have to agree to hand over, the warranties you have to sign, the endless meetings you have to sit through and the constant phone calls. It was a nightmare with a capital **"N."**

About a year later - yes, I said year - we were just about to close escrow when up pops the devil! The buyer lost their mezzanine lender - whatever that is? So they had to start from scratch and begin to look for funding all over again. By the time April 2001 rolled around, the good ole' USA was heading into a recession but the only people who knew (or admitted it) were financial intuitions and business folks who were paying attention. Banks stopped lending and investors took a hike. And our deal? Let's just say it was dead even though they didn't want to admit it. Tim scrambled to put back together two of the other offers we had earlier but they also were gone in the wind. I was alarmed and excited all over again but for different reasons this time.

Alarmed because there went the big payoff, the security, the beach house for Chocolate and worse than all that, my girl was so looking forward to retiring and getting away from the stress.

Excited because *Walter,* the selfish bastard, got to keep his stage, his company, his big income and all of the goodies that went with it. Sick, I know, but truly, I was more than a little relieved. I wasn't ready to give it all up (*yet*).

* * *

So, where were we? We finished the new conveyor system and the finishing department was now back together, bigger and better than ever. We were testing new water-based finishes constantly but nothing was working. Between our activity in the new finishing department and rearranging the whole factory after the addition, we were working a lot of hours and weekends, too. The payroll was skyrocketing and our people were showing signs of wear. I promised it would just be a little longer but then, wham, we hit our busy season.

Meanwhile, I had a brain fart and out popped the idea to build *"The Signature Series"* by yours truly. This brainchild kept Jerry and his team very busy for several months since the definition of Signature Series was *"exquisite, different and new."* We needed to out-source new doors, glass, moldings, hardware, finishes, electrical parts and many new suppliers. I wanted this line to be special, high end, so we had to have the best of everything, which was hard to find because they weren't commonly used goods.

And then, I did it again, another brain fart! We weren't busy enough, so I decided to expand our showroom for the unveiling of the new *Signature Series* line. After a month or so of negotiations and a few trips to wonderful San Francisco, I secured the showroom next door to ours and made the arrangements to *"bust through the wall."* Once we started renovating, everything had to be perfect - new carpet, paint and lights, ceiling fans, blinds, signage, props and accessories. I spared no cost. This was to be one of my company's finest hours. It had to be perfect, and it was.

We had a terrific show and sold a million dollars of this new high end line with my name all over it. **Steve Balsamo, "The Designer"** had arrived! And, with a splash.

* * *

For many years, I was designing great products and no one seemed to notice. I guess they assumed I used a designer or copied them from somewhere or maybe they thought I just pulled them out of my butt. Don't get me wrong, we got an occasional write-up, a little buzz around the industry and, heck, we sold plenty of product. But for *Walter,* this was never quite enough. He needed more!

Finally, this industry was going to notice and appreciate me for my talent. We were written up in all of the trade magazines and rags and interviewed by all of the reporters; they wanted to know what *"I had to say."* We were the talk of the show in the hallways, elevators, restrooms and, best of all, in our competitor's showrooms of all places - the ultimate insult! *"Did you see CI's new line?"* *"Creative Ideas has a real hit!" "You ought to make something like Creative Ideas' new line."* And the greatest compliment you can pay a designer, *"Creative's new line is HOT!"* These were some of the comments that made their way back to me through the gossip mill. Like the old neighborhood in Brooklyn, the industry talks and word travels fast, good or bad.

Everyone wants to be *hot* at least once in their career and no one wants to be referred to as *cold.* That's death to fashion and death to a company. It means your designs are old, passé, out of style or out of touch with what's current. For us, we were never cold but we were never hot, we were always w*arm* and you can build one hell of a company just by being warm. I did. But man, to be considered hot just once, now that's a designer's dream come true. Like a ballplayer who hits 40 home runs in one year, everyone wants and expects that he'll do it over and over again. You can ride the crest of that wave for quite a while - just check out the contracts some of these guys sign after one great year.

My competitors all seemed to drop by during the show to congratulate me (and eyeball the new product, of course). We had dealers from all over the country popping in, even ones we'd never seen before. The new orders were piling up like crazy. I still get a rush today just thinking about it. The *"ten year, overnight success"* had arrived. Gary was right.

Walter was very pleased with himself, indeed.

* * *

As we rolled into 2001, life was getting better and better and things were beginning to settle down a little. We even started to squeeze in a week of vacation from time to time. Maui was the usual destination. We'd just sit in the sun, relax, unwind and contemplate life. I even managed to take a few weekends off here and there, going to as many Dodger games as possible with my three amigos (Tris, Jim and Clint), and playing in (and running, of course) a Fantasy Football League.

And believe it or not, Chocolate dragged me all over Southern California on Sundays, our so-called day off, looking for that beach house. From Seal Beach all the way down to San Clemente, I think I saw just about every other house there is and now I know all of the neighborhoods like the back of my hand. She's relentless!

We were working hard, playing when we could, raising our kids and sometimes we even snuck out early on Fridays (at 6 p.m.) to catch a movie or go to dinner with friends. Our home was always under some sort of construction. Remodeling is like a hobby to me; I love it. Let's face it, I must bore easy. And then there was Sera Garcia (Ellie), our life-long housekeeper, who kept up after us and the house. She was always bitchin' about all of the mess from the remodeling but she got over it. She was also the nanny to my two grandkids and they stayed with her at my home until school age while Mikee toiled at CI. Ellie is like family to us and still with us to this day.

Mom, Sis and the rest of our family were all happy, healthy and enjoying life. What more could you ask for? My two nephews, Tony and Nicholas, were growing like weeds. They both played basketball, were great students and Tony was playing drums. Mike, his dad, is a musician (in his spare time) so I guess the fruit didn't fall far from the tree.

Mikee and her family loved their new house and they were doing fine. My baby girl, Mikela, was a beauty and Steven was a good boy. Nicole was in Florence, Italy. Somehow she and Chocolate convinced me that it was okay to allow her to go halfway around the world (where I couldn't watch over her) to attend school. Yeah, right! I was born at night but it wasn't last night. After relentlessly working on me, somehow I agreed. I think they both chanted over me as I slept. Actually, I never had a chance or a choice. Women…

As for the rest of our cronies, Tris, finally met the love of his life, Victoria, and they were married (I was the best man, natch). They opened a successful door and frame business of their own (West Coast Door and Frame) and lived nearby in a condo that Tris bought a few years back. Clint also lived in Orange, in a condo he bought years ago with Jana and their two girls. Clint's Tux shop (Clint's Formal Wear) was doing well and allowed Jana to be a stay-at-home mom and home school their girls. Jim married again (for the fourth time), this time to Tammy, a nice gal with a son, Ian. Jim bought his parent's old home in, you guessed it, Orange.

Sam and Chuck bought a new home in Anaheim Hills and they also were doing fine. Chuck toiled for Allied Van Lines as their head mechanic. Nancy, Dennis's ex-wife, remarried a man named Tony and they had a nice home in Yorba Linda. We kid Nancy because she has been married three times so we nicknamed her Nancy "*KesterBellFordLeoni*," parts of her maiden name and all her exes' last names. Devin, her son, (my godson) is a great kid, playing soccer and planning on college soon.

Dennis, big surprise, divorced again and was back to playing the field. He was dating a nice lady named Sonny and he bought a bar and changed the name to

Sonny's Sports Page. Dennis helped me in the early stages of my business so when he came to me and asked to borrow $10,000 for the down payment, I was glad (and compelled) to lend it to him.

Remember that saying *"No good deed goes unpunished?"* Obviously, I never learn. I lent the money to Dennis and he told me he'd pay me back *"in full within three months."* His words, not mine. I asked just three things. One, *"Please don't make me have to ask for it."* Two, *"Please return it on time, in one lump sum like I gave it to you."* And three, *"Let's not ever let money get in the way of our friendship."* He agreed.

A little over a year later, I finally got up the courage to ask him for the money. I'd been steaming for a while since he hadn't even mentioned the loan since I'd given it to him. He went off on me. *"I've got bills to pay," "I need money to run this business,"* etc. I was appalled. I reminded him that he told me *"three months"* and that it was his time frame, not mine. He also promised that I would be paid back in full before he made any improvements to the bar. I watched for a year as he bought new barstools, pool tables, remodeled bathrooms, flooring, signage, etc. Well, Dennis finally did pay me back over the next six months. I had to ask several times and I got the money in payments. But, we remained friends.

* * *

I did learn one valuable lesson, something my dad used to preach to me way back when, *"Money and friends don't mix."* Dad was right, again. I now believe that lending money to friends or family is the best way to ruin a relationship. There are more people who don't speak to each other over money than anything else, including loved ones. I don't do that anymore - lesson learned, the hard way. But of course, nine doors.

My dad also used to say, *"Your best friend is the money in your pocket, without it you have no friends."* I don't know for sure on that one, so I'll let you decide…

PART 2 – THE FALL...

As we moved through the spring of 2001 I was noticing that business was already slowing down a little more than usual. Our dealers were starting to moan and groan like they did every year at that time but that year a little more so and earlier. Two bad things happen when the dealers slow down: First, they stop paying, and second, they stop ordering. I hate both. After 20 years of doing the same thing over and over you get to know the drill pretty well. Besides, I kept statistics on everything.

Our business dropped off and increased at about the same time every year. And luckily for Creative Ideas, the drop-off usually came later and was not as severe as the year before. The increases came sooner and were more intense, just what you dream about as an owner. I worked diligently over the years to cut our summers (slow season) short. Back when I first started, summer came in April and lasted through September. That's six long, grueling months, which would never do. With proper planning, landing dealers in different states with different climate conditions and developing more new product and styles that better fit those states and special programs, we were able to trim that that down to just two months.

During those two months, we worked hard on samples for the next markets and catching up from the last rush. We also cut down on overtime which can become a habit, and we'd close the factory for a week of vacation in June.

Again after 20 years of doing the same thing over and over, you get pretty wise. I would close the factory for a week in the middle of June, dead smack in the middle of the slow season, for summer vacation. And then once again in December, between Christmas and New Years, for winter vacation when everyone was too distracted by the holidays to get much done. This worked out great for everyone. The employees got two weeks of paid time off a year and never had to wait more than six months for their next rest period. It's a good plan since after vacation, everyone's full of piss and vinegar (and broke) and ready to get back to work and their steady paycheck. Then, after about three or four months, just as they were beginning to wear down, we motivated them with talk of vacation just around the corner.

When you have 300-plus employees, scheduling vacations can be a nightmare. Everyone wants the same week off, like Christmas week. To do it the traditional way, we would've been down way too many people in certain departments. And *"fuhgettaboudit"* if you had to turn down a request, which usually came at the last minute. The toughest part of my program was getting everyone on board with a set vacation period and understanding that there were no exceptions. Like everything else in life, you have to make a few exceptions but we tried to keep it to a minimum.

As for us, we used that time to do scheduled maintenance on the factory such as painting, restriping the floors and moving machines. Whenever we bought new equipment, I'd plan for it to arrive so we could install it during those weeks. The people who did not qualify for vacation, along with my maintenance department, would work that week and take vacations later. I especially liked working those weeks so I could spend time in my factory directing traffic and enjoy the slower pace without a phone call or a page every three seconds. It was a chance to catch my breath.

I always said there were three steps into the slow season for the furniture industry. Step one: April 15th, tax season, when everyone is broke for a while. Step two: Daylight Savings when days are longer and people start to move outdoors. Instead of buying furniture, they start building pools or patios, working in yards or buying new cars. And finally, the third deadly step: the Heat. When it gets hot, nobody wants to go into a furniture store. Instead, you find everyone at the beach, park and on vacation. How did they expect us to make a living?

That particular year, I had already been clued in to the fact that we were heading into a recession. Shhh, don't tell anybody our government likes to keep that secret as long as possible. I knew because of the sale or shall I say *no sale* of our business. I'd been hearing for a few months that money was getting tight, no one was lending and the market was slipping. I could tell by our dealers' and salespeople's complaints that business was way off. With the July San Francisco Market just around the corner I was busy banging away at new product. I figured I'd better do something - we had to stay busy. I had a second mortgage on the building because of the new addition and payments on the new conveyor system. Besides, I hated going backwards; I was spoiled by so many good years in a row.

At July market, I introduced a bunch of new items in all of the lines we offered. Unfortunately for us, we didn't get quite the response we were hoping for. Summer markets were usually slower than winter markets and that year was even worse because of the threat of the looming recession. Still, all in all, it was a good market for us despite the lack of traffic. What dealers we missed at the show we picked up on the road in the following weeks. September started off with a bang for Creative Ideas. Little did I know there was a terrible explosion yet to come.

* * *

I was at home getting dressed for work when I saw the fire in the first tower, shocking! I assumed, like everyone else, that an airliner had lost control or had engine failure resulting in such a terrible accident. But, like the rest of the world, as I witnessed the next plane head into the second tower, I told my wife, *"We're under attack."* SHOCK was the only word to describe my feelings at the time. But, it just figured. For the past few years, terrorists had been bombing our U.S. Embassies in other countries. They tried a feeble attempt on the Twin Towers once before and then there was the attack on the USS Cole.

Unfortunately, we as a country didn't do enough to get these low-life killers, so their confidence grew. Finally, they did something to really capture our attention. bin laden (I won't give him the respect to capitalize his name) was in our sights many times and still we did nothing! Sorry, the truth hurts. It especially hurt the 3,000 or so Americans who lost their lives that day, and their family and friends.

Say what you like about the pro and cons of war, but at the time we all, and I mean all of us, wanted action and we didn't care. We would have signed up to *nuke* the whole Middle East. Let's face facts: Before that dreadful day, our country was heading into a recession made worse by the 9/11 attacks. Then the two wars came - Afghanistan and a short while later, Iraq. Throw in the hurricanes that devastated the Florida Coast, the massive wildfires that ran rampant throughout the West Coast, the floods in the Midwest and then Katrina and the devastation in New Orleans. These were rough times for our country and tough times to be in business.

* * *

We panicked. Chocolate and I just sat there for the longest time, dangling on every word the reporters spoke, our eyes fixated on the TV. Finally, I told Chocolate, *"I need to do something."* I needed to get to work and see what was happening there. I told her I'd see her at work and asked her to check on Nicole, who was still up in Berkeley. I raced out the door; I knew that my employees would hear the news soon enough and I wanted to be there to do something. But what? I didn't have a clue, but I knew I had to do something.

As I pulled up to my office some 20 minutes later, Mikee met me at the door. She and the staff had just heard the news and were already tuned into the TVs around our office. Word was spreading like wildfire amongst our factory people. As I walked into the office, Jerry, Mac and a few of the managers were already on their way up to see me. I flipped on my TV and watched in HORROR at the footage of the Pentagon, which was now under attack. I wondered out loud - how could this be happening and what was next? Could this be the beginning of the end? World War III? As the buildings, one by one, crashed to the ground we watched in disbelief and cried and prayed.

I told Jerry to get everyone together for a plant meeting and then I spoke to our people. I said, *"I don't know what's going on but our President has said for us to stay calm and not to panic. He wants us to go about our normal business. There is nothing we can do right now so we need to do what we do best and that's go about our business of making furniture."*

I told them to check on their families and I promised to keep them informed throughout the day as things progressed. As I looked into the faces of my people I could see fear and confusion - none of us really knew what to do. I just followed our President's advice. I told my managers to get everyone back to work and to keep things as calm and safe as possible. I called Mac into my office and told him that I wanted a flagpole erected in front of our building by morning. The rest of the day was a blur as we sat by TV sets and fielded calls from panicked families, friends, suppliers and customers. I told them all the same words I told my people: The best thing we could do was go about our business and wait until we got further word. Those were our President's orders.

Sept. 11, 2001 may just have been the longest day of my life as I'm sure it was yours. It changed me; I will never be or think the same. I had to repeat the same meeting that afternoon for the swing shift and it was no easier. By then, we knew that another plane crashed in Pennsylvania and we really didn't know what to expect next.

I still, 'til this day, can't believe it happened. I can picture the Twin Towers like it was yesterday and, when I do, I'm sad. I have a statue of the towers in my home office (my daughters gave to me) that I still look at every day in remembrance. I don't want to forget; I never want to become complacent. The things we just take for granted. Those towers and the people that perished that day will never be forgotten, should never be forgotten. I believe we should have to see that replay on TV every couple of months so we never forget.

But we're Americans; we move on quickly, we forget, we become complacent and that's our biggest weakness. Not me! I got mad, I got sad, and I got going… **but I will never forget**.

* * *

I stayed at the factory until we closed that night, walking the floors, patting people on the back and reassuring them that things would be alright. When I wasn't in the shop, I was glued to the television like the millions of other Americans or I was on the phone with family. It was just after midnight as I made my way home and I was already thinking, plotting out a strategy for the next morning. The ride home seemed to take forever; I couldn't wait to get back to a TV and home to my family.

I don't think I slept at all that night. Who could? All I could do was channel surf for more news and the next update. The image of those towers crumbling to the ground is burned into my memory like a brand on a cow. By sunrise, Choc and I were already showered and dressed and ready to go to work.

Chocolate didn't sleep much that night, either. We were scared, really scared, but we knew we had to be strong for our family and our employees. When we got to work, once again I was at a loss. It's funny just how many people look for leadership and guidance in a time of crisis. I met briefly with Jerry and the staff and gave them the same marching orders as the day before. I said, *"Our President has asked us to remain calm and try our best to go about our business as usual, so that's what we will do."* President Bush made it very clear that we all had to continue on, go to work, school, shop, do what we do *"or else they win."* That's just what they wanted, to cripple us. Well, not in America. I did just what every other American did; I swallowed hard and moved forward.

By noon, Mac called me out to see the new flagpole standing prominently in front of our factory. I was pleased and proud. I wondered to myself why I hadn't done that sooner. I called Chocolate and Jerry out to see it and told Jerry to have all of our people from both shifts meet in front of the building at 2:45 p.m. - just between quitting time for the first shift and starting time for the second. At 2:45, what I saw out in front of my building amazed me. I had given plant meetings before and assembled the shifts one at a time but I don't think I'd ever seen all 300+ of our people standing together at one time. It was breathtaking…

Not only were all of our people there but some of the friends and family members who picked up or dropped off employees also attended. There were even a few salesmen and vendors who were on site at the time. As Chocolate and I, along with the rest of the office staff, made our way to the flagpole everyone gathered around us in a giant circle. I said a few words - I'm sorry but I can't remember them - and then I gave the order for Mac to raise the American flag at half-staff.

As he slowly raised the flag, I led us all in tears. My heart was pounding in my chest and my voice cracked as I led all of our people in the Pledge of

Allegiance. Afterward, Chocolate, Jerry and I took turns saying a few words of encouragement. I told our people we would be fine as a nation and we would be fine as a company. I told them again not to worry, that *"this too shall pass."* I promised them things would work out and we'd be alright. Many were worried about their jobs and their futures. I reassured them that people would still need furniture and we were the best at what we did, so there would always be a place for us.

Trust me, I was as clueless as they were but, as a leader, you can never let your fear show through and so I didn't. It's funny, I could come unglued at the smallest of things. For example, if I dropped my cell phone and chipped it, I'd go berserk. However, in the time of crisis, I'm the one calming and reassuring everyone, that things are going to be okay. That's when the best in me shines through or maybe the best in *Walter*. *He* always thought of himself as a bit of a hero, a Superman. In my heart of hearts, I knew that this was going to be pretty tough time for all of us; little did I really know…

Over the next few days, I began to see just how much this tragic event would impact us initially. But I could never understand at that point the long-term consequences for our company, our industry or our nation. 2001 began with a bang; we had a terrific market and landed lots of new dealers and sold lots of product. So much so that that each of the first three months of the year were record months and we had our largest first quarter - in fact, the largest quarter in the history of our company. Indeed, 2001 looked as though it was going to follow the same growth pattern we had been on for years.

Monday mornings at our company were hectic to say the least. The two fax machines were overflowing with orders placed over the weekend and still ringing off the hook. All of the girls were on the phones answering questions so that the dealers could report back to their clients from the weekend. Jerry was usually in his office with one or two of the other managers barking out orders for the day, and Chocolate was grappling with a bundle of mail large enough to choke a horse searching for checks, the best part of her day.

As for me, I just loved the smell of fresh coffee and success that was always in the air at Creative Ideas. Most people hate or resent getting up and going to work. Not me. Ever since I started Creative Ideas, I couldn't wait for morning to go in and see what I could conjure up next. I was that guy who couldn't wait until vacation was over to start yakking about work, business or the next design. I was the stereotypical chief, cook and bottle washer and I loved it. Cell phone in one hand, office phone in the other, monitors blazing, with people lined up at my door and I was in my glory.

But on the first Monday after 9/11, I could already see the future and it scared the hell out of me. I watched and listened as the phones fell silent. And the fax machines? We checked them periodically just to see if they were still working. The normal chatter turned into an eerie hush that was louder than you can imagine. As I walked in, I could feel everyone's questioning eyes upon me. I pretended not to notice. I made the normal rounds asking of *"Good morning"* and *"How was your weekend?"* But eventually, the questions had to be answered.

"How come it's so quiet?" "How come there's no orders in the fax machine?" "Where's all the mail?" and so on. I said, *"Be patient, it'll come back. It's only been a few days, and people are still in shock. They're not going out and buying furniture right now."* Wow, was I ever right. I hate it when I do that.

The final quarter of 2001 was the worst we had in years. Our sales dropped significantly and money stopped coming in since no one could afford to pay us. Within months, we were already losing some of the dealers who couldn't stay afloat and the balances they owed us went with them. What started out as an extremely promising year ended up very poorly. Overall, our year ended down a whopping 15% and that was after having a record first quarter. Only once in our history did we see a drop in sales from the year prior and that was in the recession and war year of 1990. And even then, after a very rough 12 months we were only down 13%.

But, as always, *Walter* would figure out what to do next.

* * *

Earlier, I likened myself to my mom in the strength and endurance department during the worst of times. Well, as I said, you have to pick yourself up, dust yourself off and keep forging forward.

There's a country music group named Rascal Flats and they do a song called "Stand." The words go like this:

You feel like a candle in a hurricane
just like a picture with a broken frame
alone and helpless,
like you've lost your fight
but you'll be alright, you'll be alright

Cause when push comes to shove
you taste what you're made of
you might bend til you break
cause it's all you can take
on your knees you look up
decide you've had enough
you get mad, you get strong
wipe your hands, shake it off,
then you stand, then you stand...

* * *

That's just me; I can find inspiration and strength in the strangest places. I love that song because it's life in a nutshell and when things go wrong, we need to find our inner strength...

Chocolate and I with the Twin Towers in the background.

Creative Ideas flag ceremony after 911.

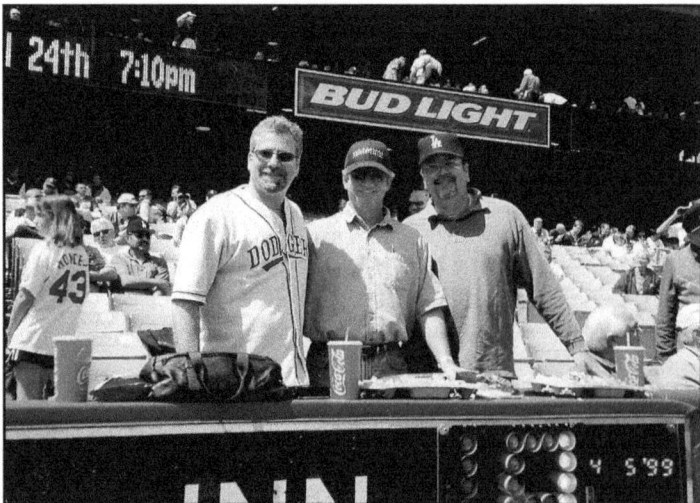

Me, Tris & Jim at a Dodger game.

STEVE BALSAMO, CREATIVE IDEAS

Steve Balsamo deserves credit for helping to create the computer-desk category that blossomed into the home-office boom of the late 1990s. Balsamo also merits recognition for adjusting his Creative Ideas strategy when SOHO cooled off earlier this decade, developing an equally feature-rich line of entertainment furniture. But his most impressive achievement may be the one he's now attempting. Balsamo is among the last of his breed, that rare bird known as a California furniture manufacturer. And he has no intention of starting an import program or of moving out his home state, where regulatory costs and taxes — combined with imports — have choked off most of what once was a vibrant furniture manufacturing sector. Balsamo is de-fiant and proud, but he's also a realist. He knows he can't get into a price war with the imports, so he's focusing on being a niche player, a specialist who offers plenty of finish and SKU options but delivers them quickly. He's lining up with retailers who get it, stores that are willing to devote the space and sales expertise to sell his highly versatile line. The jury's out on this strategy, but we're not betting against Balsamo.

Magazine article about yours truly and Creative Ideas.

My sister Jackie, mom and me out for dinner.

CHAPTER 13
THE AFTERGLOW

S ometimes, life has a funny way of trying to tell you something. There are times when the message is loud and clear like it's screaming from the mountain tops and then there are times when it's low and muffled and you have to really want to hear it *or you won't*. I wasn't ready to hear or accept the message that was beginning to echo in my ear more and more often.

* * *

After 9/11, we (in general and as a company) struggled until January, 2002 and then things started to pick up some. January market, being a winter market, was always much busier than the past summer market. That year, traffic was off quite a bit but the dealers who came were still buying. After all, everyone was down for so long after 9/11 that even with slow traffic in the retail stores, inventories were beginning to run low. Thank God.

And the million dollar question was, *"What's new?"*

This is what every dealer who has ever walked into a showroom asks first - I don't care what the business is. If you don't have something new to offer, they will politely go about their merry way. Never wanting to be outdone or fall behind, I had a bunch of new product, fabrics and finishes. My old theory, *"The more shit you throw at the wall, the more likely something will stick"* never let me down. And, indeed, we had a pretty good market, not $1 million but you can't hit a home run every time. Sometimes, a double or triple will have to do. For Creative Ideas, getting some new customers, placing new items on dealers' floors and selling some show specials always added up to a successful market and great beginning of a new year.

Unlike most years when every month is greater than the same month the year before, that January came in a little short as did February and March. Just as I started to get concerned, April came on strong, beating out the year before by a tidy sum. This continued every month for the rest of the year, so I started to feel better as time plugged along. After dropping almost $4 million in sales in 2001 (which equates to a little over 15%), that year we were back on track, up almost 10% over the year before. 2003 was more of the same, up another 4% over 2002 but nothing like the 25% growth we had been experiencing for the past 20 years.

I knew that the recession and war were taking their toll on our industry. Let's face it: Furniture is a luxury item. You can always put off buying a new desk or couch and they did. And the truth is, every industry was affected in one way or another.

The downturn in the furniture industry was evident everywhere. At the Furniture Mart in San Francisco, things were changing. Every show was a little slower than the past and attendance was dropping. The hustle and bustle of market just wasn't there anymore and the excitement was replaced with desperation. I could see it on dealers' faces and hear it in their voices. The halls weren't as busy, the elevators weren't as full and there were empty showrooms popping up on each floor when usually there was a wait, sometimes as much as a year, just to get in.

The shows died off much earlier than usual. Ten-hour days became five, and five days became two-and-a-half, or so it seemed. With slow business came much anticipation and lots of complaining. Finally, management cut the show to four days instead of five because of poor attendance. When you're busy, the days fly by and before you know it, market's over. When you're slow, all you could do is watch the clock, wait, worry and question. Where's this one? How come they didn't buy? Is so and so coming? And deep down inside, you're asking, *"What the heck are we going to do?"* When your career and business depend on these trade shows, believe me, it can be very nerve racking.

We couldn't help but notice that some of our dealers just weren't coming anymore; they couldn't afford the expense. Others just came for a day or two. Between airfare, hotels and meals, most small dealers decided it was better to stay home and tend to their businesses. The larger dealers sent their buyers but with instructions to buy carefully and only things that were really necessary or a great deal. I didn't mind all that much since I knew my reps would go out to their stores and get the business, but it still felt like throwing a party when only six people show up. It's discouraging, expensive, wasteful and devastating to the companies that don't have reps capable of going out to get that business.

It was also obvious that a few of the old factories were gone and in their showrooms were new companies with import goods from China. For my company, imports were not that much of a threat. Some years back, when California lost its mind and started to burden our factories with more and more restrictions, many companies packed up and moved across the border to Mexico. A lot of people swore that would be the beginning of the end for those of us who chose to stay.

I stayed, and we endured higher taxes, higher rents, minimum wage increases, more inspections and, the backbreaker of all, workers compensation insurance rates doubling and tripling each year. Not to mention, the string of bullshit lawsuits that Governor Gray Davis caused us when he eased the rules to favor ambulance-chasing lawyers. These lowlifes feed off the blood of hard-working people, making manufacturing almost impossible. We, as an industry, had a string of negligent phony lawsuits that cost us valuable time, energy and money. Not to mention, it just wore on us after a while.

* * *

What's the joke? *"What do you call a boatload of lawyers at the bottom of the ocean? A good start."*

* * *

I hate, Hate HATE lawyers and insurance people are not much better. My apologies to my buddies, Tim (my lawyer) and Al (the insurance man), but think about it, all of our crooked politicians are lawyers. Need I say more? That's why our country is a mess. You want to improve health care and lower medical costs? Stop allowing people to sue their doctors for nothing. The costs we pay for our doctors to carry very expensive malpractice insurance is ridiculous. Why not combine workers' compensation insurance with health care insurance and save us all a ton of money and senseless lawsuits? In my years of owning Creative Ideas, we had tons of fake back and neck injuries just to collect a few bucks the easy way. Heck, I had kids with toothaches and poor eye sight trying to collect workers' comp, if you can believe that.

* * *

But back to why I was insulated from imports: It was easy; it was my sales pitch and our company's game plan. Creative Ideas offered more styles, shapes, sizes, colors, fabrics and function than all of our competitors put together. Most companies made 10 to 20 total pieces of Home Office. We made 26 bookcases and nine file cabinets alone, before we even built the first desk. And we had nine lines with over a 100 items in each. We made accessories, hutches and matching chairs for each line - our competitors didn't. Creative Ideas was *bench-made*, it was as close to custom as you can get. Besides, we were *"Made in America"* with solid woods and the finest hardware on the market. Creative Ideas delivered on time, affordable, high-quality, innovative product with a lifetime warranty.

With quality, function and the ability to customize, who could beat us? Nobody! We gave the consumer something our competitors couldn't - *choices!*

I think you get the point. We dominated the category of home office. *"Do what you do best and be the best at it,"* and we did. I always said, *"We have no competition"* and we didn't. By the time the importers copied us and got it to our shores, we were already on floors and selling product. Besides, with us, dealers bought only what they needed for floor samples. They didn't have to tie up their cash in inventory. They could just let our catalog and website do the work and we'd do the rest. One of my reps, George, always said, *"Creative Ideas does all the heavy lifting."*

* * *

Chocolate and I were taking a steam bath one evening and reflecting on all that had happened since 9/11. It was the early part of 2002 and we were talking about how much life had changed in general. We were bemoaning the drop-off in business and the loss of some good customers and friends not to mention the drop in profits. Then, Chocolate made a statement that woke the tiger in me. She said, *"Well, I guess this means I won't get my beach house."* I responded with, *"Are you crazy? This is the best time for us to buy a house. After all, the market is flat and we have the money to do it."* I promised her right then and there in our shower that within six months we would have a beach house. Me and my big mouth...

A few months later, we were in San Clemente looking at my buddy Tony's new beach condo when we came across an open house. It was at the beach, so naturally, we had to check it out. It's there that we first met Fred Bevy, a local real estate agent, who said, *"I have a great fixer-upper for you, if you're handy."* I said, *"Sure, let's take a look."* We followed him to a house on the bluff in Dana Point, Capistrano Beach, to be exact. We pulled up in front of a 25-year-old house that needed more than a fixing up.

As we walked through the front door, all I could see was a wall of glass looking out over the Pacific Ocean, a 100 feet above the blue pristine water. The views were incredible - San Clemente Pier to the south and the Dana Point Harbor to the North. And directly out in front was Catalina and San Clemente Islands.

I didn't even bother to look around the house that much. I just asked the price and told Fred to make them an offer several hundred thousand dollars below the asking price. I instructed him that it would be a cash sale with no contingencies and we'd take the house in *as-is condition.* Both he and Chocolate looked at me like I was crazy and Fred said they had just lowered the price so he doubted they would consider our offer. I explained, *"What do I have to lose? Make the offer."* After all, I knew that I could always pay the full price and trust me, I would have for this spot.

Over the years, and having the money to back me up, I've developed a knack for negotiating things of great value. You just can't believe how much money I've saved us in doing that. The trick is, you have to be able to back up your offer right then and there if they agree so there's no time for second guessing. I always figured, *"shoot for the moon."*

Most people are aiming high with their sale price, so we often land on a star. That day, we were lucky - we got the moon. Several hours later, we were informed that they accepted our offer and had only one request, a 60-day escrow. Great news, in fact, even better for us as it would give me more time to free up the cash and plan my next move. Just as I was feeling really good about the great deal I'd just brokered, I learned that the owner of the house was in the hospital and gravely ill. Mr. Parker had cancer and the day he lowered the price on the house was the very day he learned that he would not be going home again. As luck would have it, that day also coincided with the day I happened along and made the all-cash offer.

It seems Mr. Parker wanted to be sure his wife would be taken care of and not have to worry about selling the house, contingencies, money and all that stress that went with it. He passed away a few weeks into the escrow and I was riddled with shame and guilt until I sat with Mrs. Parker. She thanked me for coming along and allowing Mr. Parker to die peacefully without having to worry about her financial situation. I still felt like crap but she assured me that he was thrilled to know that the house was sold and that she'd be okay. She stressed that it was a blessing that I came along that day and, who knows, maybe it was.

I told Mrs. Parker that I would be happy to help her in any way that I could - her wish was my command. She expressed concern with moving and deciding what to do with all of the things that she no longer needed or wanted. I offered to have my people come and move her and donate to charity anything that she didn't want. I promised her that I would take care of everything. She asked if she could leave a few items in the garage for her son to come pick up a few months later and, naturally, I agreed. I told her to put a post-it note on anything she wanted to save for her son and that we would move it into the garage until he came to retrieve it.

Time flew by and one day, I got a call from Fred that the keys were ready and escrow closed, congratulations! I asked about Mrs. Parker and he said that she'd already moved out with the help of her daughter but left a few things behind for her son. That evening, Chocolate and I cruised down to the beach and arrived at our new/old beach house with visions of a remodel dancing in our heads.

As I flung open the front door, I noticed that nothing had changed. Everything Mrs. Parker owned was still in the house except now it was all covered in pink post-it notes. Seems Mrs. Parker moved into a furnished place and decided just to take her clothes and a few personal items; the rest she left for her son or charity. Chocolate and I got quite a kick out of it and we spent the following days emptying the house and filling the three-car garage with the goodies she left behind.

Oh, I almost forgot, when I opened the garage door there was a car with a pink post-it note on the windshield. About three months and two trips later, her son finally took the last of their possessions. I didn't mind as we were busy working and planning the remodel down the road.

* * *

Some months later, a group of our friends invited us up to Big Bear (the mountains) for the Oktoberfest weekend. We booked a room at The Lodge in the heart of town and set out for a nice getaway weekend. We were having a blast; dancing, eating, drinking and just cutting loose from the daily stress and strain of work. As you may remember, I've loved Big Bear ever since I remodeled a cabin up there in my 20s and 25 years later, the feeling was still the same. That Saturday, we did what we always do when we're in a different town or city, we went for a ride. Big Bear is not that big and there is not all that much to see so we decided to cruise through some of the nicer neighborhoods. As we turned into an area called Castle Glen Estates, we noticed a new cabin for sale. Uh oh…

Twenty minutes later, a nice young lady named Donna showed up with the keys. As we opened the front door and walked in I said to Chocolate, *"This is it! I love this house."* We looked at about 25 more houses that weekend and did our due diligence but nothing else measured up. I knew from the beginning that the first house we saw was the one I wanted.

I told Donna to make a cash offer, quick escrow, etc. just as I did with the beach house a few months earlier. I guess this time I offered too little - our offer was turned down. We decided to wait and make them stew a bit before we made another offer. Besides that, Chocolate wanted us to take a breath and make sure that we weren't jumping the gun. We finished our weekend of fun and left Big Bear without my house.

I could not get that cabin out of my mind, and two days later, I called Donna to make another, more reasonable offer only to hear that the house had sold. Sold? I was heartbroken, bummed out and kicking myself in the ass for not manning up and offering a fair price for the house. Naturally, I wanted to get a deal. Well, sometimes it works out and sometimes it doesn't - this time it backfired on me. Chocolate said, *"Obviously it wasn't meant to be"* and promised that we'd go back up soon and look for another house but I still couldn't believe that I lost *my* house.

Over the next two weeks, I called Donna several times to check the status and see what else was available. On Friday morning, I got the call; the house was back on the market. It had fallen out of escrow. I couldn't believe my luck; I couldn't wait a moment longer. That night we drove up to Big Bear and, the next morning, after a little back and forth light negotiating, I wrote a check and we bought the house. Believe it or not, they came down on the price and we still got a great deal, including all the new furnishings. I guess losing the first deal made them more anxious to negotiate and the thought of losing the house did the same for us.

Twenty-five years after I fell in love with Big Bear, 25 years after I swore I'd buy a cabin up there someday, **I did.**

* * *

"Dreams do come true if you stay true to them."
Never laugh at someone's dreams;
"People who don't have dreams, don't have much."

* * *

Shortly after we closed escrow, I went into my attic and retrieved the snow-shoes, the old wooden skis, the rusted ice skates and the old jugs I bought 25 years earlier to put into my cabin someday. Today, they are displayed prominently on the walls and shelves of my Big Bear Mountain home. I often ask, *"Why the hell did I wait so long?"* Heck, we could have afforded the cabin years ago and enjoyed it for years with our kids and family but that's life. Life is passing by while we're busy making plans…plan well.

Not long after we bought our two dream homes, one at the beach (Chocolate's dream) and one in the mountains (mine), I bought a boat. Yeah, a boat - a Formula 34PC. It's a cross between a yacht, a fishing boat and a fast motor boat. We somehow decided it would be fun to have while we remodeled the beach house. This way we could spend weekends down at the beach in the Dana Point Harbor, just five minutes from our house, while we watched the progress. They say the two best days of owning a boat are *"the day you buy it and the day you sell it."* I say, *"Who are they?"* I still have mine many years later and I don't use it much but I still love it when I do. By the way, I named my boat, ***"You Gotta Believe"*** after Tommy Lasorda's slogan. It just seemed fitting.

* * *

I was walking through the airport one day on my way back from a business trip when I decided I needed something to read on the plane. I stopped at the news stand and noticed a book titled "The Millionaire Next Door" written by Thomas Stanley and William Danko. Knowing my fascination with self-improvement, money and becoming a millionaire I immediately bought this book. It was a short flight from San Francisco to Orange County but nevertheless, I read the book cover to cover.

After reading this book, I came away with three lessons of real merit. First, don't judge a book by its cover. Many people look like millionaires, living in big mansions, driving fancy cars and wearing fine clothes and jewelry. But, for the most part, the bank really owns it all and they just make payments. Most people we assume are rich are *in debt* up to their eyeballs and if things change they could lose it all. It's happening now.

Second, the truly rich people *own* things like their homes, businesses, stocks and cars, and have very little debt, if any. Also, they're usually not who you think they are. The millionaires are proven to live in normal neighborhoods, in their same home for many, many years and drive nice but not exotic automobiles. I was quite surprised at reading this since I had always wondered how so many people were so rich? Now I know - credit. Looks can be very deceiving.

Third, I realized that I had become wealthy over the years and fit the mold of the millionaire next door. Chocolate and I owned a really nice home in Yorba Linda but it was no mansion, and we had been in that home for 15 years or more. We owned and ran our own business and had our own building. We had some

244

money in the bank and a few investments. And we both drove very nice cars, a Porsche and a Range Rover, but no Bentleys or Lamborghinis.

* * *

So, after 9/11, I think we realized that life is too short and it was time to *"get busy living or get busy dying."* We chose living! We'd been working hard for many years with the promise of *"someday."* You know, we all do it…Someday, we're gonna do this or someday we're gonna do that. Someday we're gonna go here or there. For us, it was someday we'll buy a cabin or someday we'll get a beach house or someday well slow down, travel, rest, retire, spend more time with our kids, family and friends, etc.

A lot of broken promises until 9/11 woke us up.

* * *

People, Today IS Someday!

By this point in my life, this message was getting louder and clearer for me. I couldn't ignore it any longer.

Me and Chocolate out on the town in San Francisco.

Creative Ideas managers yearly fishing trip.

Chocolate and Me at Dallas Cowboy's camp.

Christmas Eve with the girls and Santa/Jim.
(Front) Chocolate and Nicole.
(Middle L to R) Carly, Cathy, Sam, Ida, Tami and Sydney.
(Back L to R) Jana, Tracy, Teri, Tiffany, Debbie and Mikee.

CHAPTER 14
THE FINAL DAZE

2004 started out like any other year. After getting through another crazy, pressure-packed holiday season and turning the big five-o (50, can you believe that?) I was trying to catch my breath and prepare for another winter market. It seems the older I got, the faster those shows came around and the more they took out of me. Since 9/11, I'd been designing like a mad man - more items, more styles, more colors and more lines. We now offered nine complete lines in three woods, 12 finishes and more than 2,000 items. That's a lot of home office, trust me. But it took more product and more dealers to do the same business as yesteryear.

The furniture business had its share of tough times in recent years. It had been up and down constantly and the old rule book just didn't apply anymore. The busy seasons were shorter and not as brisk, and the slow season was longer and more profound. I kept a graph of month-to-month sales and followed it for years. The first 20 years, you could set your watch to the ebb and flow but not any longer.

Business being what it was, that year would be especially challenging for Creative Ideas since we made the bold decision to leave the San Francisco Furniture Mart. I decided to take a chance on a new venue and move to Las Vegas where the World Market Center was being built. Many in our industry shunned the idea and thought we were fools going with this new venture but I was sure it would be a success. In fact, I boldly predicted, *"Las Vegas will kill the San Francisco Mart completely and become the main furniture market in the country within five years, knocking High Point, N.C., out of that position."*

Somehow, that quote made its way into an article in the *Furniture Today* newspaper and well, let's just say I pissed off more than a few people at both venues. I didn't really intend to but I really didn't care, either. It's what I believed. Besides, it was well known that I had already given notice and that January would be my last show in San Francisco and I didn't show in High Point. Most will tell you that if you're in the furniture business you must show in High Point. I can honestly say, I never did and never will. With all my traveling, searching and studying of our industry it's odd that I've never even so much as stepped foot in High Point (considered by most as the furniture capital of the world). In fact, it was one of my goals - to be successful in the furniture business and never do High Point.

After all, I figured I already did two shows a year and to add two more would be nuts. Besides, most factories design for one and exhibit the same goods at both; not to mention you see the same dealers at both shows. Admittedly, maybe more dealers did go to High Point, but who needed the extra work, expense and time away from the factory? That's what I had reps for, to go out and get us business and to drive their customers to our show. I proved you could be successful in the furniture business without High Point, so I achieved that goal. Success isn't always about money.

* * *

Our last show in San Francisco was very sad to say the least. Not just because we were leaving a market and city we'd been at for some 20 years but because the show was already dead - most just didn't want to admit it. For many factories, High Point gave them the bulk of their business and San Francisco was just a regional market to pick up some additional West Coast business. For this reason, many good companies were beginning to abandon their space in San Francisco and just show at High Point, which compounded the problem for owners like me. Companies like mine depended on San Francisco and its attendance for our business and for years the show had been dwindling away.

I blamed the management and made my discontent well known. I often met with them and complained that they were not doing enough to support the show. Besides poor advertising, the building was old and in need of much repair to present itself as a major marketplace. By comparison, High Point was leaps and bounds ahead in design and fashion. I'm not complaining but we paid high rents 12 months a year to use a building for ten days; the least you could do was keep it presentable and safe.

To give you a few examples, our elevators stalled and rocked and scared you to death whenever more than ten people were aboard. Not to mention, there were only four elevators servicing thousands of people and ten floors of showrooms, and they were slow as hell. There were no escalators after the second floor, and the staircases were industrial, dirty, hot and gloomy. We had no air conditioning. The windows wouldn't open due to age, and the heat was sporadic when it worked, which wasn't often. The halls needed paint, carpet, new display windows and new fixtures. And forget about food - there was none in the building other than a coffee stand on the ground floor. For about three years straight, we lived with a giant cage around the building and the promise of repairs and new windows but for two-and-a-half of those years, it just sat there with nothing going on - not a pretty site. Finally, we did get the new windows, along with a rent increase to pay for them.

As for the advertising, I often accused them of *"Selling the sand when they had the only well in the desert."* By this, I meant that they had many great factories that only showed in San Francisco and they never mentioned that in their ads or marketing. Instead, they would run ads promoting all of the factories that had showrooms in High Point. Most dealers came to San Francisco to see different companies than those at High Point so it just made sense to me that you should promote that. They never got it and, one by one, all of the good companies gave up and moved to High Point, leaving San Francisco as a shadow of what it once was. Hence, the drop-off in traffic that followed.

And they wondered why I was the first to jump ship to a new, exciting, state-of-the-art facility in the trade show capital of the world, Las Vegas. More expensive, yes; more exposure, you bet. After all, who doesn't want to go to Las Vegas?

For most dealers, it was going to be a great change of pace. They'd been going to San Francisco for 50 years and had grown bored with it. Not to mention, Las Vegas was much more attractive from an expense point of view. Vegas offers great air fares from anywhere in the world and cheaper hotel rooms, ground transportation and meals. Besides, who could beat the entertainment, golf, shopping and gambling in a city that never sleeps? I don't know about you but I was there...

* * *

The challenges in 2004 started early. Shortly after the January market in San Francisco, I was notified that the World Market Center's grand opening was going to be delayed six months until January, 2005 due to buildings delays. The detractors (and there were many) blamed the situation on financing and were already declaring Las Vegas a failure. I knew better and never doubted the validity of the show. I met with the two owners, Jack Kashani and Shawn Samson, on numerous occasions and was selected as one of the first people on their Board of Advisors along with my friend, Dan Kush. So we had the inside scoop so to speak.

However, I was a little nervous about the delayed opening because that would mean I had to forgo a summer show that year and that's a little scary. Creative Ideas had done at least two shows a year since our second year in business and we always depended on the shows to land new customers and get new products on our dealers' floors. Besides that, market was where you found new sales reps, learned new things and got the necessary exposure and publicity to make your company vital. But I thought, what the heck? Lately, the shows had been terrible in attendance and most of our order-writing happened on the road after the shows anyway. I figured maybe we'd save a little time and money and just do a big *"No Market-Market Special"* program to get the business on the road and give something back to our dealers. Lemons to lemonade, I thought.

But I had no idea just how many lemons we were dealing with. Shortly thereafter, our No. 2 account, the Woodworks in Northern California, filed for bankruptcy. Thank goodness Chocolate had been watching them closely and they were honorable old friends of ours so we didn't lose any receivables. However, we did lose a $1 million plus account, which hurt! Million dollar accounts don't come along very often for many companies, especially when you make a limited product line like ours. It takes years of doing business together, relationships, training, quality goods, timely deliveries, a great staff on both sides and great product that sells with frequency. Creative Ideas had nine such accounts at one time in its heyday and that's saying something.

Within months of losing the Woodworks, our No. 1 account Billy Bob's Home & Office, out of Detroit, also filed bankruptcy. Oh noooo, I thought. To lose one million-dollar account is bad; to lose two in such a short span of time is devastating. Needless to say, I was scared to death. What's going on?

In business, you win and lose all the time. Over the years, we had lost our No. 1 account on more than one occasion: The Barn, Just Oak, Office Depot, Fedco and The Broadway stores come to mind quickly. Each time, it's devastating but you have to suck it up and move on. There is always someone else to take their place if you look hard and long enough. *"One door closes and another one opens,"* as they say. But times were different in 2004. Many furniture stores were struggling since 9/11 and many dealers retired, closed or went bankrupt. For us, this was going to be a struggle, especially without a trade show in the summer to pick up new accounts. But, as always, I just said we can do it, we can get through this and we will. What choice did we have? They say, *"When you lose, don't lose the lesson."* Who the hell are *they* anyway and what's the lesson here?

Billy Bob's had been with for us for many years and was our company's very first million dollar account. Something both Bob Seroka, the owner, and I were very proud of. In fact, I created our *Million Dollar Club*; trophies, award party and all because of his company and Bob was the first member. Bob and I had become pretty good friends over the years and I trusted him with the largest receivable allotted to any of our dealers. Many will say that was a mistake but not me. Because of Billy Bob's and the exposure of the award parties, many other dealers saw that doing a million dollars at wholesale was possible and they wanted to join the club.

With great reward comes great risk. No pain, no gain. Bob was always a man of his word and did exactly what he said with me. I can't speak for what he did with others. At the time Bob filed for bankruptcy, he owed us close to $400,000 and we had truck-loads of furniture on the dock and in transit earmarked for his company. After speaking with Bob, Chocolate and I put him on a COD basis with payments to reduce his balance with each delivery. Fortunately or unfortunately for us depending on how you look at it, Bob was able to stay afloat for long enough to get the balance down to $185,000 and then he was forced to close his doors. A few bad decisions, a divorce, too many locations or poor money management - you can pick his poison. I think it was all of the above.

Within a six-month period we lost almost $3 million of sales and $185,000 of receivables. I would rather lose the cash than the customers any day. I could always make more money but building dealers up to the million-dollar plateau was going to be very tough.

* * *

When it rains it usually pours and 2004 was starting to be a very wet year indeed. Within weeks of the Billy Bob's fiasco, I received a certified letter in the mail. It seems an ex-employee who was suing us for a workers' comp claim got kicked to the curb by our carrier. He decided to get a lawyer who was filing a class action lawsuit against our company for wage and hour infringement, whatever that is.

This young man had worked for me for a little over five years and quit one day for a new job. After about four months, he somehow got canned. Well lucky me, he decided that out of nowhere he had hurt his back over a year earlier at Creative Ideas. Our insurance company looked into the case carefully as they should and found no evidence that he ever injured himself at my company. No reports, no claims, no witnesses, no doctor visits, absolutely nothing to substantiate his bogus claim. So basically, the insurance company told him to go pound sand and turned down his claim.

This must have angered him so he found another lawyer and they made up this wage and hour claim and filed a lawsuit for $2 million against my company. Thanks, Gray Davis for easing all of those regulations. Needless to say, I was shocked and scared to death. I had to go out and find a top-notch wage and hour attorney to handle my case.

Enter Richard Simmons, the lawyer, not the exercise guru. Richard came highly recommended by another high-priced attorney who I had just used to defend us in a patent lawsuit (which we beat, thank God). For a while there, I was paying four different lawyers for different things at the same time. The bigger you get, the more people want a piece of you - to get what you have (money) without working for it.

By the way, Richard Simmons (the attorney) opposed Arnold Schwarzenegger for governor of our great state and wrote most of the California law books on wage and hour issues so I felt like I was in good hands. He also had great seats on the floor at the Lakers games, which he often shared with me. Heck, the tickets were free but it cost me about a $100,000 to attend a dozen Lakers games that year.

Nothing in life is free - Somebody is paying the bill, trust me.

* * *

So here I was without my two largest customers. I was being sued for $2 million. My receivables were slow and we were out $185,000 from Billy Bob's. Oh, and summer, the slow season, was just around the corner. The World Market Center just informed us that they were having some other problems and delayed the grand opening another six months until summer, 2005. This was getting very scary.

I had no real way of getting new business without a trade show and in this environment, it was getting tougher to replace what we lost. To compound my problems, July 1, 2004 was the deadline for all factories in California to comply with the AQMD's new finishing regulations. The year was only a few months old but it was already off to a rocky start.

Its times like this that you have to really reach down inside and see what you're made of and call on the *Walter* within to help you through. *Walter, **Walter**,* where are you?

* * *

Remember when I mentioned the new finishing line, equipment and the water-based finishes and I said they would come up again? Here is where that all comes into play.

Creative Ideas, along with all manufacturers who use paints and stains in California, had about four years to get ready for the new regulations that passed in 1999. Unlike most companies, I was proactive; I went out and brought in a water-based finishing supplier that touted themselves as a specialist in this field. As you may recall, I listened to their advice on purchasing and installing the new finish line to meet the requirements for their water-based products. The only problem was, here we were four years later and none of their water-based products worked even though we tried and tested them over and over again.

I was in a state of panic when they informed me not to worry, that they would have AQMD-compliant stains for us to use by the deadline. By now, after years of testing failed water-based products from them, you can see why I was concerned about making the deadline. Many promises and deadlines had already been broken and missed over the years. Oh, by the way, the fines for not being in compliance were up to $10,000 a day. They can shut your doors, press charges and throw the owner in jail - me. And you may recall, I swore I'd never do that again.

* * *

I mentioned earlier that I had just turned 50 in December, 2003. That year, Chocolate threw me another big birthday party. It was fun. Everyone I knew was there, including a few of my dealers, employees and some of my suppliers. I was honored and pleased that they all took the time to show up. However, I never gave much thought to turning 50. To me, it was just another birthday like 30 or 40. Milestones in life, yes, but not much else. I felt great, the same as always.

A few years later, I wrote a short story titled, ***"I Woke up One Day and I was Fifty."*** It was kind of a funny satire about all the things we *miss, do and feel* after we turn that magical number. I've been told that to sell my book I will have to create a *web site* for myself and, when I do, I will post it on there for all to read. I'm sure somewhere on the cover or jacket of this book you will find the Web address. I hope you'll read it. It's funny, true and eye opening at the same time. Especially if you're near or at that age.

There is a great song called, "100 Years" by Five for Fighting - John Ondrasik that comes to mind every time I think of aging. It's a glimpse of how quickly life goes by. *"I'm forty-five for a moment, the sea is high, and I'm heading into a crisis, chasing the years of my life..."* Great song!

As I came to grips with turning 50, I began to look back more often and forward less. It seems most of the good times were behind me and all that lie ahead were aging and the fear that I might follow in the footsteps of my dad's family, which meant I'd be dead long before I hit 60. I also feared that I would die behind my desk or in my factory toiling away. I know that sounds crazy, but it makes sense when you examine my family's history.

Grandpa died at 44 of throat cancer. Grandma died at 49 - heart attack. My dad and Uncle Joey died at 55 of lung cancer (and they both had bad hearts) as did Uncle Sally, who kicked the bucket at 56. Uncle Dominick was the lucky one; he made it to the ripe old age of 59 before his heart gave out.

So, you see where my head was going with this? I was 50 and stressed to the max. I didn't eat, sleep or exercise properly, I worked too hard and way too many hours and the last time I took a vacation was three years earlier. I had an incredible wife and kids and I didn't spend as much time enjoying them as I should have. I knew this pattern had to stop, but when?

"Ask and you shall receive" or ***"Be careful what you ask for."***

* * *

The only way I knew how to run a business was to run it full tilt, all out, all work and no play (which makes Steve a dull boy). I had been doing it that way for 20-something years and I had always enjoyed it. No, I loved it. I managed to work hard and long and still have my family and friends, play some and enjoy life. I did it all. I had my cake and ate it and then some. I balanced a career, family, life, business, homes and friends. All while growing wealthy along the way. The true great American rags-to-riches success story, that's me. I'm not bragging, just giving you the facts. I was an underdog who beat long odds.

But I always thought it was our choice and we could change things whenever we wanted or at least that's what I wanted to believe. Chocolate always told me, *"We have choices and we make choices."* All of a sudden, I was feeling like I no longer had a choice. I felt trapped by the very thing I built and loved.

* * *

Throughout the chapters of this book, I speak fondly of *Angels*. However, there are always *Demons* to offset them, the good old yin and yang. Demons, like

Angels, come in all shapes and sizes and can overwhelm you if you allow them. They can be persons, places or things and I had my share of all of them throughout the years - the dumbwaiter, fire escape, bums and bullies. But, for me, my largest demons always existed between my ears.

First, I'm a *neurotic*, a bit of a neat freak, a perfectionist. My whole life, everything had to be in its place at all times or it would drive me crazy. My shirts are always hung on wooden hangers and they have to all face the same direction, sorted first by style and then by color. My car always has to be clean, my hair trimmed and tidy at all times. I couldn't come home from work and notice a weed in the yard without tending to it. Sooner or later, I'd find myself out there pulling weeds for the rest of the evening. Everything I did had to be perfect and I've been known to drive myself and those around me a bit crazy at times. Poor Chocolate.

Second, were the *Voices* in my head and they were not kind. They were nothing like my friend, *Walter.* No, these voices were the worried voices, the kind that torment you. The kind that question and worry about everything. What if this happens? What if that happens? What will I do about this or that? The kind of voices that can cripple you, force you backward and keep you from ever amounting to anything. The kind that can cause you to doubt yourself and rob you of your confidence and ability to forge forward. We all have some of these. However, most people find a way to overcome them.

Well, thanks to *Walter,* Tony Robbins and the book, "The Power of your Subconscious Mind" I learned how to deal with them most of the time. *Walter* allowed me to dream big things; Tony taught me how to drive forward with passion and never give up. The book taught me to use my subconscious in positive ways instead of allowing the negative to creep in.

Today, I still hear the voices from time to time but now I can control them and they don't scare me as much anymore. I learned how to change the channel, how to drown them out. I still like things neat and my shirts are still on wooden hangers, but now I mix the colors. Sometimes, I don't shave for days and my car is usually filthy when I'm in Big Bear.

We all have demons. I had to face them head on and overcome them, I couldn't let them win. I had to beat them or at least learn how to work with them so I could maintain control. This is the only way to go through life, head on with your chin up, moving forward. This is what I do, the key to my success.

This brings to mind something I heard recently: An old Indian chief was talking to his grandson and telling him *"There are two wolves that live inside all of us.*

One is good and the other is evil and they battle all the time." His grandson asked, *"Who wins?"* The old warrior answered, *"The one you feed."*

* * *

The highs were great but I was up to my eyes in buildings, employees, machines, customers, products, inspectors, lawsuits and problems. Not to mention, most of my family worked for my company, which was added pressure. And, all of a sudden, for the first time, we were beginning to have some real quality control issues. Our finishes were failing at the stores and in consumers' homes. *"Now what?"* was all I could think.

At first glance, I didn't think much of it. I knew we were changing out chemicals in order to comply with the new laws and I expected some problems for a little while. Besides, I had my hands full with the lawsuit and such. But, as time marched on, the problems and complaints began to mount and the last thing I could afford was a major quality problem. I met with my crew and the finish company's people constantly trying to figure out what the problems were and how to solve them.

I was informed by our supplier that we needed to change out some equipment to make the new chemicals work properly. Days turned to weeks as we acquired new pumps, spray guns, drum agitators and heat lamps. We spent thousands of dollars, but, the problems continued. Weeks turned to months as we added more heat lamps, fans, a furnace and swamp coolers for make-up air and invested tens of thousands of dollars. Again, the problems grew worse. Months turned into a year and still no fix, even though we rebuilt and enlarged our heat tunnel and added on to the finish line. The bills began to mount; the cost was staggering. The problems were reaching a critical state, and we tried everything our supplier recommended. Still, with no end in sight the demons grew louder.

By now, it was just before summer, 2005. The World Market Center was going to be done in time for our July show. Thank God, was all I could think. I had reserved a 7,500-square-foot showroom on the tenth floor. It was a prime location - the best in the building - but all I got were four white walls, windows and a door, the rest was up to me. Most companies hire a designer and a contractor to build out their showroom, not Creative Ideas. I wore those hats. I designed the layout and showroom and had our factory build the walls, partitions, moldings and wainscot. Chocolate and I picked out the lights, paint, carpets and decorations. Jerry, Mac and I made several weekend trips to install everything and we saved our company about a hundred grand by doing it all ourselves.

We had no choice. After losing the $185,000 to Billy Bob's and all of the finishing problems and expense that came with them, cash flow was a little lean. Besides, I still had to pay the deposits and rent ($17,000 a month) along with about $125,000 worth of samples to fill the room. Then there was the cost of signage, rugs, a bar, wall décor, props, accessories and plants and trees. Not to mention the air fare, trucking and hotel rooms and meals for our crews. It was very expensive. However, we spent a fraction of what most did and our showroom was one of the best looking in the building. That's a fact. And yes, I'm bragging.

I was working diligently trying to keep a lid on the finishing nightmare. I wanted to fix it and design a new Signature Series line that would knock the socks off our customers at our "Grand Opening" in Las Vegas. I came up with *Mio Retaggio* (My Heritage - My Legacy) and it was sensational, if I do say so myself. It really was the most beautiful and complex line we'd ever designed or built. And the most expensive, as it should be. I was spitting in the face of the Chinese imports and the flood of cheaper home office products that were showing up in our marketplace at an alarming rate.

The Chinese couldn't and wouldn't ship solid-wood desks over the ocean because there were too many quality issues. The importers couldn't and wouldn't stock 2,000 items in nine styles and 12 colors and they wouldn't bother with all of the accessories. It took too much space and was way too expensive. We did all that as well as custom, matched colors and shipped within six weeks - another thing our competitors couldn't do, so we had our niche well carved out.

Besides, we were the Cadillac of office furniture at a Pontiac price. Our quality was second to none and our service and delivery were the best in the business. Everyone loved Creative Ideas because we *over-delivered*; we made them money without all the hassle and price matching. We stood by and for our dealers and took great care of them. Loyalty, a lost art in business...

While getting the showroom ready, I had a few hobbies on the back burner. I was building a 5,000-square-foot house at the beach. I guess I forgot to mention that I decided to tear down the old one. I figured, to hell with the remodel, let's just start from scratch and build a new one. I found myself there two or three times a week (that contractor thing again) only this time it was 45 minutes away, not so convenient. Along with that, I decided to save a few hundred thousand dollars and build all the cabinets, doors and woodwork for the house and install them myself. Why not? I had nothing else to do with my spare time.

Running a big company was never enough for me. I always needed more, other distractions, other projects. Don't ask me why, I'll just blame *Walter.*

* * *

The finishing issues were beginning to cause expensive problems. They were also damaging something that took us 25 years to establish - our reputation. Over the years, I worked hard to be the best, to create the best and to build a solid company with a reputation for quality and service second to none. We succeeded! Our dealers, customers, reps, suppliers and even our employees loved us. Because our customers trusted and depended on us, they were willing to give us a break or 20, but enough was enough. The problems continued for a year-and-a-half and the industry was beginning to lose patience with us.

The word on the street was that we were having major finishing issues, which is death to a furniture company. No dealer in their right mind wants to sell product to consumers only to have it returned because of faulty finish. Dealers have their own reputations and businesses to protect and no one likes to return money and lose a customer who just waited six weeks for his desk. Our competitors were having a field day spreading the bad news and we had to defend ourselves by denying the problems and pretending we shipped too soon or shipped wet product. If our dealers really knew that the problem was in the chemicals they would have had no choice but to jump ship.

Most dealers were starting to get really disgusted with us and the threats of cutting us off were growing. A lot of our dealers were already cutting down our floor displays and not buying new product from us until they saw improvement in the finish. They were returning product for credit or repair at an alarming rate. I was losing my mind and so were my poor wife and all of our reps and customer service staff.

Just when you think things couldn't get worse one of our largest customers, Star Furniture in Houston (owned by Warren Buffet – Berkshire Hathaway Group), called in a panic. They had major problems. Warren Buffet owned four of our major dealer chains in the United States and they talked to each other regularly. I tried to explain that this was just an isolated problem and that we would stand behind our product and fix it but the buyer would not hear of it. He'd already notified all nine stores in the Star Furniture chain to stop selling Creative Ideas product immediately and he turned back a truck-load of our goods on his dock. He informed me that he had a warehouse full of product he wanted to return and for us to stop shipping the open orders in our system.

I was freaking out; I'd never encountered a problem of this magnitude in my career. I got on the phone to my supplier and had them rush out to my office. I called my rep, Ben, and instructed him to go straight to Star Furniture and calm down the buyer and explain we'd have a fix for them by morning. How? I hadn't a clue just yet but I knew I would figure something out. I always seem to come through in the toughest situations. That is truly when I'm at my best.

My supplier agreed to fly their crew out to Houston and go to Star's warehouse. He was to open every package and check each piece and make any repairs on the spot. Star agreed to the plan so they were en route the very next day. Next, I had Chocolate contact the trucker and get the truck that Star refused back to the factory ASAP so we could do any repairs necessary.

Well, we got all of the product fixed, reshipped the original truck load and Star ordered us back on sale in their stores. But somehow this all took a few weeks to straighten out. In that time, we lost the confidence of the buyer and his 500 or so sales associates on the floor. Orders were canceled, shipments delayed and customers grew angry and wanted some recourse, which cost us plenty. Star's salespeople had to take a lot of flack over that. The bottom line is, we never could regain the sales department's confidence in our products again so after a few months, we started losing our samples from their floors.

The buyer promised he'd see me at market to restock the floors but he never showed. Within six months, we lost a $500,000 account which was on its way toward a million and never got it back. Worse than that, we couldn't hide the problem anymore. It's a small industry and people talk, especially your competition. And believe me, after so many years of being on top, they loved having something to use against us. That's business.

It wasn't long before our floor samples were disappearing from the other Berkshire Hathaway stores. Many of our other dealers also had hit the breaking point. Many quit, but most just cut back their inventory enough to hurt but not enough for us to go sell their neighbors. I guess they figured if we could straighten this out then they could restock and not lose us as a vendor. No one wanted us to fail. Every one of our dealers was behind us but they had to do what was best for them and that was to slow down and make sure we made the necessary improvements. It got to the point where we couldn't be trusted anymore. A business that took me 25 to build was damaged in about a year. Trust and reputation are hard things to earn back.

The furniture business is a lot like real estate. The more real estate you have (floor space), the more business you do. If your product is good and sells, it's very hard for a dealer to consider replacing you on their floor. Why take a chance with someone or something new? Keep in mind, if you lose your space to someone else - say a cheaper import - and it sells, it's hard to regain your place, especially if your reputation as a quality, problem-free company has been damaged. This is where I found myself, in between a rock and a hard place.

It got to a point where I called our furniture "*Surprise Furniture*" because you never knew what you might get or what the problem might be. Every time you opened a box of our furniture it was literally a surprise. Some loads would arrive perfectly and others not so much. Sometimes, the packaging was stuck to the furniture; other items would turn white and milky. Sometimes, the perfect loads would fail weeks later in the consumer's home, even ruining their carpet at times. We had to replace many a carpet in way-too-many homes. That's very expensive and very unsettling to the consumers and to our dealers. These were just the beginning of the complaints we received.

Creative Ideas spent hundreds of thousands of dollars over a two-year period fixing, replacing, and refinishing furniture. We unloaded and reloaded many a truck, packaged and repackaged many a desk and refinished about 35 pieces a day. The repair bills, credits, returned goods, freight bills and discounts to keep and mark down product were all new to our company and they were overwhelming.

Our overtime payroll was killing me. Our employees were tired, disgusted and short of patience. Our office staff was running out of ways to apologize and our sales reps, our very lifeline to our customers, were beginning to lose confidence. In fact, a few even resigned. Even Chocolate had reached a point of no return and she is always a can-do, confident, upbeat person.

But through it all and with blind faith, we pushed on. Market was right around the corner and I believed that sooner or later we would get the problem resolved. Someone had to have faith and lead us through this debacle and that had to be me. The World Market was running behind schedule, big surprise. They assured me that all they had left to do was install our carpet, windows and some electrical and finish the painting and then we could do the rest when we arrived on Thursday.

Jerry and our crew pulled into Las Vegas with two truck-loads of furniture and accessories and went straight to the building. I had flown in earlier and met them at the door. I wanted to check out the showroom before morning to get a game plan together. We had just two days to get everything finished, unloaded and set up before our long journey home Sunday morning. It was a big job but I had promised our guys they would be home early Sunday to get some rest. As we stepped off the elevator I could see right into my showroom. The sign man hadn't arrived yet, the carpet was still in giant rolls on the concrete floor, none of the electrical was finished and they were still painting. The phones weren't hooked up and the lighting I ordered wasn't anywhere in sight. Great!

Needless to say, I got a little upset. After about an hour of yelling and screaming at anyone who would listen, the superintendent on the job assured me that by 9 a.m. we'd be ready to move in. I wasn't so confident. I told Jerry and the crew to go check into the hotel, eat and get some rest. I stayed behind and tried to track down my lights and the sign man who promised we'd have our windows done by morning. Once I was confident that everyone was on site I went a caught a few hours sleep.

When we arrived the next day, the carpet people were just finishing up; they had worked through the night. As for the painters, they must have left early so I assigned that to a few of our guys to finish up. Our lights finally arrived that morning and Mac and his helper got busy with them right away. Jerry and I started hanging the wainscot and moldings and the rest of the crew began to unload the trucks and unpack the furniture. This was a monumental task and we got it done in two 12 hour days. Jerry and our crew were headed home Sunday morning after breakfast as promised. We had a week left before the first day of market, but still no sign man.

The following weekend, Chocolate and I drove to Vegas and met up with Jerry and a small crew to finish up the showroom. We still had no phone service, no window signage and somehow, the carpet in front of our showroom was wet and damaged. It was Chocolate's job to get all of the props and accessories unpacked and displayed. She has a natural touch when it comes to making everything look just right.

By Sunday morning, everything was done except the window signage and the plants. My sign man was busy all over the building but he promised me that my windows would be done by morning. Finally, he delivered. Chocolate and I spent the rest of the morning buying plants and trees and making sure the leak in the air conditioner and the carpet were repaired. Then, I started preparing for our afternoon sales meeting.

I've done many shows and held many sales meetings but this Sunday was different. Once all of our sales reps arrived, looked around, got a beer and settled in, I started our meeting. Normally, this was where I'd go over new product, show specials, the latest news from the factory, pricing, etc. It was usually very upbeat and positive as most were ready for a great show and anticipated making a lot of sales and lots of money. However, this meeting took a different tone right from the start. The first question out of everyone's mouth was, *"What's happening with the finishing?"* followed closely by *"What do we tell our dealers?"* and *"Do we really have it fixed this time?"*

There was an uneasy feeling in the air and we all knew it. My job as their fearless leader was to instill confidence and get them excited about our new product, our incredible new showroom and our bright future. I guess I did okay but I'll say that I swallowed hard as dealer after dealer came up to me throughout the show to express their displeasure in our performance over the past year. I apologized more times for my company in those five days than in all 25 years before. I did a fabulous job of reassuring them that all was well but, truthfully, in my heart, I knew that we were far from it.

We had a great show and sold a ton of the new Signature Series line, *Mio Retaggio.* In fact, it looked so good that it took everyone's mind off the past problems, at least temporarily. After five long days of selling, entertaining, apologizing, explaining and trying to convince the world our problems were behind us, Chocolate and I went in on Saturday morning to clean up. After vacuuming, straightening up, dusting and taking inventory, it was time to close up shop and hit the road.

* * *

As we drove through the desert, I couldn't stop talking about the show. All the excitement about the new line, how great the showroom turned out, what an incredible location we had in the building, how awesome the new facility was, what a great place for a show and on and on. I was really wound up with excitement (and Starbucks) for the first hour or so but as the drive wore on I began to come down off the high (and the caffeine). *Demons...*

I began to talk about all that was ahead of us. Now that the show was over, it was back to the grind of daily business. The euphoria was gone. The AQMD's July, 2005 deadline had already passed and our finish supplier had not yet formulated a legal top coat lacquer for us. So as we drove, we were out of compliance and running illegally. Our annual inspection from the AQMD was due at any moment. Although I told everyone that our finishing problems were behind us, I knew that there was still no real, solid answer, just hope.

Then, I started to rehash all that had to be done to get this new product line off the ground - the brochures, price lists, new supplies, the newsletter, new tooling, training and on and on. It was a major investment of time and money to create a new line and get it shipped in four weeks like we promised. I also started to dread going back to the overtime, bills, lawyers, factory and all the employees and the demands of my daily duties. The demons grew louder...

* * *

By the time we hit Fontana, about two-and-a-half hours out of Vegas and an hour from home; I turned to Chocolate and said the words I never believed I'd utter,

"I'm done, I don't want to do this anymore, I want out."

Chocolate turned to me and said, *"You're just tired, you don't mean that. You love this crap and you'll be fine in a few days once you're rested and back in the swing of things."* I repeated,

"I'm done, I'm over it, I don't want to do this anymore." Again, Chocolate reminded me that I was just tired and that I should get some rest and then think about what I was saying when I had a clear head.

I agreed and we continued our journey home.

The Signature Series "Mia Passione" and its creator.

Inside the factory - The Assembly Dept.

The Finishing Dept.

The Final Assembly Dept.

The Warehouse.

CHAPTER 15
MOUNTAINS

Once home, I put aside the thoughts and fears I expressed in the car. Once again, I beat back my demons and pushed forward. Like a machine, I went about my business as usual. After unpacking, settling in and getting a couple of good night's rest and a day off I was ready to rock-and-roll Monday morning. But somehow, I knew the bounce in my step just wasn't the same anymore. I started noticing that I wasn't as excited to go in and face the world as I used to be. The days just didn't seem to go by as fast and the simple troubles seemed to bother me much more than they did in the past. That burning desire to expand and grow just seemed to dissipate. Something was missing: It was the *Passion!*

The past 25 years had taken their toll little by little and I never noticed. But the past few years, well…the passion was gone and for me, that was not good. I always said that without passion you have nothing. I believe life, business, marriage, success, family, friends - everything is based on passion. I knew in my heart and brain that something was missing but I convinced myself that this too shall pass and that I would get it back. After all, I felt this way about things before and it always passed. I just needed some time and a few things to go my way for a change so I forced myself to get my head out of my ass and move forward.

Creative Ideas and my life seemed to go in cycles. There were times when I felt like I could do no wrong and I was on top of the world. Invincible. Everything I touched turn to gold. Then there were times when everything I did just seemed to turn to shit. Believe me, I have hit some ruts that lasted weeks or months at a time with one thing after another going wrong or blowing up. To be successful, you have to plow through those bad times and make the best of the good times. Over the years, I endured fires, floods, strikes, a stabbing, a kid almost dying in my arms and almost dying myself, customers lost and dollars, too. We've had our share of deaths in the family, sickness and disagreements, problems with our kids and all of the stuff you go through at one time or another as a family and as a business. But somehow, I always came out on top. Lemons to lemonade, I reasoned and a strong woman behind me. And who could forget *Walter,* my secret friend.

Chocolate and I have been together since I was 19 years old (that's 36 years now). Over the years we've have had our ups and downs. In fact, one of my girls recently asked me, *"Have you ever stopped loving mom?"* I answered a resounding *"**No,** but there have been times where we didn't like each other very much."* Still, our love for each other was always stronger than any obstacle that came our way and the *passion* we had for each other always helped us endure. Tony Robbins preached *"Live with Passion"* and I'm a perfect lab rat for that.

My point is, I believe you have to push through the tough times. You can't quit just because you don't like the way things are going today. You have to battle through, keep the faith and let that burning passion inside drive you forward. *"You can't measure the future by what's happening right now."* Heck, if I did that, I would've quit my business sometime within the first five years when it was just barely staying afloat and I was working for free. But then, if I had, I never would have reached the success we've enjoyed. I might have left my wife (or her me) when things got too rough. But, instead, we hung in there and we've had a wonderful marriage, better than most will ever have.

Take my family, for instance (no please take them - yuk, yuk). I could have disowned my parents for all the trouble we had in our lives; many do, they just walk away. But not me. I hung in there, stayed loyal and always did my best by them.

That's passion…

* * *

Over the next few months, not much changed. The finishing problems continued and became a daily way of life. We revised the process over and over. We even let the furniture sit at the factory longer so fewer problems occurred at the stores. Meanwhile, our supplier continued to blame the finish failures on our factory, our people or our process.

It was later that year that they finally admitted that their chemicals were failing all along and offered us a mere pittance to settle with them and move on. I was insulted and refused since I felt they'd been lying and taking advantage of us for over a year. The damage they caused was irreparable and a few bucks weren't going to fix it. They were afraid I might sue them and, believe me, I thought about it. I figured there was no way they could ever repair or repay us for the reputation and goodwill lost, the customers and floor space lost, not to mention the time, heartaches and dollars.

People have asked me time and again why we didn't just dump them and start over with a new supplier. Well, it's not that simple. First, there weren't that many good companies still out there. But, we only needed one, you might say. Well, we used more than 20 different chemicals that all had to be compatible with each other or else they would fail. This process takes time, effort and lots of patience, which we didn't have. Finally, it would be suicide to have two companies in your factory at the same time, since each would blame each other for any product failures and no one would take responsibility.

Besides that, it would take a new supplier six months, if not longer, to get up to speed. It's quite difficult to come in cold and figure out all of our finishes and develop a program that would work for us. Even if they could, it would still be just a test and then it could take months to find out if it really worked. And there was always the promise that our supplier would finally fix the problem. Maybe I just wanted to believe…

I read an e-mail the other day that said, *"Don't believe all you hear, spend all you have, or sleep all you want."*

* * *

Along with all of the finishing problems, the import business finally caught up with us. It didn't affect our sales or displays directly. However, it affected our dealers' state of mind. They thought they could buy and sell an import set for half the price of the domestic one and they convinced themselves (foolishly) that they would sell three times as many. Well, even if they did - which they didn't - they never realized until it was too late that the expenses were three times as much as before and the profit margin was thin at best. Not to mention, the competition on these look-a-like imports was fierce. Everyone was trying to beat the next guy's price to get the sale.

It didn't take a rocket scientist to figure out that even if they sold double the product at half the price, they were losing their shirts. I could plainly see this and I shouted it from the mountain tops but it fell on deaf ears.

Let's face it: Dealers had to drive twice as many customers through their stores, which took more advertising dollars, and they had to make twice as many sales, which took luck. They needed to place two orders, receive two deliveries, and unpack and dispose of twice the packing material, which took twice the labor and space. Then, they needed to inspect, deluxe, load and make two deliveries, which took twice the manpower, fuel and delivery trucks. And that's assuming nothing went wrong. If all goes perfect, they'd still lose money on twice the sales and rarely does nothing go wrong in the furniture business.

The imports were less than perfect and the distance they traveled increased the likelihood of quality issues or damage. Besides that, most of the Chinese factories were still new and inexperienced at this game, so mistakes were constant. I won't even go into the problems caused by the language barrier.

Our dealers were finding this out the hard way. They were working harder than ever and losing money at an alarming rate. As Chocolate and I tried to collect our receivables, they told us that the only product they could make money on anymore was Creative Ideas. However, most still couldn't pay for our goods. Everyone was getting further and further behind on their payables. Our receivables were growing and our cash flow was dwindling away. For the first time in over 20 years money, or should I say the lack of it, was beginning to haunt me. Over the last two years, Creative Ideas lost 15 of our top 40 accounts to either bankruptcy, stores closing or finishing problems. With them went a lot of cash.

Add it all up and we were down 6% in 2004 and then another almost 18% in gross sales in 2005. The worst two years in a row for us ever and no recession to blame. From our peak year in 2000, we had gone from over $26 million to just under $20 million in 2005. Still a tidy sum and a nice sized business but heading in the wrong direction.

Warning! Danger! Danger! The signs were everywhere.

* * *

By the time September, 2005 rolled around, we had finally settled the nuisance lawsuit. We settled out of court since it was costing way too much to fight. Richard Simmons came to my office one day and dropped a wage and hour law book larger than most Yellow Pages on my desk. He explained that it was big company against small employee and that sooner or later they could find something in this book to build a case on. Right or wrong, when you get sued you've already lost, even if you win. By now, the opposing counsel had dropped their demands down to $250,000 and Richard wanted to offer them $65,000. I reluctantly agreed and we finally settled at $125,000.

The legal fees and the lawsuit combined ended up costing us about $225,000. Oh, and the real kicker: they finally settled the workers' comp claim for $15,000.

Had they done that a year earlier, I would have probably saved the $225,000. Thanks a lot.

Then there was a flood in our new Las Vegas showroom that damaged our carpet, paint and caused a lot of the solid-wood furniture to warp or crack. The time and money it took to fix it might not have been so bad had we been notified sooner but management somehow forgot to call us for weeks. We had to make a several trips back and forth to repair it all. It's always something! It took months of headaches but the World Market Center's insurance company finally covered most of the cost. These days, it seems everything is a battle, or maybe it's just me?

* * *

One day I was heading into Chocolate's office to bitch and complain about something (which I did often just to vent) when I noticed she was crying. My girl doesn't cry often, so when she's crying I know something is terribly wrong. I immediately forgot what was on my mind and sat down in front of her and asked, *"What's wrong?"* My stomach was already upset and in knots from the look on her pretty face.

Like always, Chocolate tried to make light of the situation but I continued to push her. It took some prodding but she finally handed me a stack of papers: requests for credits, returned goods orders, return authorizations and parts requests. It just went on and on. And then she told me that two more of our large dealers had threatened to cut us off if the finish problems continued. She reminded me of the looming new immigration laws and minimum wage increase that were coming down the pipe. She'd finally had it up to here with all of this. And to make matters worse, she knew I needed a hundred grand to make payroll the next day and nothing came in the mail and no one was giving any indication that much was on the way.

I looked at my girl, upset and crying, and I thought, *"Is this what we've come to? After 25 years of working so hard…"* Then I heard myself say,

"This is it, from this day forward I will do everything within my power to get us out of this business by the end of the year even if it means just closing it down. We're done."

And then I promised…

* * *

Tony Robbins always says, *"In life, you need inspiration or desperation."* I now had both.

From that day forward, I did just that. I called my old buddy, Tim McDonald, the business broker, and asked if there might be any takers for my company. He had nothing to offer - the market had dried up completely. I called another broker out of High Point that had chased me around for years and asked him to look into a potential sale. He did but nobody wanted to pay much for an American manufacturing company based in unfriendly California, especially one that had finishing issues. I began to give up hope for a sale and started to plan on breaking up the company and selling it off in pieces for whatever I could get, the sooner the better.

But this too would take time. I put together a six-month basic plan in my head and then presented it to Chocolate. I figured we would have to give our employees and customers at least three months notice. By state law, we had to give the State of California and the City of Corona three months to prepare and the employees three months to find new jobs. You can't even close a company without rules and regulations and added expenses. I also wanted to get through the holiday season so we could avoid laying people off around Christmas. I just didn't have the heart to do that. After all, this wasn't their fault and Lord knows I'd been there and done that.

I was at peace with my decision and I was determined to make the best of a tough situation. I also figured that by taking our time and giving everyone fair notice, maybe our dealers wouldn't be too upset and pay us off. That's a big maybe. I also figured we could try to use up some of our raw materials and eliminate as much of our stock as possible. The two really big obstacles were going to be our building and the new showroom that I had just signed a five-year lease on. I got on the phone and called Tim Hawke, my real estate broker, and asked him what he thought my building was worth. He agreed to come out and give me his assessment.

Next, I called my old friend, Dave Palmer, president of the World Market Center, and asked if there was any possibility of getting someone to take over my showroom. Surprised as he was, he understood and assured me that my showroom was in big demand and that they would have no problem getting someone off the waiting list to take it. I thanked him and asked him to keep this confidential as nothing has been decided yet.

Things were happening fast. Monday morning rolled around quickly and Tim showed up as promised. After a quick walk-through, he and I decided on a price although he thought it was high for the market. I asked him to put out some feelers and he told me that he had someone who recently sold some property and had to do a 1031 exchange right away to avoid the capital gains tax. The next day they showed up and toured the facility. The following day, Tim presented me with a close to full-price offer and a quick escrow. The very next evening, we sat in my conference room and signed the papers. We sold our building in one week from the time I first made the call. One week, seven days, I didn't even get a chance to reconsider.

After the papers were signed, Tim left and Chocolate and I cried. It was as if we'd just pulled the plug on a loved one and, for me, it was. Reality had set in, we were really doing this. Selling the building set the wheels in motion; there'd be no turning back now. We'd given birth to this child 25 years earlier and now we were going to let it go. I think we were both in shock, glad to have the building sold but totally confused about our future. Fortunately, we had the weekend to recover some and collect out thoughts. I know for Chocolate it was bittersweet. She was sad but relieved that we could soon retire as planned.

As for me, this was the beginning of my worst nightmare…

* * *

I pushed forward; there was so much to do and so little time to do it. The buyer agreed to let us lease the building back from him until April, 2006 - just five short months. The next few months were a whirlwind, November and December always are. Between birthdays, holidays and the busy season it's enough to drive you crazy. Oh, and I was still building the beach house in my spare time.

But now I had a whole new agenda to deal with. Somehow, I had to run business as usual, keep this all under my belt and prepare for the inevitable. It's hard to keep a secret of such a great magnitude. If word got out, customers would quit buying and paying, reps would quit selling and just collect checks and employees would slack off and look for new jobs on our time. Not to mention, the fear of fake accidents and the lawsuits and theft that could follow and our suppliers pulling the plug out of fear that they wouldn't get paid.

It's a delicate balance trying to run a business and close a business all at the same time. That's putting it mildly, it's impossible!!! Yeah, that's better. But add a few four letter words in front of impossible and now we're getting closer.

* * *

Chocolate and I decided to start by putting a credit hold on any dealers who were consistently delinquent or likely, to go out of business, which were many. We also started turning some of the slower dealers to COD which pissed off a lot of people. This immediately put a strain on our backlog, shipping department and the whole operation and we couldn't explain why to our staff or reps. We knew that to ship risky dealers would be foolish because we had to buy the raw materials, pay the labor and commissions and then take the chance of never getting paid. It was going to be hard enough to get our money out of our good dealers because everyone would feel betrayed and entitled to some form of financial retribution.

Furniture dealers have a funny way of taking it upon themselves to justify undo credits for floor samples and future business lost. All of a sudden, there are so many more customer service issues, credit requests and goods returned with no justification. Trust me, I've seen this scenario play out with more than one manufacturer that closed over the years. The dealers stop paying, the reps stop selling, employees, materials and tools start disappearing, suppliers stop shipping and the banks stop lending. It's like rats diving off a sinking ship. But I had a plan and I was going to see this through, even if it killed me.

Next, we notified our management staff to cut down on buying new inventory and to start using up the materials on hand. I blamed it on slow receivables, losses and cash flow. We even cut down on buying the tons of office supplies that we used like they were free. I also ordered a freeze on all new equipment and tools. A company like ours was constantly retooling and re-sharpening to the tune of thousands of dollars a month and that's just on small stuff, not the big equipment.

Chocolate started to pound away for our money like never before. We knew that if we didn't collect it now it would be very difficult once our little secret went public. I, on the other hand, attacked our payables and tried to bring them down so that we could pay everyone off in the end. We didn't want to burn anyone. I've often said, *"I came into this business a gentleman and I want to go out the same way."*

Besides running the day-to-day business and trying to keep up a good front, I had to start the daunting task of figuring out what to do with all of the people, equipment, fixtures, permits, trucks, inventory and crap we had collected over the years. You'd be surprised how much stuff you can put into a 130,000-square-foot building.

I spent endless hours calling, meeting and interviewing auctioneers, suppliers and companies who'd buy anything and everything from machinery to inventory to raw materials. There were forms upon forms to be filed with the Federal Government, State of California and the City of Corona. You can't just lay off hundreds of people without warning them and notifying all of the agencies. The things I still had to do and learn were overwhelming. But I pushed through. Mikee was working with our attorney and making sure we took all necessary legal actions and looking into how to shut down our profit-sharing plan, a major job. Some of these things take weeks and months and years, if you can believe that.

As the holidays rolled around, things were hectic as usual so I don't think our people noticed all of the new faces coming and going and I didn't bother to explain. Tim wanted to show the building to new suitors often and that was quite uncomfortable. Over the years, I have always been busy but I was always an open book when it came to my people so it was very difficult to keep this all a secret. The pressure was mounting and it was coming from everywhere.

We were hard on credit so that made our backlog dwindle and warehouse inventories rise. Many of the dealers we put on hold or COD got mad and went away, which was to be expected but hard to accept. Our vendors wanted to get commitments on our future purchases so they could plan and order for the coming new year but how could I do that? When you're a company of our size, your vendors have to think and plan months in advance since our hardware is made overseas, shipped and stocked here. Lumber is cut, bought and dried in advance according to your needs, so all of this was very challenging.

Along with that, I had to figure out how and when to have an auction for our equipment, a warehouse sale for our finished goods inventory and how to handle Christmas and our annual vacation and bonuses. I also needed to off-load the Las Vegas showroom and everything in it and resign my post on the advisory board, which broke my heart. I had put in years of time supporting, planning and flying to meetings so this too felt like my child. And what about my people? How do I tell them and what were they going to do? I was losing my mind; I was praying for help. *Walter* was doing all he could but, for once, it wasn't enough.

* * *

One day, I was sitting in my office and staring into space when a voice came through the intercom, *"You have a call on line one. It's Dick from XYZ Furniture Company."* Dick was an old business acquaintance, someone I ran into at the occasional trade show or talked to once in a while to compare notes. I'd known Dick and his fine company for many years and I think we had a mutual respect for one another.

On this particular day, he called to chat about a bullshit lawsuit he was dealing with thanks to our user-friendly state laws. Seems some lawyers had gotten together and were suing some California firms for using the term *"solid oak"* in their marketing materials, saying it was false advertising. The whole time we were talking I was racing through all of our literature making sure we were very clear about what our products are made of. Making solid-wood furniture is almost impossible; there is always some plywood or particle board or other species of wood mixed in for cleats, drawers and inside parts. Luckily, I had always been very clear about the raw materials we used and I felt we were covered, whew! That was close.

This is exactly the kind of panic we lived with for years, always the threat of another lawsuit or rule change on the horizon. After bitchin' for a while, I mentioned to Dick that I was getting tired of the business and thinking of calling it a career sometime soon. He expressed the same frustrations and then said, *"We ought to merge our two companies into one larger company and share the load and expenses."* Needless to say, this innocent conversation would become the start of something big.

For the next hour or so, we tossed around ideas of just how something like this might work. We could sell half the equipment and keep the best, we could move my company into his larger factory, cutting our overhead expenses because it was bought and paid for. We could run both product lines independently and then design his bedroom and my home office together. We could still keep all of our employees and our profits would rise because our combined sales would push us over the $30 million mark, a place neither of us had been before. We figured that since he and I shared some customers and reps we'd benefit from the ones we didn't share. As we spoke, all I could think was, *"I've got to make this happen."*

What Dick didn't know at the time was that I was already on the way out. I'd already sold my building and made plans for my great escape. Over the next few days and weeks, we started to put the deal together; we were going to merge our companies and become partners.

How exciting was this! Chocolate could retire, my employees and reps could retain their jobs and we could keep our company and product lines alive. Meanwhile, I'd get rid of our largest risks - the building, our machinery and the showroom. I figured I'd only be responsible for 50% of things so that might mean some relief and time off.

Dick and I even figured out the best way to split up our responsibilities. He loved the factory, machinery and hanging out in his office and disliked sales, marketing and traveling, so he would take care of the internal duties. I would handle the sales, marketing and new product design from my home office. I loved this because these were the things I still enjoyed doing. And the stuff I began to dread

- collections, dealing with employees, vendors, machines and government agencies - were now his.

As we began to put the deal together, I had to do an about face. All of a sudden, I found myself back in business. I had to plan for the January market, create new product, order raw materials, restock our factory and still have the auction and inventory sale. Along with that, we still had to make this announcement to the world and move our company into his, which was no easy task. Moving, the very thought sent chills down my spine. I also knew that this change was going to disappoint many people but what they didn't know was that I just saved more than 200 jobs and saved our dealers the aggravation of finding a replacement for us, a very costly expense for them. All in all, I felt pretty good about the decision.

Time flies when you're having a blast. It was late December and I had just met with my mom, sister and brother-in-law to break the news to them. I wanted them to be the first to know so they would have plenty of time to adjust. Needless to say, they were very concerned.

Meanwhile, Dick changed his plans on me. Out of nowhere, he hired a consultant named Jack and they devised a plan where I would take more of a back seat role. When we met, Jack did all the talking while Dick stared into space. I learned that Dick wanted to buy me out completely. He planned to give me a royalty for three years while I stayed on with the company overseeing the sales, marketing and new product development. According to their plan, there would be no cash exchanging hands except one dollar to consummate the deal. I was instructed to sign a no-compete agreement for the next three years. Dick planned to buy (at a discounted price) only the machines and tools deemed necessary and enough raw materials for 60 days. And the kicker…my family was out. Mikee, my mom, Mike and several other top managers were too expensive and duplicated in his operation so they were deemed unnecessary.

It went on and on like this for quite some time. I was shocked and appalled - angry as hell, but I tried to bite my tongue. Chocolate sat across from me giving me the look to keep it under control. Finally, I couldn't take it any longer. I lashed out. I said, *"What the hell happened to our deal and who the hell is this guy (Jack) and where did he come from?"* I wanted to know why everything changed and why Dick couldn't speak for himself. I argued that this was a mistake and that we couldn't afford to lose all of these people.

After a while, calmer heads prevailed and we agreed to look over the contract and talk a few days later. I really wanted to just kick their asses out and tell them where to stick their proposal. I didn't like or trust this Jack character from the first time I laid eyes on him (something about a snake oil salesman) and now I had my doubts about Dick and his character also.

After they left, Chocolate and I discussed everything that had transpired. Once I was able to calm down and really think things through, I realized that maybe this new plan wasn't so bad after all. Let's face it, I was used to running the show and not very good at playing with others. Also, by doing this deal I would be completely free of all of the responsibility and liability of the company, showroom, etc. Hmm, not so bad. After further review, we figured that we could find jobs for Mikee, Mike, Mac and the rest and maybe it would be a nice time for mom to retire and enjoy the rest of her life. After all, she was 73 years old and she'd been complaining about getting tired.

Lemons to lemonade, I figured a way to make this work.

* * *

A friend once asked me, *"How do you know you're ready to retire?"* Another asked, *"How can you give all this up - the power, money, perks and success?"* And still others asked *"Why?"* *"Why would you want to retire so young?"* And *"Why would you give up that kind of income?"* Some even asked *"What will you do with yourself?"*

To outsiders, we made it look easy for years. But for anyone who knew us well, they knew that manufacturing was really hard and challenging. I lived, breathed, ate, slept, wept and watched over this company long enough. I started from nothing but a dream. All I ever wanted was to be my own boss and make a few bucks along the way. I finally came to realize that, at 52, I'd had enough, I'd done enough and I'd made enough. I had my day in the sun and it was glorious but it was time to move on and let someone else have the stage.

My answer to their questions…

"I've spent my whole life climbing mountains and each time I reached the top, the dust settled and the fog lifted and there was just another mountain to climb, another peak on the horizon.

I've decided this is high enough, I don't want to climb anymore mountains, this is the top for me…"

* * *

Most people never know when to quit, they never know when enough is enough. They spend their whole lives working, stressing, chasing that rainbow, trying to keep up with the Jones' and looking for that pot of gold at the end of the elusive rainbow. But I've come to realize that no matter what you do, there is always someone bigger, better, smarter, richer, prettier, thinner and younger, who has more hair, a bigger house or a fancier car.

We've all heard of the person who waited all their life to retire and then when they finally did they dropped dead a year later. Not me, the voices were loud and clear now.

* * *

There is no peak, it's just an illusion.
Mountains…

Chocolate and Me on vacation in Sicily.

A street named "A. Balsamo" in Italy.

My boys: Godson Tony (left), nephew Nick, Nicole and grandson Steven.

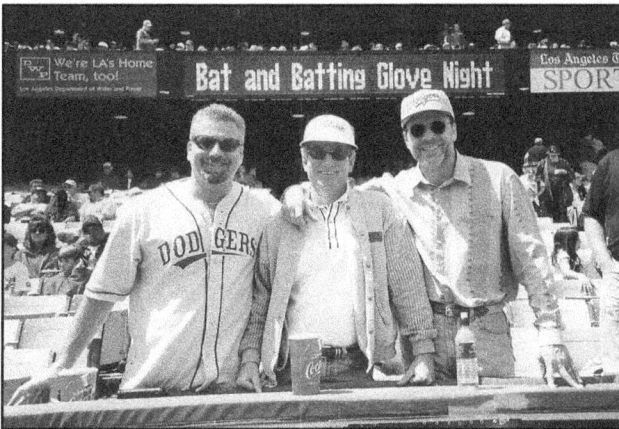

Me, Tris and Clint (right) as a Dodger game.

Godson Devin (left), Choc, Me, and Godson Chayson.

CHAPTER 16
THE DAWN

They say, *"It's always darkest before the dawn…"*

* * *

The final days at our company were very tough and very long. I could spend the next 40 pages trying to describe just how sad and how tough it was for Chocolate and me and, I still don't think I'd give it justice. I liken it to having your child grow deathly ill and finding there is no hope of recovery, nothing you can do to save him. The helplessness of standing by watching and suffering as he grows tired and weary, all the while waiting for the final day, knowing it's inevitable. The lack of sleep and countless hours worrying and somehow feeling like it's your fault. The guilt, the shame, the pain…

Our hearts were broken and our spirits were down. We were tired, worn out and physically and mentally exhausted. I tried to be strong and cover as much as I could and not put too much pressure on Chocolate and I know she did the same for me. We were both at our wit's end but we had each other's back. Somehow, we dug deeper and comforted each other and reminded each other that *"this too shall pass."* Brighter days were right around the corner but we still had a ways to go. We counted down the days to help keep our sanity but it seemed like an eternity.

They say *"What doesn't kill you makes you stronger."* But they say nothing about those things that nearly kill you. There were times when I think I was having a nervous breakdown and, as I look back now, I'm sure I had some form of a breakdown. It took me a long time to recover and get back to my old self but I fought and eventually made my way through it.

* * *

I accepted the deal with Dick and his company and tried to put on a happy face. I realized that this was my last true battle and that time would heal all the wounds but Jack and Dick made my life a living hell. Their demands and requirements were unreasonable considering my compensation ($1) and what they were getting in return (almost $19 million in sales, a product line, brand name and a trained crew to build it and sell it). Not to mention, me at the helm for three years. They asked for and received as much information as the company that offered me $14 million just five years earlier and they were buying everything.

* * *

I balked and thought this was crazy. After all, they weren't buying our corporation or any of its liabilities or responsibilities, just some of the assets. At this point, Creative Ideas was still in much better standing in our industry and we were still doing much more in sales than they were. Our reputation, though damaged, was still strong enough to repair if we continued to produce without the finishing issues. I still had a great product line and sales crew and an outstanding relationship with our customers. Creative Ideas was still relevant. I couldn't understand all the bullshit they were putting us through.

They constantly changed their minds and constantly broke their promises and didn't live up to most of our verbal or written agreements. Some of it was just small, petty, irritating stuff and others were large, expensive issues. They beat me down on all the machinery and tools they needed to make the transition and they haggled over every penny they had to pay. I gave them all the tooling to go with the equipment and threw in lots of little things because I knew they would never pay for them and they were vital to our success.

Jack was unbelievable; he was relentless in his pursuit of a better price and a better deal for Dick. I guess that's why Dick hired him. Jack caused arguments, distrust and much dissension between the two companies' management crews. It's a shame but I was the only person who tried to work with Jack and he did everything possible to alienate me. Jack may have been good at crunching numbers and having Dick's ear but his people and management skills left a lot to be desired; no one wanted to work with or for him.

We ended up selling them about a $500,000 dollars worth of raw materials and allowing them some time to pay for them. That wasn't exactly the original deal. Originally, they were to buy only 60 days worth of raw materials and pay us in full when they were used up. After the 60 days had passed, they wanted to renegotiate the price. Again. The problem is, they took weeks just to get up and running and they never got up to full speed. So, at the end of the 60 days they still had much of what we had sold them left. It got ugly and ended up in a battle. Finally, we agreed to take much less for the merchandise and they agreed to pay us the remainder over the next several months. Every one of these battles took a little more out of me and damaged our relationship further.

I sold them crown molding worth $2 a foot for 50 cents. Later, I needed some of that molding for my home and they sold it back to me for $3.50 a foot - nice.

* * *

January 2006 was no happy new year at first. I had so many things going on, so much to learn, so much to do and so many things popping up that I was out of control. With our building sold, Chocolate and I found ourselves in the unenviable position that many had been in - looking for a 1031 exchange to protect ourselves from capital gains tax. This is no easy task because of the strict requirements and very short time allotted. There's a lot to learn, rules to follow, properties to see and major decisions to be made and they needed to be made quickly. To complicate matters, we had virtually no experience at this.

I also had to prepare for a major show on short notice. This is a big job, what normally takes months of preparation had to be accomplished in just weeks. And here we were combining two companies, two lines and two sales forces into one showroom. Somehow, I had to pull it off without the control I normally have. Instead, I had Dick, Jack and Wally (their sales manager) looking over my shoulder and questioning my every move.

At the same time, I had to give our people, customers and suppliers the low-down on the deal that was transpiring. The news did not go over well with our employees. Most were very sad and a few were angry and felt we had somehow betrayed them. They never knew all the fights and battles I had with Dick and Jack to save their jobs, maintain their rate of pay, and honor their time served and vacations earned.

Dick didn't want to pay the wages we had established for our crew because he felt it would compromise him with his lower paid factory and management people and it did. I refused to do the deal unless he took all of our people, including Jerry (which he was reluctant to do), and kept their wages, vacations, etc. I felt Jerry was crucial to the operation because, without me, our people would need a leader, someone they could trust. This was the only battle I won although he didn't take about a dozen of our employees, all of whom Chocolate and I found other jobs for through business friends and associates.

Two of our oldest and dearest managers, Al and Pancho, decided they would rather resign than make the transition. This was not good; they were our assembly and mill managers and, between the two of them, they had served some 40 years and knew more about my company than anyone else. They were going to be missed and now my argument for keeping Jerry was even more relevant.

For the most part, our customers and sales reps were nervous and skeptical. They feared I'd phase out and that would be the beginning of the end for Creative Ideas. Dick and I agreed to keep the sale to ourselves and let the world believe it was more of a merger and partnership (like the original plan) for the sake of the business and a smooth transition. Lord knows, we didn't need anyone panicking and jumping ship. But somehow, Dick's people started telling our reps and customers they had bought us out. This made me look like a fool and a liar. Here I was going around talking about merging and here they were telling anyone who would listen that I was out. Dick and Jack denied the leak but it was obvious and the gossip mill was in full bloom.

Shortly after the new year, our finish supplier showed up and made me an offer I couldn't refuse. I didn't get a horse's head in my bed but what transpired was just as criminal. They offered me a mere pittance for their mistakes and it was a take-it or leave-it kind of deal. Once again, I refused and proceeded to tell them where to stick it but this time they didn't accept my refusal. Instead, they threatened to cut off my finish supply immediately and file a lawsuit against me for the balance I owed. They made it clear they would screw up my deal with Dick. In 25 years of doing business, I was only so threatened and helpless once before and that time a drug-crazed kid held a gun on me.

Left with no choice, I was forced to take the deal although I hated doing so. It paled in comparison with the amounts we had previously discussed but I knew that if I didn't take it we would risk losing everything. Cutting off our finish supply would shut us down completely within a few days and they knew it. In fact, they informed me that we had shipments on their dock that they had already put on hold. If word leaked out, it would spread like wildfire and Dick, who was already having second thoughts, might have just nixed the deal since nothing had been formally signed. Not to mention, our dealers and sales reps were already nervous as hell; most had large floor displays and open orders that meant big money to all concerned. Time was running short on our lease and market was just weeks away. I was overwhelmed and tired of fighting, so I caved.

* * *

We had decided, under protest from Dick, to keep the Creative Ideas showroom provided I pay half the rent for a while and I secure a new tenant for his smaller showroom. Great, another task for me as if I weren't already busy enough. However, I accomplished it thanks to my friend, Dave Palmer, and my role on the advisory board. The Creative Ideas showroom was in a prominent spot and large enough for both lines to share though it was much more expensive, which really bothered Dick. We managed to lay it out and set it up so it looked and flowed very well, thanks to no small effort from *Walter*.

All in all, the whole show was very weird. We quickly discovered that trying to sell office and bedroom in the same showroom with two different crews was uncomfortable. Sales meetings and conversations were strained. Neither crew knew if this was their last show but knew that sooner or later we would have to combine forces and someone would be left out. Then, we had dealers who were curious about all that had transpired and spent more time gossiping than buying.

There are *three* words you never like to hear as a salesperson - *"I'll be back."* Over the years, this had never been much of a problem for Creative Ideas. Our dealers would come in and see what we had new to offer early and then go out, shop and compare. Once they realized that no one had what we had, they always came back and bought. But this show was different; many didn't return. If that weren't enough, it amazed me that Dick didn't even want to attend the show. He did so only because Jack, Wally and I convinced him that it would be in his best interest and it wouldn't look good if we weren't seen in the showroom together.

I couldn't believe that after 20-something years of doing business with these people, he barely knew his reps and hardly knew our customers. Dick was a behind-the-scenes type of guy and his old partner, Barry, was the front man who did all the work and got most of the glory (before he died). Maybe this time around Dick didn't want another guy (me) out in front getting all of the credit while he stayed in the shadows. I don't think I'll ever know for sure.

After the show, things went from bad to worse for everyone concerned. Dick was having second thoughts and wishing he hadn't gone through with the transaction - not a good way to get started. Jerry, my production manager, grew bitter and was hardly talking to me - not a good way to end and certainly not a good way to complete the move and get us rolling in the new facility. Dick's managers were angry over my employees' pay and they were all threatened by each other. Each thought it was just a matter of time before they would be eliminated. No matter how many times we told them that was not going to be the case, it fell on deaf ears.

As for the rest of our office, Dick decided he only wanted a few of our staff now and, lo and behold, none of them wanted to go. All of a sudden, their new workplace was too far, and the building old and ugly and they didn't like it, Dick, Jack or their staff. Now Dick was coming unglued. He knew he needed a certain amount of our people to make the transition successful. He started crying foul and accusing me of nixing the deal. It was crazy but it gets worse. Chocolate and I had to meet with each of our staff and beg and bribe them to go over and give it a try for at least a while. We ended up securing three people by giving them either raises or fewer hours or both. Can you say blackmail? I was hurt and sick over this; I worked so long and fought so hard to keep their jobs and this was how they repaid me.

My dad always said, *"The money in your pocket is best friend"* and without it you will see just how many friends you have. This was only one of the many tough lessons I would learn in the days to come.

* * *

The final week arrived but not soon enough. It was time for us to move our factory into theirs and transfer all of our employees over to them. The move was tough, and the pain was almost unbearable. I wept often when no one was looking while we tore down my factory, my baby, my brainchild. Originally, we had agreed that we would load the trucks on our end and Dick's people would unload on their end and we would split all the costs of truck rentals, fuel and overtime. Somehow, that didn't quite work out as planned. Big surprise! Our people did most, if not all, of the work on both ends and it ended up taking a lot more time and costing me a lot more than I ever expected. But this was how everything was going lately.

Meanwhile, I had finally selected a company to run our machinery auction and we planned the date: April 19, 2006. There was a lot to know and do to prepare for this event: We had to price the product, tag everything, conduct inventory and clean and touch up the machines so they looked their best. And then there were safety issues, security, advertising, online bidding, etc. I had several friends who had gone through this process before and they clued me in on how to get the max for the minimum. I even managed to sell several pieces for a very fair price to a few industry friends beforehand, which was very beneficial since I had no costs involved.

The day of the machinery auction was heartbreaking. It took so many years to buy and collect all of this fine machinery and I took very good care of it and kept it like new. There were times that I waited and waited to buy a piece and made sacrifices in order to afford it. Over the years, we had put together about $4 million worth of machinery, tools, fixtures and vehicles. That day, I watched as each item sold for peanuts compared to its original price.

But I knew this would happen and I tried to mentally prepare. I set a goal of a million dollars when it was all set and done. Lord knows I'd been to enough of these auctions over the years and made some pretty good buys in my time. I can honestly say that each time I went, I always came home feeling a little sick to my stomach, knowing another man's dreams had been shattered. My buddy, Tony, and I went to many auctions together and we'd always kid each other, saying one day we'd be at each other's auction. That too came to pass. Be careful what you say - words become deeds. I was told it would be best if I stayed away that day but I couldn't. I had to be there. I had to see for myself; I think I needed the pain for closure.

I watched as people snatched up my prized possessions at low-ball prices. I was amazed that some items actually drew pretty good prices and others went for damn near nothing. Some items, like our 11 spray booths, sold for only $10,000 combined; that's less than each cost by themselves. And that $400,000 conveyor system…well, a cowboy from Texas bought it for $35,000. Now, that's a deal, and it was enough to make me sick. Oh, and the $10,000 we got for the spray booths turned out to be fake; the auctioneer had pretended to have a $10,000 starting bid when actually nobody bid on them at all. Three weeks later, we demolished them and sold them off for scrap metal. I got about $2,000.

After the auction, we walked the floor one more time; it was the last time Creative Ideas would look like the factory I had worked so hard to build. And we cried. This dream started way back in Brooklyn as I roller skated by an old lumber yard and now some 40-something years later it was over. Nothing lasts forever…

The following day, the trucks started to arrive and everything was gone within three days. Three days? Amazing. By Saturday, the only thing left was my memory. $4 million worth of stuff, give or take a few bucks here and there, and we cleared about $1 million. I was pleased that at least I hit my goal and believe it or not we were lucky to do so in this business climate. Let's face it: There was no one opening or expanding furniture plants in the United States anymore and we were fortunate that our equipment looked great and the home building industry was still on fire. We made a lot of cabinet shop owners very happy and one lone furniture manufacturer a little sadder that day.

* * *

In the following weeks, Chocolate and I scrambled to get everything done but we were drastically shorthanded and running out of time. We still had so much to do and even more with all of the moving, close-down procedures and the pending sale that followed. I asked Tim for another month on our lease to help ease the burden and pressure so we had until May 1 to be out of the building. I didn't want to extend it any longer since it was expensive and I didn't want to prolong the agony.

Once our people transferred over to Dick's, all that were left was a handful of staff in the front office. Three to be exact. Mikee took a job with my friend, Warren, and was working half of the day with each of us. The transition was very tough on Mikee both physically and mentally, since she had become a major part of Creative Ideas and watching it come down was very hard on her. Not to mention, the pressure and emotion of watching the pain her parents had to endure, which was killing her. I know she felt helpless and desperate to aid us and she did an incredible job and put forth an outstanding effort. We couldn't have pulled it off without her.

Jack had agreed to let DeAnn, my assistant, and a few factory workers stay on with me until we closed completely but like most things, that changed. Because so few of our staff went over, I was allowed to keep DeAnn for just a few hours a day for two weeks. And the others? Well, he couldn't spare them at all.

Seeing how we started Creative Ideas early in the year way back when, all of our contracts, permits and insurance policies were now up for renewal and had to be dealt with, which is a lot of work under normal circumstances. Problem is, no one wanted to write a short-term policy. However, we still had a few months to go and needed the coverage. In most cases, we had to buy a year's policy and then cancel early and pay the penalties, which were extreme.

As for contracts with our vendors, we worked them out with Jack and Dick. Most of my deals with my vendors were always verbal and I was always true to my word. Somehow, that was no longer the case. Commitments and promises were made and broken and I looked like the fool but sadly, I had no control. Chocolate worked diligently with our bank, which was getting nervous about our credit line. Who could blame them? No one wants to get left holding the bag.

As for the permits, as each came up for renewal I wrote and called letting them know that *Balsamo Enterprises Inc.* (aka Creative Ideas) was no longer. I had to agree to allow Dick to use our AQMD permits for a while until all of the paperwork to transfer them could be accomplished. This process could take up to a year and it was a risky business since I had no control but all the responsibility.

* * *

Out in the factory, all I had left was Mike (my brother-in-law and shipping manager), Mac (our maintenance manager) and his helper, Benito, and one laborer. Jack left a few guys with Mike in the shipping department to load the final shipments before they also reported to Dick's. Mike, Mac and Benito had agreed to stay on with me until the bitter end before reporting to their new jobs. And a few of my old crew would drop by after work and help me for a few hours each night. (Thanks Damacio, Freddie and Ben.) However, after a few weeks, they tired and quit coming and who could blame them? They'd already worked a full day and this was hard, dirty work.

We still had about a month to go after the move but so much to do. There were walls and doors to patch and paint, spray booths and heat tunnels to take down and hundreds of barrels, pallets and other stuff to get ready for recycling. There were big holes in the ceiling and concrete walls and floors to patch and fill after the dust collector and spray booths came down. We also had to deal with all of the leftover benches, furniture and fixtures that had to be disassembled and trashed or readied for sale. There were miles of pipe and wire to be removed and hundreds of screws and bolts that had to be cut off and filed down. I had told the new owner that I would clean up the building and leave it in perfect condition, and I was going to keep my word even if it killed me.

I would work in the office and shop all day long and then work well into the night in the shop after everyone left. For two solid months, Chocolate and I worked seven days a week and about 15 hours a day. We went home only to eat and sleep and then came back to it. We were relentless, tired and sore but we knew the only way we could get the job done was to push through the pain, and that's what we did.

What kept us going was the light at the end of the tunnel, the countdown of days left, an end in sight. I likened it to being in prison and knowing we'd eventually be set free. Eventually, our sentence would soon be up. It was that light at the end of our tunnel they kept us going.

* * *

Once all the shipments were gone and Mike's crew had left for Dick's, Mike popped into my office and told me he was done and extended his hand and said he was leaving. *"Leaving?"* I said as I shook his out-stretched hand. He explained that he wanted to take some time off between jobs to rest and that this would be his last day. I was crushed since we still had weeks to go and so much to do but I thanked him for his time served. Then I called Chocolate and asked her to cut his final check and pay him through the week even though he was leaving on Monday, without any notice. Life is full of little disappointments and for me this was a major one. I never expected that of family. I thought he would be the last man standing beside me in the end. I guess I was wrong…

Shortly after, our laborer found another job and never came back. With a few weeks to go, the days got longer and the work got harder and dirtier for the three of us still left. Finally, Benito's patience gave out and he quit. He reported early to his new job because he didn't care much for the hard work and long hours. That left just Mac and I and still so much to do.

* * *

We were closing down the office, cleaning up the building and property and readying for the final warehouse sale. Each day, I would grab a few day laborers off the road on my way in and use them wherever I could, mostly sweeping and cleaning. Mac was filling in the concrete, patching the roof and wrapping up the electrical, and I was pulling and prepping the stock furniture for the sale. Chocolate hired a man named Ken to help run the sale since I had little time or patience to deal with consumers.

Chocolate and Mikee were still trying to collect our money and pack up the hundreds of boxes of files we had collected over the past ten years. As a corporation, you must save and store seven years of records, everything from payroll to sales, in case of an audit. For this, I bought a 30 foot trailer and we loaded box after box by year into the trailer where we would store it for the next seven-and-a-half years.

We ran the warehouse sale for three weekends in a row starting Thursdays at 9 a.m. and going till 7 p.m. Sunday evenings. Ken and his crew did a nice job selling almost everything at wholesale or above, which was quite a pleasant surprise. Each evening after the sale, Chocolate would take care of the accounting and I, with the aid of a helper or two, would package the furniture for pickup the next day.

When the sale was over, we still had about 20 sets left, which I either gave away to my helpers or sold on a consignment basis to two of my dealers. For this, we got maybe 25 cents on the dollar when it was all said and done but at least the stuff was gone. The factory was completely empty and it was an eerie feeling to walk through. Each night, as I would go around shutting off lights and closing doors I'd visualize the place when it was up and running and that made me sad. For years, I'd walk the floors at night after everyone went home and I'd always say out loud, *"Thank you, Creative Ideas, for all you have given me, my family and crew."* Well, this would be the last time I could say that.

Creative Ideas was now officially and completely gone.

* * *

One morning, Chocolate and I were in the office packing when the press came by for an interview and I reluctantly agreed. It was so weird walking through the factory and trying to explain what we did there and how we did it when all that was left was a big empty hollow building. The writer was doing a piece on manufacturing in our country and why it was slowly but surely disappearing. I told him about all the trials and tribulations we had endured over the past few years with finishes and the AQMD as well as higher insurance and workers-compensation rates, utility bills, lawsuits, taxes, imports, etc.

Shortly thereafter he wrote a nice article about me and my company's demise. It was *Walter's* last claim to fame.

* * *

It was Friday morning, May 5, 2006, and we had just finished packing up our three cars with our personal things when my daughter suggested we take a final picture in front of the shop. Some 25 years earlier, Chocolate, Mikee, Nicole (in her PJs with feet) and I stood in front of the first Creative Ideas factory and took our first family/company picture. Back then, we were full of anticipation, hope and promise - excited to start on this journey into the unknown.

Today, we stood in front of Creative Ideas for the final time and once again took what would be the last family/company photo. We forced a smile and even took several photos, including some with our grandkids. But this time I can honestly say I wasn't excited about the journey into the unknown. I was too busy thinking back.

I walked back inside with Chocolate as if to say goodbye to an old friend. The factory was dark and empty; you could hear a pin drop. The office was still, all the chairs lined up at the desks we were leaving behind for the new owner. I wanted to cry but did my best to hold back, not to get everyone started. I just didn't want to leave...

As I put the key in the door for the last time, my heart just sunk and I was overwhelmed. I couldn't hold back the tears any longer and then I cried - we all cried.

* * *

And then we drove away. It was over...

**Creative Ideas final day family photo:
Mikee, Me Chocolate and Nicole (squatting).**

Mikee, Steven, Chocolate, Nicole & Mikela.

THE FINAL CHAPTER –
HAPPILY EVER AFTER...

The ending words of a fairy tale usually go, *"And they lived happily ever after."* This is my story. Through my Eyes!

* * *

It's been three years since I drove away from Creative Ideas (I know, enough with the three's). It's now 2009 and I'm 55 years old. I started this book last year and here I am about to finish it, closing yet another chapter on my life. Like the final days at Creative Ideas, I find myself a little anxious, a little sad and a little nervous and scared about my future. Will anyone buy this book? Will anyone like it? Will anyone read it? And of course, what will I do next?

Walter says it will be a best seller. Maybe we'll write another book (he already has a title) or maybe we'll buy a piano and learn how to play.

That *Walter,* he never stops *and I never want him to.*

* * *

Once we turned the company over to Dick and Jack things went from bad to worse pretty quickly. I've never seen so much confusion and disorganization in a company in my life. I would go in a few times a week and try to lend a hand or an idea but no one cared to listen. Amazing. I built Creative Ideas from nothing and now I had virtually no say in it or its future at all. Dick would ask my advice or opinion on things and then do the exact opposite. Crazy, I thought.

He was also so tight on credit that customers couldn't afford to buy new samples even if he could deliver them. Everyone at the factory, including the reps from both sides, were backbiting and gossiping. I tried to tell him and Jack that somehow we needed to bring the crews together and make them realize that we had become *"one company and one team"* and that we rise or fall together. However, he never bothered to take control so it never worked out and each crew refused to work with or for each other. No one wanted anything to do with Jack the one running the show. Dick preferred to blame me, for what I don't really know, but I do know that he resented giving me a check for the royalties each month. No, he flat out hated doing so and even this became a battle each and every month. Dick is a pretty wealthy man and owns a ton of property so money was not an issue. I think he just enjoyed having me twist in the wind and, somehow, making me wait and wait to get paid gave him some deranged pleasure. But truth be told, in the end, he still wrote the checks.

At least I was smart enough to know when to say enough is enough. He, on the other hand is pissed that I got out of the business and resents me for it. Not my fault. Today, I often hear how lucky I was to quit when I did and to get out before this major recession - that luck thing again. I'd like to think it was a little prophetic on my part. *Tony Robbins* says, ***"Successful people ask better questions and, as a result, they get better answers."*** I couldn't agree more. I looked at the whole package: The business, the industry and the economy and I was honest with myself and I decided it was time. If that's luck, then lucky I am.

* * *

Within the first year, the new Creative Ideas was having so many troubles with the finishing, quality and production that the four-week lead time stretched to eight weeks. Our reputation for great quality? Let's just say it wasn't the same. Customers began to complain and no one had any answers and, worse, no one bothered to pick up their calls. Sales started to drop off and more and more customers started to leave. I was getting calls daily from reps, employees, customers and suppliers wanting to know what was going on. The finishing problems were as bad as ever and now the quality and lead times also were failing. I had no answers but tried to calm the waters.

Dick grew angry and disgusted with each passing day and kept threatening to close down. He worried more than anyone I've ever seen run a business but did little to help himself. The company joke was that he would need a flashlight and a map to find the back door to the factory. He complained that he invested over a million dollars into this venture and it wasn't making him any money. I reminded him that he needed to give it a chance; it had only been a short time. I pointed out that it would help if he could get to full production and that he was way overstaffed with his regular people and understaffed with the Creative crew.

I went into the factory one day and noticed that he had some 40 people sanding bedroom parts (in slow motion, no less) and they weren't even building any bedroom at the time. I complained to him, Jack and anyone who would listen that they had way too many people and he was just throwing away money. The office management was out of control as well and I often pointed this out but, like everything else, it fell on deaf ears.

Dick had some $2 million of bedroom furniture stacked in the warehouse and no orders for most of it. *"So why build more?"* I pleaded. I also told him that the space and manpower that he and Jack allotted for the Creative Ideas line was too small and we needed more people to satisfy the customers and orders in house. Deaf ears…

They held meetings constantly, meetings to advise you of the next meeting. Long, tedious, get nothing accomplished meetings. While I was in the factory one morning before a meeting, I noticed that one of our finishes wasn't the right color. I immediately called over the line supervisors and told them they had a problem. These two guys had worked for me for years and I wanted to advise them on what to do to get it corrected quickly.

Once back in the office for the meeting, Dick informed me in front of everyone that he no longer wanted me to talk to the people in the shop. I had to follow the *"chain of command"* as he put it and talk to either Jerry (fat chance) or his plant manager, Dwayne (who couldn't care less), if I noticed a problem. This enraged me and after the meeting, I let Dick and Jack know of my displeasure. I told them it was ridiculous, reminding them that these people worked for me for years and there was no reason for me to get an interpreter to tell them when I see a problem. I told them that I thought this was counter-productive. Deaf ears…

A few months later, Dick and I got into an argument over the money he owed me for the inventory. He pissed me off so much that I slammed my hand on his desk and broke his glass desk top. I think this must have scared him. I may have told him that had this happened years earlier, when I was a young hothead, that instead of breaking his desk it might have been his neck. Shortly thereafter, Jack informed me that Dick didn't want me to come to the shop anymore. Big surprise! From that point on, whenever we met it was at a restaurant or a coffee shop, somewhere in public.

One afternoon I got a call. It was Dick. He wanted to meet with me in the morning for breakfast. *"No problem,"* I said. I arrived and we had a casual breakfast while Dick explained that he was thinking of getting rid of the Las Vegas showroom and wanted my advice. Well, we discussed this for probably a half hour, all the while I was giving him a hundred reasons why this was a terrible idea. Worse than that, he wanted to hand the showroom off to a fierce competitor of ours who had the showroom next door. I told him this would be suicide, that every one of our customers would show up and our competitor's reps would bury us.

Why he even bothered to ask or listen to me, I'll never know because he then proceeded to tell me he had already given up the showroom and our competitor was moving in. I was both confused and angry. I asked him, *"Why are you wasting my time if you've already made the decision and given up the showroom?"* He didn't answer.

Then he informed me that he wanted to terminate a few of our reps. Once again, I pleaded with him. I told him without a showroom, it would be hard, but without the reps, it would be impossible to maintain any business. He said he had already made up his mind and proceeded to give me a list of who was out and who he wanted to keep. Out were Gary Tripp, George Arbeiter and all of the best earners on both sides. In were only the reps that made very little money and very few sales. I explained that this made no sense - that he wanted to fire our best reps and keep some of the worst performers because of their salaries. He was ignoring the fact that they only get paid if they sell and we needed the sales. Deaf ears…

I asked him when he was going to move forward and he replied, *"Soon."* The next morning, Jack told me that he was going to call all the reps on the list and fire them, today. I jumped into my car and raced to the factory. I burst in on Dick and Jack and pleaded with them to reconsider. Jack explained that he had nothing to do with this decision and that he agreed with me. Dick said his mind was made up and that he couldn't afford them any longer, he was losing too much money. The writing was on the wall - he was closing Creative Ideas down.

I asked if I could call them and break the news to them and he agreed. I also asked if he would honor all of the open orders in house, which is customary (but not mandatory), and he said that he would only pay them through the end of the month. Needless to say, we argued. I felt this was unfair and wrong. These people toiled for me for years and now he was going to fire them abruptly, with no real reason or warning, and screw them out of the orders they'd already written and monies I felt they earned. I said, *"Fine, I'll call them all and I will take the lead at getting them together and filing a lawsuit against you."* He softened and agreed to pay them for all of their open orders and, like a gentleman, he did.

I returned home and called my troops one by one and explained Dick's decision. I thanked them for their years of service and wished them well. I also told them that I would do my best to make sure they received every penny they had coming and I did. And to Dick's credit, he paid them all off in full.

Shortly before this transpired, word somehow leaked out that Jerry was going to get fired. Funny how that happened around there - leaks. The next morning, Jerry went in and resigned. He gave his two week notice before they could cut him. Good for him.

When Dick fired Wally, his sales manager, after some 20 years of service, it was abrupt and callous or so I'm told. Wally was in tears when I walked into his office. I, too, was in tears as he informed me of his termination and how bad he felt. According to Wally, there was no, *"Thank you for all the years"* and very little else but I wasn't there so I don't know what exactly transpired.

Next up was me. Dick wanted to buy out the remainder of my services with one final month's check and be done with me. He gave me the written 30-day notice that was called for in our contract and I agreed to move on. I still informed him that I would help him and, if he needed me, he could call. What the hell, I actually felt sorry for him. This whole thing was such a mess and I just couldn't believe it was happening all over again. For me, it was like a reoccurring nightmare.

A few months later, Jack called me from his home and informed me that he, too, was gone; his services were no longer needed. Gee, big surprise. I guess what goes around, comes around. I wished him well and we never spoke again.

One by one, people quit, got fired or laid off until there wasn't much left. It was very sad. I had agreed to help Dick until the end and I offered up as much as I could. I gave him advice and the names of my auctioneer, who did a great job for me, and Ken, the man who ran my successful sale. He used neither and his auction didn't go very well. I never could understand why he would ask me for my advice or opinion and then always do the opposite. Crazy and a waste of time. But Dick is resilient. He sold some of his buildings, bought back some of his own equipment at his auction and rented back part of his building. As far as I know, he's still making a few bedroom sets and selling a group that he imports from China. God bless him. I wish him well. I guess he never knows when to quit. *Mountains*...

* * *

As for me I now have a new *Stevism* and it goes like this:

* * *

"I live in a little place called happily ever after. Everyday is Saturday and we're always on vacation. Thank God."

* * *

Over the years, I have been so lucky to have lived, loved and learned so much, to have experienced so much and to have touched so many as they have touched me. My family and friends mean the world to me. My life has been fuller, richer and more successful than I could ever have imagined or even wished for. *Walter* did okay...

* * *

Creative Ideas opened up the world to me. It enabled me to employ people, meet and understand people and travel. I was fortunate enough to start a business, build it and have great success seeing it to fruition. Having it come to an end was heartbreaking, but owning Creative Ideas was my pleasure, it helped make me the man I am today. The *library* of life has served me well. I came to realize that anything is possible if you believe, set goals and always keep trying.

Creative Ideas was me; it was my stage. It will always live in my heart but it's not me anymore. Now, I'm just plain, old Steve Balsamo and that's okay. I'm just a guy, just a person, maybe just like you. Someone who worked hard, tried harder and made it to the top. An underdog who beat the odds, who shot for the moon and maybe landed on a star.

You make the call...

* * *

If there is a moral to my story, it's just this:
"If I can do it, so can you. Never give up, never give in."

Me and Chocolate living "Happily Ever After."

THE CAST:

Steve: I'm just pleased as punch at how my life turned out. I always say, *"No Regrets."* I have lived a life with *Passion.* I've toiled and played, fought and loved, clawed and slid on the ice, laughed and cried.

I really have done it all and I have ***everyone*** to thank for it. A special thanks to my mom and dad. Without you, it could not have been possible. And thanks to my wife and kids for always loving and supporting me.

Today, I live with my beautiful wife, Chocolate, whom I've been with now for 36 happy, wonderful years. If you can believe this, I often wish I had met her sooner and I was just 19 when I did. We have three lovely homes here in California - the one in Big Bear, our family home in Yorba Linda and the house I built for her on the bluff in Capo Beach. Yes, I finished it and it turned out great. We travel back and forth, to and fro, with our new baby, ***Bella Boo Balsamo,*** a cute *Maltese* puppy and the new love of our lives.

I write, go to *Dodger* games, watch my *Cowboys*, travel, take care of our properties and investments and basically, do as I please. How many can say that? Today, my mountains are ant hills and I like it that way. Call me *Lucky #3…*

* * *

Walter: Ah yes, *Walter.* Where would I be without *Walter?* He helped me through the worst of times and brought me to the best of times. It was *Walter* who was always there for me, even when I was the Invisible Man as a kid and the Incredible Hulk as a man.

Walter always gave me ***Hope*** and always kept me ***Dreaming*** - two things you must have to *survive* and to really *live. Walter* was by my side when I was scared as a kid and lonely as a teen; he guided me to the light in my 20s and helped me survive the 30s. It was *Walter* who kept me grounded in my successful 40s and helped me to a soft landing in my 50s. *Walter* built houses and companies and made some bucks. He wrote a book and ***he never let me forget where I came from***.

It was always *Walter* and I took all the credit. We all need a *Walter* in our lives. I thank *God* for giving me mine…

* * *

Chocolate: The love of my life. She often says, *"I love my life,"* to which I answer, *"And I love my wife."* Today, she spends her time just doing whatever she feels like doing at the moment. She, too, has no regrets and no more mountains to climb, not even any ant hills. She's happy, healthy and just the most wonderful person I've ever been so lucky to meet, know and love. Chocolate loves to e-mail, shop, exercise, talk to our girls, laugh, travel and spend time with her pals. And best of all, she still loves me and being with me???

Go figure…*My personal **Angel!***

* * *

Mikee: Our Mikee girl is still living just down the street with my two beautiful grandkids, ***Steven*** (15) (on his way to high school and playing the guitar) and ***Mikela*** (8) (the ball player and scholar in the family). Man, have they grown and so fast. Mikee has done a fabulous job raising and supporting them as a single parent and I couldn't be prouder of her. She still works for Baghouse, the company she went to after we closed. She loves her co-workers and has several close friends that she spends time with. She, too, is quite happy but still searching and has *mountains* yet to climb. We are always close by if she needs us…

* * *

Nicole: Our baby Berkeley girl is all grown up and got married last August. Happy anniversary! We can't talk politics since we're on different sides of the aisle for now but we share many other interests, such as our family, the *Dodgers* and now home improvements since she and ***Mike Winn*** (her hubby) just bought their first home. Mike is a great fit in our family and we can talk politics and just about anything else since we get along great, I have a new friend. He and Nicole seem to be made for each other. Poor boy, he has his hands full since Nicole, like her mom, is an independent woman and ready to take on the world and any charity that comes her way…

**Nicole's Wedding - Walking her down the aisle to the tune:
"Over the rainbow/What a wonderful world"**

* * *

Mom and **Dad:** As you know, **Tony,** my pop, died of lung cancer some 22 years ago. The time has flown by. I miss my dad from time to time and wish things could have been different but as I said, *"no regrets."* I don't have the nightmares anymore either. Chocolate and I drop by his burial site every now and then to say hi as does Nicole. I can't speak for anyone else but I know that I will never have a Thanksgiving dinner again without thinking of my dad.

Mom, **Noreen,** is doing great. She is happy, healthy and still full of vim and vigor. We are amazed at how great she looks and how young she still acts and feels. She is blessed to have great genes and I only hope and pray I take after her in that regard. Mom got me from A to Z and who knows how I might have turned out without her. Mom still resides in Corona with my sister, Jackie, and her family and is living life to the fullest…

* * *

Jackie and **family:** Jackie and *Mike* are doing great; they have raised two fine young men, my nephews, *Tony* and *Nicholas.* Jackie works for the school district and she loves her job. Get this, she works with handicapped and mentally chal-

309

lenged children, go figure. Mike is still in the furniture industry and he's running the shipping department for his company. He loves his job and surroundings. As for the boys, Tony (the brain) is now a freshman in college and Nick (the jock) is a junior in high school. I'm very proud of them as they are both bright, fine young men...

* * *

THE SUPPORTING CAST:

I have always wished the best for all of my friends and family and these days, they all seem to be doing well and are happy. Many friendships grow apart over the years - it's only natural. Somehow, we have maintained a strong relationship and bond. I will always try to maintain that; I will be the glue.

* * *

Tris and **Victoria** have a beautiful home in Orange and their door business is doing very well. Times are a little tough right now but that's to be expected. They both are quite busy with their home, business, dogs and family. But still, Tris and I remain the best of friends and get together as often as possible, even if it's just for dinner or a Dodgers game. Tris will always be like a brother to me...

* * *

Clint and **Jana** are enjoying their life together with their two girls, and the tux shop makes them a good living so they're happy. You can always find Clint and his family down at the beach on Sundays riding bikes, soaking up the sun and enjoying life in general. Clint and I don't go a week without talking and we see each other often for a baseball game or a play and dinner. His girls, *Carly* and *Christa,* are a couple of beauties and Clint and Jana have done a great job at raising and home schooling them. They really are a wonderful family...

* * *

Jim and **Tami** are doing well. Jimmy quit drinking and has been sober for more years than I can remember. Jim got his Master's degree and is now teaching so he's achieving his goals. Like the rest of my buddies, Jim and I see each other often and we get together with the guys for ball games, fantasy football or any excuse we can come up with. Jim and Tami are at all of the family events as are the rest of our gang…

* * *

Sam and **Chuck** have a nice home in Anaheim and Sam owns her own escrow company. It's a struggle as it is with most businesses these days but she'll make it because she's a real go-getter. Chuck is rebuilding old cars, following the Dodgers, and riding his Harley whenever he's not working. And my Godson, *Chayson,* is working and going to college; he is a fine young man and I'm proud of him. Sam and Chocolate have been best of friends for more years than we care to talk about and they also see and talk to each other weekly, if not more.

* * *

Dennis sold his bar a few years back and moved near the Colorado River, where he plans to build another bar and live out his dreams with his new girlfriend. Sadly, Dennis has drifted away from the crowd some but, hopefully, he will see the error of his ways and come back to us soon enough. I hope so, because we miss him. I miss my old friend…

* * *

Nancy and Tony have gone their separate ways and sold their home in Yorba Linda. Nancy works for the AQMD, if you can believe that, and she moved back into her old condo in Yorba Linda. *Devin,* my godson, just got married to a lovely gal named Felisha and they have a son, Dustin, with another child (Blake) soon to arrive. Chocolate and Nancy go to church together and they e-mail or phone each other often. Chocolate has the girls down to the beach house from time to time for a weekend of eating, drinking and hanging out together sun-bathing or watching movies…

As for the rest, there are too many to mention but that's life, what can I tell you? I love them all…

The gangs all here:
(Top L to R) Tris & Victoria, Jim & Tami, Jana & Clint, Sam & Chuck,
Pastor & Wife, Debbie & Pat, Jackie & Mike.
(Bottom L to R) Kelly, Mikee, me, Chocolate, Nicole, and Mom
(Noreen).

Oh, I bet you thought I forgot *Vito*, my brother. Silly you, I didn't. I just thought he deserved more than an honorable mention so if you'll indulge me a bit longer…

* * *

On Feb. 6, 2008 I awoke very early and went to my office. It had been a long sleepless night and I was so troubled that I didn't know what else to do. I sat down at my computer and sent this e-mail message to everyone in my address book and asked them to pass it on. I titled it:

* * *

VITO BALSAMO

Yesterday was 55 years and 52 days from the day my beautiful brother was brought into this world. Life for my brother has not been kind. He was born mentally retarded, was sick a lot and not given much time to live - ten years at the most experts thought. Vito fooled them all; he passed ten and was institutionalized around the age of 11. When we left Brooklyn, New York, mom was very poor and she, my baby sister and I came to California to live with my grandparents. Vito was left behind to fend for himself in a pretty terrible place called *"Willowbrook State School."* It would make most prisons look civilized. Over the years at Willowbrook, Vito would have his nose and other body parts broken many times and more scars on his face and body than you can imagine.

But he never complained. He just wished he could go home…

* * *

I was just 14 when we left Brooklyn and Vito was 15. Vito was already losing his hair and his sight and was considered legally blind. It would be many years later that the state of New York would have mercy and declare Willowbrook State School unfit and close it down for good. Vito, now a man of 24, was transferred to California and put in a place called *"CLIMB,"* a small health care facility in Pasadena. Vito spent most of his life there and over the years he would lose the complete use of his sight and eventually, his legs.

But unlike most, Vito never complained. He never asked for much or needed much, just to go home…

* * *

Vito, though blind, could tell you the color of his socks in his drawer by feel and he was always neat as a pin. Sometimes, it would take him five minutes just to tuck in his shirt and he loved his long Beatle-like haircut. Vito always said *"black was beautiful."* He loved and cared about everyone, yet we called him retarded?

As time passed, Vito would get sick from time to time, each time taking a little more life out of him. But still, he never complained. He was always just happy to see us and just wanted to come home…

* * *

Most of you never met my beautiful brother and that is your loss because you missed out on meeting the best our family ever had to offer. Vito spent most of his life never having or knowing the wonderful things *we all take for granted every-day,* such as: home, sight, family, freedom, how to drive, your own bed, work, a girlfriend, shopping or just going to the fridge for a snack. He was *never* in control of his heat or air or bedtime or even the food he ate, and he had to ask to use the bathroom.

But Vito never complained he just wanted to go home…

* * *

Vito loved TV and the movies even though he couldn't see them anymore and could barely hear them over the recreation room noise. Vito loved music and was never too far from his cassette player. Some of his favorites were the Beatles, Stevie Wonder, Elvis and anything Motown and he knew all the words. He danced! With all the things that went wrong for Vito over the years, the only thing that ever really disturbed him was losing his hair. Go figure, the poor guy just never got a break.

In recent years, Vito was wheelchair bound and his legs and feet were deformed and rotting from lack of circulation. He was blind and losing control of his arms and hands. He could no longer eat his favorite food, a hamburger and fries, because he could no longer swallow solid foods and has to be fed with a spoon.

But still, he never complained. He just wanted to come home…

* * *

Yesterday the good LORD finally took mercy on my beautiful brother, Vito. After a long and gallant fight,

"VITO FINALLY - GOT TO GO HOME."

He passed away at 7:10 p.m. on Tuesday, Feb. 5, 2008. Vito was 55 years and 52 days old.

Vito beat all the odds, but Vito deserved better. He deserved a better life and a better family. A better brother...

* * *

I always say, *"I live in a little place called Happily ever After."* Well, it's a little darker here now. I only wish I could have and would have been better to my brother. But I was too busy climbing mountains and it was all too painful for me to see. I spent the first ten years of my life sleeping with Vito in his bed because I was scared at night and he protected me. I wish I could have protected him.

* * *

I live by the standard of *"No Regrets"* because I know that if you turned left instead of right everything may have turned out differently. I'm selfish in the fact that I'm happy the way my life turned out but if allowed *"just one regret"* for me, it would be Vito.

* * *

I know most of you didn't know Vito, but now you do.

* * *

His name was:
"VITO STEPHEN BALSAMO" (12/15/52 – 02/05/08)

And he lived. I just want as many people as possible to know that Vito lived. He lived and he never had much (but hope) and he never complained. He took it on the chin...

If you can find it in your heart to think a good thought or say a prayer for him or just pass this around the Internet so he can live on in our thoughts, I would forever be grateful. Who knows, maybe there's another Vito out there and someone

315

will realize by reading this that…
   "Time is of the Essence."

   You're home now, Vito…
   I love you. May you finally rest in peace.

                              Thank you so much.
                              Steve Balsamo

Email dated Feb. 6, 2008

SO, THAT'S IT...

I wrote a book. I set a goal, I got to work and I put my mind to it. And I did it. It was tough at times. I hadn't a clue what I was doing and I was a little intimidated with the thought of writing a book, trying to publish it and then the horror of trying to sell it. I wrote this book with passion - not skills. I wrote it from the heart - not the brain - and I'll do my best to get it published and into stores like I always do, with hard work and sheer determination.

* * *

You just read my book so I want to thank you so much for putting up with me. I hope you found something meaningful, insightful or inspirational within these pages. If not, I hope maybe I just entertained you a little or made you smile or think about your life, your family, your friends...

The Yin and the Yang.
You can't have one without the other

I want to thank you and leave you with the lyrics from another song. "My Wish" by the Rascal Flats.

I hope the day's come easy and moments pass slow
And each road leads where you want to go
And if you're faced with the choice and you have to choose
I hope you choose the one that means the most to you
And if one door opens to another door closed
I hope you keep on walkin' til you find the window
If it's cold outside, show the world the warmth of your smile,
but more than anything, more than anything...

THROUGH MY EYES

My wish for you, is that life becomes all that you want it to
Your dreams stay big, your worries stay small
You never have to carry more that you can hold
And while you're out there gettin' where you're gettin' to
I hope you know somebody loves you
And wants the same things too
Yeah, this is my wish...

For You...

AFTERWORD

While I'm unable to comment on the events of my father's life before he entered mine, I know that through his tumultuous past, he now stands before me as this incredible human being; loving, caring and with flawless character. I was almost five years-old when the relationship between my mom and Steve became the spark that is this eternal and breathtaking love I see every time I gaze upon the two of them. The road they traveled was hard and full of challenges (some of which are not addressed in this book), but the lesson here is to be brave in your mistakes and that love will guide you through all. Dad gave of himself and made it known he would remain a part of our lives until the end; a truly unbelievable commitment to make at the tender young age of 19.

As life sped up with the move to Pedley, it also slowed down. The pressure of purchasing a new home and beginning a new business was crazy for my parents but the abundance of time and bonding of our small family unit during that period has and will always last a lifetime. I watched my parents struggle and work grueling and unbelievable hours, sometimes with me and my sister at their side (an experience I can only be thankful for). The work ethic they instilled and the ability to accept each and every day as it comes was a major part of what my parents taught my sister and me. They also taught us love, generosity, perseverence, hard work and to never forget where we came from. Without a doubt, it has been a tough road for them. But it was worth the labor - I know each and every person who has been touched by them would agree.

I watched my dad take their company from infancy to adolescence, into adulthood and through its final breath. The empire my father built with my mother standing beside him, supporting and guiding him every step of the way, provided some of the best times of our lives. Dad and mom reminisce (sometimes forlorn) as they look back, but I am happy to report that they are living well in retirement.

My heart leaps and a tear of joy spills down my cheek as I write this, knowing they finally reap what they have sown so meticulously all these years. They now live their lives at the pace of their choosing and not the pace of the everyday rat race the rest of us run. I was shocked when, in retirement, my father called me from jury duty and reported that "It's no biggie" and explained, "What's the big deal? It's a beautiful day out." Back in the day, although he was always happy to do his civic duty, it would have been a burden with no beauty to be found anywhere because it was taking away from what was necessary – working hard and with a purpose. When I heard his calm words over the telephone that day, I found it amazing… Amazing that my hard working dad ACTUALLY had the time to notice the day around him and how beautiful it was. UNBELIEVABLE!

Today, mom and dad spend their time traveling between their beautiful homes and enjoying their communities. My dad is perpetually busy but has a smile on his face; he has fewer wrinkles and an easygoing swagger. My mom, beautiful and as strong as ever, has a smile on her face, has actually grown two inches taller (as the family joke goes) and she actually has a memory now (from the lack of stress). I am proud of them and their accomplishments. I am, as I'm sure the entire family is, forever indebted to the most important people in our lives for all they have sacrificed, all they have taught us and for the love they have shown us each and every day no matter how much was going on in their lives. I am forever grateful and appreciative. Dad, Mom… your "legacy" may not be what you thought it was going to be, but I assure you of this… you have left your mark in this world and it shines brighter than the brightest star ever could.

Daddy, thank you for being EVERYTHING you never expected, everything you aspired to be and all that you are. You are the first man who taught me how to love. You are the standard that no one has lived up to. You ARE my hero - always have been, and always will be.

MIKEE

SPECIAL ACKNOWLEDGMENTS

100 Years

Words and Music by John Ondrasik

Freedom Never Cries

Words and Music by John Ondrasik